AMERICAN GOVERNMENT
A Brief Introduction

AMERICAN GOVERNMENT
A Brief Introduction

Max J. Skidmore

Marshall Carter Wanke

ST. MARTIN'S PRESS   NEW YORK

Library of Congress Catalog Card Number: 74-78169
Copyright © 1974 by St. Martin's Press, Inc.
All Rights Reserved.
Manufactured in the United States of America.
For information, write:
St. Martin's Press, Inc., 175 Fifth Avenue, New York, N.Y. 10010

AFFILIATED PUBLISHERS:
Macmillan Limited, London—
also at Bombay, Calcutta, Madras, and Melbourne

CONTENTS

Reproduced by permission of Johnny Hart
and Field Enterprises, Inc.

AMERICAN GOVERNMENT
A Brief Introduction

1 | INTRODUCTION

We can be educated for freedom—much better educated for it than we are at present.

Aldous Huxley

The Study of Government and Politics

Whether in the form of the postman delivering the mail, the policeman on the corner, the functionary at the district office of the Social Security Administration, the drill sergeant, or the agent conducting an investigation into the beliefs and behavior of some citizen or group, government touches virtually all of us each day in one form or another. Sometimes its effects are beneficial, sometimes they are detrimental; they are always important. Where government is popularly elected, the people potentially have some control over the broad outlines of the policies that affect them so greatly, but they will fail to exercise their influence effectively if they are not adequately informed about basic issues and about the ways in which the government operates. The study of government and politics is therefore an essential part of every citizen's education.

To begin to understand politics, one must become familiar with the basic structures and processes of American national, state, and local governments, but this is merely the beginning of knowledge. Beyond the basics are formal and informal relationships, differing approaches to the study of government and politics, and the frequent divergence of reality from appearances. Above all, one must develop the ability to analyze critically and to determine when it is appropriate to accept political statements, when to reject them, and when to remain skeptical until better information is available. If this is difficult, it can also be exciting.

1

Politics is everywhere. Much of what may seem at first to have little to do with politics is in truth intensely political. Politics is related directly to our view of life, our relations with others, our judgments of right and wrong, and our perceptions of the world. Politics is the means by which human beings collectively organize their affairs. It centers on the ways in which the person adjusts to the group and, conversely, the manner in which the group accommodates persons who differ vastly from one another. Aristotle described politics as the "architechtonic science," the one that is fundamental to all others. It is through politics that societies determine what can be done, what should be done, and what is done; participation in political life can help each person realize his own potential by helping to shape the larger community.

Politics in America is both collective and individual, concerned with the group and with each person. It deals with the rights of the individual as fully as with the duties. Similarly, it deals with the obligations of the community, as fully as with the rights. The task of the democracy has always been, and remains, to establish a society in which rights of the individual and those of the community are recognized and protected, and the duties of both are observed and fulfilled. Because of the constant tension between these needs no political system has ever fully succeeded in performing the task. However, the goal is not to achieve perfection but to seek it, to do the best that is possible.

In a popular government, political participation is not only a right of the people but also their responsibility. Unfortunately, in the United States the latter too often is ignored. Two thousand years ago the ancient Greeks recognized that human beings are fundamentally social animals. Political life is the foundation of the social order; by failing to participate, a person loses a major dimension of his human potential. The fundamental civil right of the American citizen is the right to vote, yet voter participation in this nation is shockingly low. Presidential elections routinely bring about a higher vote than other elections, but the 1972 contest involved only about 55 percent of the potential voters. The effects of such a situation are readily apparent when viewed against the setting of majority rule. Any candidate receiving 60 percent or more of the vote has won by a landslide. Richard Nixon won 61 percent of the vote, one of the greatest landslides in American history. Nevertheless, because of the low voter turnout (in this election even lower than usual), only about one-third of the potential voters cast their votes for the winner. What effects might this have upon American democracy?

Our political system has been beset by a series of urgent crises during the last decade as well as by more subtle but no less dangerous difficulties, such as the increasing loss of privacy, the tendency among many to reject the political process, and an increased willingness to accept authoritarian measures. These increasingly highlight the delicate balance between personal rights and public needs that is the essence of politics. The overriding political reality of these years was the involvement of the United States in a war in Indochina. The involvement not only brought about innumerable difficulties, and intensified countless others, but itself became an immeasurably complex phenomenon. It led to a discussion of America's role in the world; of the nature of communism; of the uses, limits, and dangers of power under modern conditions; of the role of war and the conduct of warfare; and even of the purposes of domestic policies. It led to troubled thoughts about the nature of the state and government and reopened the historical American questions of selective conscientious objection or civil disobedience, on the one hand, and revolution, on the other. Certainly there has been no "radicalization" of mainstream American views and beliefs, but it is significant that the questions receive any attention at all.

None of the questions has brought a clear answer, but each has required thought and judgment. Historically, military conscription, the draft, has been thoroughly unpopular in the United States, even in time of all-out war. In peacetime it was unthinkable. Since the early 1950's, however, it burst upon the American scene as a full-blown segment of the "American Way of Life." The questions surrounding the Vietnamese War directly stimulated a reexamination of its desirability. On the other hand, the conscription of middle class young men was one reason why the war was questioned. Without it, assuming that the war could still have been conducted, the deaths of young and old Vietnamese might have gone unexamined. Related to the war, but less directly, are such questions as urban blight, poverty amidst affluence, racism, and individual liberties that long have troubled the American political system but took on new urgency in the 1960's. Technology, wealth, and good will, alone, have proved unable to provide the answers, even when they have been applied.

If, as it has been said, the people get the government they deserve, then clearly it behooves the people to inform themselves and involve themselves. Enlightened involvement, an enlightened citizenry, can exist only as the result of individual decisions and actions. Each person must be aware of the potential for participation, and this begins with an under-

standing of the form and functions of government, and of the substance
of the foremost political questions of the day.

The Political and Cultural Background of American Democracy

The roots of American political ideas and the American
governmental system reach far back, even beyond the beginnings of the
Colonies. The notion that men are created equal can be traced to ancient
classical thinkers as well as to the beginnings of Christianity. The writings
both of Plato and of Aristotle generate the idea that an ethical government must operate according to law; this principle has developed through
the years into the modern doctrine that the government should be one of
laws, and not of men. The ideas of limited government and constitutionalism long were prevalent in the English traditions, dating most dramatically from the Magna Carta in 1215, when the King was forced to accept
limitations on his power, and were transplanted into the new American
environment.

The earliest voluntary settlers came to America's shores largely for
economic or religious reasons. Of those coming because of religion, the
Pilgrims arrived on the Mayflower to found the Plymouth Colony in 1620,
and the Puritans settled in Massachusetts Bay a decade later. Both groups
sought religious freedom for themselves, but they did not in turn extend
freedom of worship to others. The Puritans drove Roger Williams from
the Massachusetts Bay Colony, for example, because he challenged the
prevailing orthodoxy by denying that the state should have the power to
control religion, by advocating freedom for other religious beliefs, and by
denying the right of white persons to seize Indian lands. When he established the colony of Rhode Island, he attempted to put his beliefs into
practice, and Rhode Island led the way toward democracy for the rest of
the colonies. Even the Puritans, however unwillingly, made their contribution to the development of democracy, because their beliefs regarding
church government led to congregational control and freedom from an
ecclesiastical hierarchy. This had political implications far beyond the
confines of the churches.

Others came because they could not advance themselves in the old
society. Such persons as fourth sons, black sheep, convicts, and debtors
flocked to the New World, where many flourished. Of those immigrating
primarily for economic gain, merchants, tradesmen, and farmers settled

mainly in the middle and northern colonies, and planters established large plantations for commercial agriculture in the South, and rapidly developed a labor system based upon human slavery. Subsequently, many German and Scotch-Irish farmers moved into the western backcountry, reflecting a westward movement that, almost from the beginnings of European settlement here, seemed to encourage independence and individualism.

From earliest times, Americans sought to defy authority and promote individual gain. Because of their memories of European despotisms, they designed their new governments carefully to limit the exercise of political power. The basic principle dominating the discussions that led, ultimately, to revolution and the breaking of ties with England, was that all persons have a right to self-government, that no government has the right to rule without the consent of those who are governed. Thomas Jefferson captured the intellectual impetus for the revolution in words that sound radical even today, when he wrote the Declaration of Independence. In it, he asserted that all are equal, that government legitimately can receive power only from the people, and that the only justification for government is that it is to secure the right of the people to life, liberty, and the pursuit of happiness. These sentiments were an extension of centuries of English tradition and had been embodied most fully in the writings of the English theorist John Locke. As shaped by decades of American experience and expounded by Jefferson, they became the keystone of American political thought. The primary principle, then and now, is that the government is the servant of the people, not their master.

There were, of course, striking contradictions in practice to the principles that Americans professed to follow. The most notable was the forcible exclusion of some groups from the framework of rights, as seen in the system of slavery and the murderous Indian policies. Similarly, although Americans designed the system to restrict the exercise of governmental power, they were unconcerned with restricting the exercise of private power. The Founding Fathers could hardly have foreseen the huge concentrations of private power that would soon come from the development of the corporation and the industrial state.

With the coming of the twentieth century, the most prominent features in American society were cities, social and geographic mobility, and industrial enterprise. No other people in history have rushed so quickly into cities, and away from the countryside, as have Americans. Many basic American attitudes, however, developed when the United States was

Copyright © 1957, 1961, 1962 by Walt Kelly.
Courtesy Publishers-Hall Syndicate.

a white, Protestant, rural, Anglo-Saxon nation and have persisted with little change. Many Americans still approach politics with orientations suited for simpler times. For example, many tend still to agree with Jefferson that cities are places of evil and corruption, and that virtue attaches to rural living and the agrarian life, at the same time that they enjoy and are dependent upon the advantages of urban living. In practice, Americans demand urban life, but in theory, we have developed a mythology that tends to condemn it. This may account partially for some of our urban problems today. Similarly, we venerate the settled life although we no longer live it. Other paradoxes abound. We are individualistic and nationalistic; we are humane and belligerent; we prefer small government and adopt big government; we are contemptuous of authority and elect officials on platforms of "law and order," which often signify governmental repression.

Constitutional Democracy

The basic principles of the American system of government are equality, government only by consent of the governed, and protection for minority rights. It is a simple matter to identify instances in American history that are in sharp contrast to the tenets of American political thought. In addition to the aforementioned policies that approved of slavery and systematic injustices toward the Indians, there have been the most blatant violations of human rights and dignity, such as racial segregation and the relocation of Japanese-Americans during World War II. There have been similar violations of the protection listed in the Bill of Rights for white Americans, as well, as a result, for example, of the Alien and Sedition Acts of 1798 and the Sedition Act of 1917 that severely restricted the exercise of free speech. There have been numerous violations of procedural rights and basic courtesies committed by the House Committee on Un-American Activities (presently titled the House Committee on Internal Security) and the late Senator Joseph McCarthy. Examples must also include the murders by governmental forces of both black and white students on college campuses, and the brutalization and harassment of peaceful protestors by governmental agents in many parts of the nation. Government lawlessness, in fact, however little recognized, constitutes one of the major "law and order" problems in the United States. Nevertheless, a political system cannot be evaluated fairly by examining only its failures. The task facing the student of politics is to determine the suitability of America's political goals and the degree to which American government is achieving its goals in general, and to propose and work for improvements whenever they appear to be needed.

Much of the world today lives under various forms of authoritarianism, in which such rights as exist are granted to the people by the government, rather than being inherent in the people. In the American system, the power ultimately is lodged in the people, and they grant power to the government, which, at least in theory, exercises it within strict limitations. Two components are necessary to establish and maintain a popular government that observes limitations on the exercise of power: democracy and constitutionalism. These two components may, at times, even be at war with one another. Democracy implies consent by the governed and popular control of the government expressed through majority rule; constitutionalism implies limitations on power, even democratic power. In other words, the majority should rule—but not to the extent that it oppresses the minority. A democracy without limitation could be chaotic and destructive of the minority; a constitutional state without democracy could be unfree. A constitution comprises principles that allocate power to various agencies and strictly limit its exercise; democracy is the instrument of popular control. Both components are vital. The most convenient term for the government including them both is constitutional democracy.

Pluralist Democracy—the Controversy

There are various "models," or frameworks, that political scientists use to analyze and interpret a governmental system. As for democracy, some might contend that it is based on mass participation, with the people retaining the power and directing the policies of their government. This is the model that tends to be presented to public school pupils and probably is responsible for much of the disillusionment that develops when young adults come to recognize how little relation it bears to reality. There is the power elite model, on the other hand, which sees the American system as dominated by a fairly small group of persons who control industry, the military and civilian wings of government, the professions, and trade and labor organizations. Members of the "power elite" may move from one segment to another, but there is an interlocking directorate, unresponsive to the people, that determines policy and controls the details of national life.

The model that most political scientists tend to accept as the best description of the workings of American constitutional democracy is the pluralist model. "Pluralism" does not mean, as the word might imply to many, a society that is free for diversity. Rather it is a group theory of politics. According to the pluralist model, American society is dominated by powerful organized groups, and the government serves essentially as a broker, or referee, among them and also frequently participates as an interest group itself. Each group works for its own interests, and the government serves to coordinate and facilitate compromise, so that the most powerful groups will obtain most of what they desire while they will be antagonized as little as possible. The people may have access to power through these groups, causing some observers to emphasize their popular nature, while critics view them as channels for elite domination. It is, of course, an oversimplification to speak of the "government" as a monolithic force, because government agencies are powerful interest groups that often lack coordination with other agencies and sometimes even work at cross purposes. The Public Health Service, for example, works to discourage smoking, while the Department of Agriculture works for subsidies to tobacco farmers and spends money to encourage smoking abroad.

Many of the writers on pluralism argue that it is not only an accurate description but also desirable. They see politics in a pluralist system as "realistic"—that is, based upon self-interest rather than moral or idealistic considerations. The proponents of pluralism believe that attempts to base politics upon principle would result in a multiplicity of warring factions that would tear the social fabric asunder, and they contend that the compromises of self-interest are the best guide for society just as the "invisible hand" was to have ordered society's economic progress in Adam Smith's view of capitalism. Pluralism reflects the contentment of the great majority (silent or not) with the *status quo* that emphasizes material possessions, conformity, and political apathy. Pluralists imply that apathy is actually a good thing, that it sustains the system, because the masses, if they were to participate fully and make use of their political potential, would tend to be hostile to diversity and civil liberties. Although the "middle class life style" that is the essence of pluralist politics often is the object of scorn, the mediocrity, conformity, and materialism that the critics see seem to the pluralist writers acceptable as the price to pay for a comfortable and stable society. Many believe that this is all that the polity is capable of providing.

It is difficult to quarrel with those who maintain that American politics tends to operate as the pluralist model describes it, although the system does upon occasion rise above the operation of pluralist politics. Possible examples may be the Test Ban Treaty and the civil rights and voting rights acts of the 1960's. In general, however, the pluralist model seems accurately to describe the day to day workings of American government.

The opponents of the idea of pluralism generally do not deny that it presents a reasonably accurate view, but they challenge its desirability. They argue, for one thing, that it places extreme emphasis upon organization. The only group powerful enough to participate in pluralist politics is the organized group. It leaves the unorganized out of account, except insofar as they share interests with the organized. Of course, it may be argued that the unorganized should therefore organize, but the critics contend that circumstances often make organization difficult, if not impossible. Another inadequacy charged against a pluralist system is that the process ignores individual citizens, who theoretically are the primary units of a democratic society. They are unlikely to be heard, even if correct, unless they succeed in uniting. This means that pluralist politics has produced a radical, and in some ways substantially unexamined, change in democracy. It has shifted from individual emphasis to group emphasis. Admittedly a society of more than 200 million persons has little chance of placing primary emphasis upon unorganized individuals, but this should itself increase concern about population size. Moreover, pluralism provides only a rudimentary conception of the public good. It defines the public good only as that which flows from accommodation and compromise among competing powers. The general public, like the individual, is left out of account.

The critics of pluralism charge that its value judgments are openly elitist and that they center on power alone and ignore ethical considerations. It is cynical indeed, they say to conclude that the people are too foolish to have an effective hand in governing, or that the only ethics that is "realistic" results from selfish competition among the powerful. However unintentionally, this would lead to open repudiation of the' principles of the Declaration of Independence. The justification for government under pluralism shifts from the protection of life, liberty, and the pursuit of happiness to the protection of the right of powerful interests to compete with or to cooperate with other powerful interests. Political equality is dispensed with in favor of open acceptance of political inequality. Government by consent of the governed becomes government by the power of the governor. The opponents of pluralism thus see it as a repudiation of the American Revolution.

So proceeds the controversy.

2 THE CONSTITUTION

Unrestrained political authority, though it be confided to masses, cannot be trusted without positive limitations, men in bodies being but an aggregation of the passions, weaknesses, and interests of men as individuals.

James Fenimore Cooper

Origins

The situation in the new American states after they had gained their independence from England seemed to call for some form of federal union. Because there was as yet no American nation and each state was independent and jealous of its prerogatives, unanimous approval of all thirteen was required if they were to be bound together in any semblance of a federation. It therefore is not surprising that the first ties binding the states to one another were loose and placed hardly any power with the central government. These ties were the Articles of Confederation, and they left the states as the primary centers of power.

In September 1774, prior to the outbreak of hostilities, delegates from twelve of the colonies met to form the Continental Congress. Its resolution had no effect on British policy. The Second Continental Congress met in May 1775, after the war had begun, to coordinate and direct the military efforts of the colonies. All thirteen sent delegates, and each colony had one vote. This Congress adopted the Declaration of Independence on July 4, 1776, and quickly began work upon what came to be the Articles of Confederation, which it submitted to the states for ratification in November of 1777. By 1779, all of the states had ratified the document except for Maryland, which delayed its approval until March of 1781, when other states had ceded certain western lands to the nation. With Maryland's approval, the Articles became effective.

The Articles established a central government consisting solely of a unicameral Congress in which each state delegation had one vote. Important actions required the approval of nine states, and amendment of the Articles required the assent of all thirteen. There was no separate executive or judiciary, although Congress was given limited judicial functions regarding marine matters and interstate disputes. Initially Congress created committees as needed for executive actions but soon found it necessary to appoint permanent departments under its control. The "president" was not the chief executive but rather the presiding officer of the Congress. The Articles declared that "each state retains its sovereignty, freedom, and independence" and that the states had entered into a "league of friendship with each other" (Articles II and III).

Clearly, the government that the Articles established was more a consultative council serving to reflect the views of the states than it was the government of a nation. The arrangement was a league of largely independent units, not a nation state in the modern sense. The greatest difficulty appears to have been finance. The Congress could place levies on states for funds to operate, but there was no way it could enforce payment. All attempts to enact a tariff to provide a source of national revenue failed. Such an action required unanimous approval of all the states, and at least one state or another always would oppose the tariff. Moreover, Congress had no authority over citizens, who were subject only to the governments of their respective states.

Considering the circumstances, a good deal was accomplished under the Articles. Such agencies as the departments of Foreign Affairs, War, and Finances, all of which Congress created in 1781, could well have evolved into a cabinet government. This parliamentary form might have been more efficient in many ways than the present government. With the cession of western lands to the nation, moreover, the United States came to be something more than a mere league of sovereign and independent states; there now were national lands. The most significant governmental action of this period was the adoption of the Northwest Ordinance of 1787. This act prohibited slavery in the Northwest Territory (the national lands north of the Ohio River) and established an orderly procedure for the admission to the confederation of states created from the region. Ultimately, the Territory became the states of Ohio, Indiana, Illinois, Michigan, and Wisconsin. This innovative approach to the handling of territorial areas not only set a precedent for future development of states carved from other national lands, but also for the evolution of colonial units into self-governing nations elsewhere in the world. Additionally, the Ordinance provided a bill of rights guaranteeing contracts, jury trials, freedom of religion, and the right of habeas corpus for inhabitants of the Territory. When the new government took charge of the nation after the adoption of the Constitution, it re-adopted the provisions of this great Ordinance. The prohibition of slavery in the Northwest Territory was one of the most important actions of the Congress under the Articles of Confederation. It set the tone for much of the future development of western lands, and, if Congress had gone further and had adopted Jefferson's suggestion that slavery be prohibited in all western lands, north and south, it might have averted much of the severe sectional strife that later developed. Unfortunately it did not.

Despite the accomplishments, definite inadequacies were apparent in the political arrangements. Because it had been granted so little power, it would have been difficult for the central authority to function as a true government under the best of circumstances, and the circumstances were not the best. Moreover, one flaw in the Articles of Confederation was fatal. Congress had no way to enforce sanctions upon either citizens or states and thus could not exercise effectively even the limited powers it was supposed to have. Many leaders, especially those who favored strong central power and a greater national identity, concluded that the government was far too weak to continue unchanged.

Delegates from all of the states except Rhode Island met in Philadelphia in 1787 to discuss the Articles of Confederation and to suggest changes that would remedy the weaknesses and encourage a viable national government. Despite the limited purpose of the Convention, the delegates quickly concluded that the nation's difficulties could be eliminated more effectively by a new governmental structure than by one that attempted to preserve the arrangements of the Confederacy. Just as the new nation had come into being with a violent reaction against authority that led to a revolution, so the first stable and enduring government grew from disobedience to authority. The delegates ignored the orders that they had received and produced one of the most remarkable documents in the political history of the world, the United States Constitution.

The Constitution was the result of a series of hard fought compromises as well as basic agreements. Ultimately, all thirteen states approved the new document, but only after considerable debate with fierce, often bitter, controversy over ratification in several of the states, and only after those who were skeptical of the new proposals exacted a promise that the First Congress under the new government would propose a "bill of rights" for ratification by the states. The Bill of Rights, in the form of the first ten amendments, thus became a part of the new Constitution. The entire period was characterized, not only by dissension, emotion, and factional interest, but by political speculation and theorizing of an extraordinarily high order by a group of remarkable men. It was a period of ferment that produced many profound political writings and codified many enduring principles of political wisdom and morality.

In recent decades there have been persistent questions regarding the accomplishments of the Founding Fathers and their motives. In 1913, Charles A. Beard published his famous study, *An Economic Interpretation of the Constitution of the United States,* in which he contended that the prime purpose of those who designed the new government was to limit democratic tendencies and insure financial security and gain for themselves and the wealthier classes. Certainly it appears at first glance that the Constitution may be a conservative repudiation of the radicalism of the Declaration of Independence, but further consideration suggests that Professor Beard's argument overstates the case. Unquestionably, the Declaration is more "radical" and more democratic in spirit than the Constitution. The Constitution is full of checks upon the power of the people. Its rigid requirements for amendment, for example, require more than a majority and do not permit popular participation in the process. It establishes a powerful Supreme Court that is composed of appointive justices with essentially life tenure. It requires affirmative action on all legislation by a Senate that originally was not subject to popular election and that still represents areas rather than population. The Electoral College and many other features incorporated into the Constitution are far from the radical individualist spirit of the Declaration.

Nevertheless, some of the anti-democratic provisions of the Constitution can hardly be classed as reactionary. Appointive judges with lifetime tenure, for instance, enable the courts to defend liberty in situations when a democratic body might restrain it. The Constitution reflects a profound fear of concentrations of power. Its general function is to limit the power of the state, whether democratic or not, and this is, in the historical sense, profoundly liberal. The authors of the Constitution undoubtedly were influenced by personal considerations and by economic factors. Beard has performed a service in calling attention to the role of economics, which should no longer be ignored, but it seems incorrect to charge that economic issues were the sole criterion by which the authors of the Constitution shaped the new government. Similarly, it is true that the Constitution is more conservative than the Declaration, but it hardly seems to have been a "sell-out" of the principles of the Revolution, as some have alleged. The Constitution was, by the prevailing standards throughout the world, uniquely liberal, and it provided for a government that, although it was not thoroughly democratic, was based on the power of the people and was more democratic than any other.

The men who created the Constitution and worked for its adoption had faith in institutions. They believed that their goals of a just and free society could be achieved if the proper institutions could be established. Power was necessary, but it was also dangerous. Only the right balance of institutions could permit the necessary exercise of power and simultaneously prevent abuse by its wielder. The system that they designed incorporated their conceptions of what American society should be. On the fundamental questions, there was agreement. There should be a national government, and it should have sufficient power to govern adequately. But that government should also be limited. The ultimate power must rest with the people, who would exercise it through directly and indirectly elected representatives and through appointed officials. The system must in some manner be federal, permitting the existence of both national and state governments.

Such agreements on matters of fundamentals reflected a shared background and the wide acceptance of the basic tenets of American political thought. There were, nonetheless, extreme divergences of opinion on matters of specifics. There were tensions between the wealthy and the workers, between large states and small, between tidewater and backcountry, between small agriculture and large, between manufacturing and agriculture, between debtors and creditors, between slave-holding interests and the rest of the nation, between nationalists and those whose allegiance remained solely with their states, between advocates of various religions or none; in short, the variety of sources for conflict was astonishing. The Founders recognized this and worked to accommodate it. The Constitution to a considerable degree reflects both the myriad tensions and antagonisms that were prevalent and the process of compromise that gave it life. Some of the tensions have dwindled, others have arisen. Despite the national uniformity of freeways, hamburger chains, and television entertainment, the United States remains a very diverse nation. On balance, the potential for conflict probably is greater today than before. It is a testimony to the practical wisdom of the founders that their creation, splendid but not perfect, has survived to this day.

Principles

LIMITED GOVERNMENT.   The foremost principle of constitutionalism is that power shall be limited. Any constitution is a set of restrictions on the exercise of governmental power, and any nation that observes such a set of restrictions can be classed as a constitutional state. It is the performance that counts, not the form. The Soviet Union, for example, has a written constitution, but because the Soviet rulers ignore its requirements when they deem it to be in their best interests to do so, the U.S.S.R. cannot be considered a constitutional state. On the other hand, Great Britain has no single written document that could be identified as a constitution, yet it has a definite set of principles, developed in centuries of struggle, that strictly govern practice; Great Britain is, therefore, a constitutional state. Every provision of the U.S. Constitution makes explicit the notion of limitations on governmental power in general and on the power of governmental agencies in particular.

All constitutions are worthless unless the people and the officials of the government think that they should be observed and work to protect and preserve them. Although there have been numerous instances in which constitutional principles have failed to guide action in the United States, the general record is good. The pattern has been to uphold the Constitution and to observe limitations on governmental action. Limited government thus remains, as it must, the key principle of the U.S. constitutional system. The government, therefore, must respond to the values of the people and protect individual rights, not create or interpret values. Anything else would be a severe blow to the principle of limited government, hence to the Constitution itself.

POPULAR SOVEREIGNTY.   Another key principle of the American constitutional system is popular sovereignty. The people have the ultimate power, if they should choose to exercise it. They create the power and delegate it through the Constitution to the government. Of course, the people do not control the workings of the government directly, even through elections. In addition there are those checks already noted that prevent the people from controlling decisions. Nevertheless, under the Constitution the government does not create power and grant rights to the people. It is the people who permit the government to act and who are the theoretical holders of power. The basic theory that is consistently threaded throughout American political thought, and upon which the Constitution and the government are based, is that the government governs only with the consent of the people. If the people were to withdraw support from the government, it could no longer rule legitimately. This problem has not yet confronted the nation. From the beginnings of government under the present Constitution, the people have consistently supported the system. Although the Civil War may seem to be an exception, both sides even then sought to preserve what they considered to be the system that the Founding Fathers intended. They may turn against a particular party or administration, but they have never turned against the system of government.

SEPARATION OF POWERS.   One of the most basic principles of the U.S. Constitution is one that devised the "presidential" form of government, separation of powers. The Constitution provides for an elected executive, the President, who heads the executive branch with its administrative agencies, and who is chosen independently of the legislative branch, the Congress, and is not responsible to it. These two branches are supplemented by a third, the judiciary, headed by the Supreme Court. Many persons consider the three branches to be equal, but the constitution clearly gives the Congress the central power if it chooses to exercise it. Nevertheless in recent decades the presidency has overshadowed Congress, and the courts are a distant third as holders of power. Each branch has powers of its own and checks over the other two branches. There is some overlap formally, such as the role of the Vice President, who sits as President of the Senate even though he is a member of the executive. And there is considerably more informal overlap, such as the quasi-legislative and quasi-judicial functions assumed by many executive agencies in issuing regulations and hearing disputes, the holding of military reserve commissions by many members of Congress (a practice now under attack in the federal courts), and the assumption of quasi-judicial functions by Con-

"It's Called Separation Of Powers — We Separate You From Your Powers"

Copyright 1973 by Herblock in The Washington Post.

gress under certain circumstances such as the trying of impeached officials. Nevertheless, the branches retain considerable independence. The classic description of the operation of the separate branches is that they provide "checks and balances."

The Founders designed the government so that all legislation must originate from the Congress. Even here there are checks, because the Congress is bicameral—that is, divided into two houses, the Senate and the House of Representatives—and both houses must approve all laws in identical form. The President is responsible for administering the laws, and the courts adjudicate disputes and settle questions regarding matters of law. This is in contrast to the parliamentary form of democracy, in which the executive is selected by the legislature and serves at its pleasure and in which there may additionally be a considerable mixing of roles in some institutions such as the House of Lords and the Privy Council. (Each of these bodies retains certain judicial functions, although the former is a house of the legislature and the latter is essentially executive in nature.)

Many political scientists dislike the principle of separation of powers because checks and balances lead to considerable inefficiency. For example, one political party may control the presidency at the same time that the other controls the Congress. It is even possible for the Congress to be divided, with the House of one party and the Senate of another. In the parliamentary system, if the executive cannot work with the parliament, there immediately are new elections. In the presidential system, the situation continues until the next regularly scheduled election, which means that an impasse might continue for as long as four years. Even so, the system was designed deliberately to limit power, and if it raises the likelihood of inefficiency, the Founders considered this to be a small price to pay. Their purpose was, as James Madison put it in *The Federalist*, No. 51, to insure that "ambition must be made to counteract ambition." Too many have lost sight of the wisdom of this principle and have allowed ambition to feed upon and to support ambition.

In recent years, the power of the President has increased tremendously. In foreign affairs, despite the existence of separation of powers and checks and balances, he is probably the most powerful, and least accountable, official on earth. Even some of the political scientists who a few years ago criticized the possibility of governmental inefficiency resulting from checks and balances now complain that there are too few checks. Historically, the President has had a freer hand in foreign affairs than in domestic. Recently, however, the Congress appears to be finding many of its traditional checks ineffective, even where domestic matters are involved. It begins to appear as if too much power, rather than an inability to exercise power, is the greatest defect of the presidential form of government. The controls are weak, and even impeachment is so cumbersome and so serious that it has seemed virtually impossible to use successfully, especially against a president. Unless the situation were so extreme as to be critical, any threat of impeachment would be idle. The "Watergate" scandal and the accompanying revelations of political espionage and sabotage directed by the White House have caused discussion of impeachment and even introduction of impeachment resolutions into the House of Representatives.

Whether or not this results in the removal of the President, it clearly indicates the gravity of the situation.

JUDICIAL REVIEW.   Although nowhere mentioned in the Constitution, the power of judicial review must be considered one of the foremost principles of the U.S. constitutional system. Judicial review is the power of the courts to declare acts contrary to the Constitution to be void. Chief Justice John Marshall's decision in *Marbury* v. *Madison* (1803) first asserted the power to declare an act of Congress to be unconstitutional. Not only did this decision become a firm principle of American constitutional law, but there is considerable evidence to indicate that the Founding Fathers assumed that the courts would have this power by virtue of the fact that all actions must be consistent with the Constitution to be valid. If a law were inconsistent with the Constitution, the courts simply would refuse to uphold it. This is the argument that Alexander Hamilton advanced in the seventy-eighth *Federalist* paper, and it is discernible in the records of the Constitutional Convention.

Judicial review is an American development that followed logically from the existence of a written constitution. Other nations have copied the practice, until today in one form or another it is fairly widespread, in the sense that in most new nations with a written constitution based upon American or British governmental principles, the courts will be asked to exercise judicial review. Few nations, however, give the power specifically to the courts, and very few high courts have shown much willingness to exercise it, especially if it would require overruling the government. Of course, it should be pointed out that even in the United States, where judicial review is a time-honored principle, the Supreme Court has very seldom declared an act of Congress or of the federal executive to be unconstitutional and usually will go to great lengths to avoid doing so. This is because the Court must rely upon persuasion and leadership, since its power falls far short of that of the President or of the Congress. Not only does the Supreme Court lack the power to enforce its own decisions, but the Constitution gives Congress control over the Court's most significant power—the ability to hear cases appealed from lower courts. The Court is much less reluctant to strike down state laws or executive actions.

FEDERALISM.   The Founding Fathers demonstrated their originality when they devised the framework of American federalism. They saw as their urgent task the strengthening of the national government and the development of a nation state, but they did not intend to obliterate or even to weaken severely the existing states. Their solution was to provide a geographic distribution of power between a strong central government and strong constituent units, the states, with each level exercising power directly over the individual citizen within its prescribed sphere of action. The resulting federal system has served, in varying degrees, as a model for other nations throughout the world. Although the term "federal" was not a new one, the innovations of the Founding Fathers gave it new meaning. Previously, it denoted what we would today call a confederacy (see Chapter 3).

Constitutional Change

INFORMAL DEVELOPMENT.   Students of government frequently divide constitutions into two classes, rigid and flexible, depending upon the ease with which they can be amended. The Constitution of the United States is difficult to classify in these terms. Although it clearly is rigid in form—that is, it is most difficult to amend—it has been relatively easily adapted to changing conditions merely by differences in interpretation made possible by judicial review. This is partly a result of the tradition of constitutional interpretation as it developed, but it is also a function of the language of the Constitution itself. The Constitution is extraordinarily brief; it deals with broad statements of principle rather than with the details of governmental operation. It is the Fundamental Law of the nation, and the Founding Fathers were wise in limiting it, therefore, to the fundamentals. Probably no document that required constant amendment could command the lasting respect that the U.S. Constitution has enjoyed, and if it had specified government operations in detail (as, for example, the constitution of India does), even a minor change would require a formal amendment. The U.S. Constitution, in fact, has permitted considerable evolution of governmental practice with little change in the document itself, and without violation of its basic principles.

Judicial review has been responsible for much of the development, along with presidential practice, congressional action, and custom. For example, the Constitution clearly grants to the President the power of veto over legislation passed by the Congress. Until the presidency of Andrew Jackson, however, presidential vetoes were rare, and many were of the opinion that the veto would be exercised only in narrow and clearly defined cases. But President Jackson infused new power into the veto by using it whenever he desired. This changed constitutional practice without changing the Constitution as a document. Both interpretations of the veto power were consistent with the requirements of the Constitution, yet Jackson's precedent had a major effect upon the subsequent operation of the government.

Similarly, in the last few decades the Congress has adopted many pieces of legislation giving quasi-legislative powers to certain executive agencies. No formal constitutional amendment was involved, but there has been radical revision of the structure of the government and the traditional conceptions of the powers and duties of the executive and the legislative branches. The force of custom may also be seen in the position of political parties in modern America. They are so fundamental to the operation of American government that they may almost be thought of as a fundamental part of the constitutional system, yet the Constitution itself contains not one word about political parties.

So potent have some of the unwritten traditions of the presidency been that formal amendments have been passed to insure their continuance. The original Constitution, for example, specified that the powers and duties of the office of the President "shall devolve on the Vice President" in case the President dies, resigns, or is unable to "discharge the powers and duties of the said office." President William Henry Harrison died in 1841, shortly after having taken office, and for the first time this provision of Article II of the Constitution had to be applied. There was question whether the Vice President, John Tyler, actually became President or was merely to be "Acting President." Tyler settled the issue by insisting that he was President, and subsequent vice presidents who succeeded to the office were not even faced with the question. The Twenty-fifth Amendment, ratified in 1967, made this long established tradition part of the written Constitution. Section One reads, "In the case of the removal of the President from office or his death or resignation, the Vice President shall become President."

An opposite example is the case of presidential terms. After having served two terms as President, George Washington declined a third term, thereby establishing a precedent that continued until the time of Franklin D. Roosevelt, who not only broke the tradition by running for a third term but won and continued on to win a fourth. After his death, the Congress proposed the Twenty-second Amendment, placing into the language of the Constitution the two-term limitation that had existed, by custom, until 1940. The amendment was ratified in 1951 and so restricts any President after Truman.

CONSTITUTIONAL AMENDMENT.   The process of formal amendment is long and difficult. In order to be adopted, an amendment to the Constitution must first be proposed by a national body, and then ratified by three-fourths of the states. The Constitution specifies two methods of proposing amendments, but the only one that has ever been used is proposal by Congress, requiring a two-thirds vote of both the House and the Senate. The other method is by a national convention, to be called by Congress if it is requested to do so by two-thirds of the state legislatures.

Ratification must be by three-fourths of the states, and here also there are two methods. Congress specifies which is to be used. With one exception, all amendments have been approved by the state legislatures in three-fourths of the states. If Congress directs, however, the states call conventions to consider an amendment, approval by conventions in three-fourths of the states necessary to ratify. This latter method has been used only once, in the case of the Twenty-first Amendment, which repealed the Eighteenth (Prohibition) Amendment. The rural, fundamentalist forces that had supported Prohibition in the first place still were dominant in many state legislatures, and ratification by the legislatures thus was unlikely. The Congress, therefore, in this case only, specified conventions rather than legislatures for ratification, recognizing that conventions would be more reflective of the overwhelming public desire to eliminate Prohibition.

The Bill of Rights.   The first ten amendments to the Constitution form the Bill of Rights, one of the most important features of the American system of government, yet probably one of the most misunderstood. Contrary to popular opinion, the courts have consistently held that the Bill of Rights was designed to protect a citizen against actions by the national government only, not against actions of a state. The Supreme Court first ruled upon the applicability of the Bill of Rights to the states in the case of *Barron* v. *Baltimore* in 1833; Chief Justice John Marshall declared for the Court that the first ten amendments had never been intended to limit state governments.

Throughout their history, Americans have tended to fear the power of the national government and to be less concerned with the power of the states. Apparently they feel more comfortable with state governments because they believe, rightly or wrongly, that the states are easier to control since they are closer or are less dangerous because they are not as powerful. This feeling certainly is reflected in the history of the Bill of Rights, which was adopted because of fears that the new national government would encroach upon the lives of the citizens and the functioning of the states. Not all Americans shared these fears of course; the Convention avoided including a Bill of Rights at all, and many believed, Hamilton among them, that it would be superfluous to include one. Those of Hamilton's persuasion felt that since the purpose of the Constitution was to limit governmental power, the Constitution was, itself, a Bill of Rights. So pervasive were the fears of Big Government, however, that those who opposed a Bill of Rights had to agree to include one in order to persuade the states to ratify the Constitution. Chief Justice Marshall's opinion was probably consistent with the intentions of those who devised the first ten amendments (James Madison attempted to secure passage of a bill protecting citizens against state action, but it failed), and the Court has never overruled *Barron* v. *Baltimore*.

The result was that for years there was a great discrepancy between those rights that were national and those that were state. Fortunately, the situation has changed even though the first ten amendments in themselves still do not limit state action. The breakthrough came with the ratification of the Fourteenth Amendment in 1868, shortly after the Civil War. This amendment prohibits a state from making or enforcing any law "which shall abridge the privileges or immunities of citizens of the United States," from depriving "any citizen of life, liberty, or property without due process of law," or from denying "to any person within its jurisdiction the equal protection of the laws." It defines citizens as "all persons born or naturalized in the United States." For more than half a century the Court interpreted the Fourteenth Amendment so narrowly that there was no significant change in practice, but in the period of reaction during and following the First World War, when many states placed severe limitations upon freedom of speech and the press, the situation became potentially so oppressive that the Court finally was induced to act. In 1925 in *Gitlow* v. *New York*, the Court held that the freedom of speech and of the press, which the First Amendment protects from abridgment by Congress, are so fundamental to American life that they are "protected by the due process clause of the Fourteenth Amendment from impairment by the states." It is therefore the Fourteenth Amendment that protects a citizen from state action, not the Bill of Rights so far as the U.S. Constitution is concerned.

Most of the protections of the Bill of Rights have now been extended by action of the Fourteenth Amendment to limit state governments. The late Justice Hugo Black believed that the Fourteenth Amendment extends the entire Bill of Rights to protect a citizen against state action; the nearest the Supreme Court came to agreeing with him was in the case of *Adamson* v. *California* (1947), in which a minority of four justices so ruled. Of course, the state constitutions themselves contain bills of rights, most of which are similar to that in the U.S. Constitution, but the people of a state can usually amend their constitution relatively easily, so a state bill of rights is inadequate protection against inflamed public opinion. On the other hand, it is noteworthy that states on many occasions have been in advance of the federal government on a variety of issues. The Virginia Declaration of Rights, for example, was a model for the federal Bill of Rights. The present situation is that state practices with regard to freedom of speech, religion, assembly, association, search and seizure, and self-incrimination must meet the national standards set by the Supreme Court, and that the right to counsel (if necessary, to be furnished by the government) is guaranteed in both state and national criminal proceedings. The practices of the states vary from state to state and also differ from federal practice in such matters as jury trials, grand juries, and standards of procedural fairness.

It is difficult to predict what the future of the Bill of Rights and Fourteenth Amendment protections will be. Many citizens seem unconcerned, or even hostile to them. In addition, several members of the Supreme Court as constituted during the Nixon Administration have expressed disagreement with the theory that has extended the limitations to state governments. They will certainly not support additional extensions and might perhaps vote to rescind some of the extensions that now do limit the states.

The Bill of Rights includes those limits upon the central government and guarantees of individual liberty from governmental encroachment that the citizens of the early republic believed to be necessary to the maintenance of a free society, and for which they fought a revolution.

The First Amendment protects the core freedoms, freedom of worship, speech, press, and peaceable assembly. It also provides for the separation of church and state and for the citizen's right to petition the government. The Second Amendment secures the right to a citizen's militia, which illustrates that there was a widespread fear of a standing military force as a threat to a free society. Constitutional authorities deny that it guarantees that individual citizens may purchase, own, or bear firearms. Despite this there is often more outcry over the "sacred" guarantees of the Second Amendment than over infringements of other rights listed that truly are basic to a free society.

The Third and Fourth Amendments deal with the right of privacy. The Third protects against requiring citizens to provide food and shelter for soldiers in peacetime and limits such requirements in time of war. The Fourth secures the rights of the people to protection against unreasonable searches and regulates judicial procedures.

The Fifth, Sixth, Seventh, and Eighth Amendments set forth the rights of persons accused of crimes and require strict procedures to protect both persons and property from arbitrary actions. These amendments establish the basic rules of fairness in judicial proceedings, specifying that no person shall be required to testify against himself, that trials must be speedy, that the accused must be permitted to confront his accusers, and that he must be able to compel witnesses to testify in his behalf, as the state can do for prosecution witnesses. It protects against double jeopardy, so that the person acquitted by a federal court cannot be brought to trial in another federal court on the same charge. This prevents an unscrupulous or over-zealous government from continually retrying those persons whom it wishes to condemn until it finds some court that is willing to convict. As interpreted by the courts, these amendments limit officials from obtaining confessions by trickery or coercion, they require jury trials in all criminal prosecutions and most civil cases and fairness in the selection of jury members, and they establish the right to consult with a lawyer at any stage of the proceeding. These amendments have been subject to detailed interpretation because they set forth some of the basic protections taken for granted by Americans. Consider the implications, for example, of being tried after having been accused of a criminal act, without the right to confront accusers or to compel witnesses for the defense to testify, while the prosecution has full powers of subpoena. Such things have occurred in the past in state courts and were frequent in colonial days.

The Ninth Amendment takes care to insure that the mere fact that a liberty is not mentioned in the Bill of Rights does not indicate that it is not a right of the people. It could be cited, for example, as a device to protect the people from governmental damage to the environment. The Tenth was added to protect the states from the accretion of too much power on the part of the central government.

The Other Amendments.   Although the Constitution is nearly two hundred years old, and political and economic conditions are unbelievably different from those existing at the time of its writing, by early 1974 there had been only twenty-six amendments. The first ten amendments came so soon after the Constitution itself that they may almost be considered a part of the original document. The remaining sixteen produced considerable changes, some major and some minor.

The Eleventh Amendment, ratified in 1798, was the first adopted after the Bill of Rights and is designed to prevent a person from bringing suit against a state in a federal court without the consent of the state involved. This was a reaction to the Supreme Court's ruling in *Chisholm* v. *Georgia* (1793) that federal courts could accept a suit brought against a state by a citizen of another state, which the states feared would give the federal judiciary too much power over their affairs. The Twelfth Amendment was adopted in 1804 to prevent a repetition of the confusion that occurred in the presidential election of 1800 when there was a tie vote between Thomas Jefferson and Aaron Burr who were candidates for President and Vice President of the same party. This occurred because the original constitutional provision required the Electoral College to vote for President and Vice President simultaneously without distinguishing their votes. The election was thrown into the House of Representatives where there was considerable unpleasant maneuvering before Jefferson finally emerged as the winner. The Twelfth Amendment established a new arrangement that provided for separate votes for President and Vice President, thus preventing the inevitable tie votes and adapting the Constitution to the rise of a party system with each party offering a slate of candidates for both offices.

There were no more amendments until after the Civil War, which resulted in three more. The Thirteenth, ratified in 1865, abolished slavery. The Fourteenth came three years later and is one of the most important parts of the Constitution. Among other things, as discussed earlier, it established a national basis for citizenship and provided protections for civil rights and liberties against state encroachment. Its major purpose was to insure the freedoms of the newly freed blacks and to extend citizenship to them. The year 1870 saw the last of the Civil War amendments, the Fifteenth, which prohibited restrictions on the right to vote based upon race or color. As history indicates, it takes more than a constitutional amendment to insure action; black citizens were routinely denied the right to vote throughout much of the South until at least the mid-1960's.

The next two amendments, both ratified in 1913, were the result of the ferment of the late nineteenth and early twentieth centuries that had brought forth strong third parties, such as the Populists, and led to the Progressive Movement. The Sixteenth Amendment secured the right of the national government to adopt an income tax, and overturned the 1895 Supreme Court decision that had denied the government this power, *Pollock* v. *Farmers' Loan and Trust Co.* The Seventeenth took away from state legislatures the power to elect senators and provided for their direct popular election.

The Eighteenth Amendment of 1919 was the disastrous Prohibition amendment, which led to the beginnings of truly organized crime in this country and greatly increased the national disregard for law and order.

The ratification of the Nineteenth Amendment in 1920 guaranteed to women that they would be admitted to the vote on the same basis as men and was the largest single extension of the democratic principle in the history of the Constitution.

The Twentieth and Twenty-first Amendments were both ratified in 1933. The Twentieth revised the beginning dates of presidential terms and congressional sessions; it shortened the period after an election before the new office holders assumed power to eliminate the long "lame duck" situation, and it clarified certain points pertaining to presidential succession. The Twenty-first repealed the Eighteenth Amendment and thereby eliminated national Prohibition, but (probably as the price of adoption) it guaranteed any state that wished the right to prohibit the importation, transportation, or use of liquor.

The Twenty-second Amendment, restricting a President to two terms in office, did not come until 1951. The next amendment, the Twenty-third, came a decade later, in 1961, and granted the right to vote for President and Vice President to residents of the District of Columbia by providing the District for the first time with electors in the Electoral College. This extension of democracy was followed in 1964 by the Twenty-fourth Amendment, which denied the states the right to restrict voting in federal elections through the use of a poll tax.

The Twenty-fifth Amendment, adopted in 1967, empowers the President to fill the office of Vice President, if it becomes vacant, contingent upon the approval of his choice by both houses of Congress. It also provides procedures—rigidly restricted, of course—by which the Vice President may exercise the powers of the President under certain conditions in which the President may be physically or mentally incapable of exercising them himself.

The latest amendment, the Twenty-sixth, was ratified in 1972. In yet another great extension of the democratic principle, it lowered the voting age to eighteen. In early 1974 the proposed Twenty-seventh Amendment, prohibiting legal, economic, or political discrimination on the basis of sex (the "Equal Rights Amendment"), was under consideration by the state legislatures.

The Constitution Today: Shield Against Arbitrary Government?

As the press of population and the call for increased security, both domestic and external, become greater, the likelihood of arbitrary government increases considerably. The judiciary generally is the thin black line between the citizen and improper actions by his government. This is not to imply that the government is filled with persons eager to stifle liberty. Most officials of the government, elected, appointed, or career, are decent persons who desire only to perform their tasks well. The more subtle and more frequent difficulty stems from insensitivity to the demands of constitutional procedures on the part of both government and governed. The measures that lead to arbitrary government may be the result as much of popular demand as of a desire of ambitious officials for more power.

The task of a free society is always to insure the rights of the community without violating the rights of individual citizens. In the wake of increasing concern over airline hijacking, for example, every person who flies on a commercial airline is now subject to personal search. The average citizen probably favors this practice, believing that the increase in his personal security outweighs the invasion of his personal privacy. However, Senator Vance Hartke of Indiana, for example, considers the searches to be a violation of constitutional rights, as does the columnist William

Shadowed

from Herblock's State of the Union (*Simon & Schuster, 1972*)

Buckley. This is the kind of judgment that continually faces free societies. How much protection is necessary, and how much may liberty and privacy be restricted to achieve it? Many interest groups are actively involved in this struggle over security and rights.

The airline example is a small instance and one over which there is not very much controversy. But the important question is: How concerned are the people and the government about constitutional protections when they are not immediately affected? Unless there is general concern, and unless the issues are recognized for what they are, the protections of the Constitution may quietly and slowly be eroded. Such erosion may result from the people's fears as much as from the government's desires. Not that any given action is bad, or is unjustified, but small actions create a pattern that could lead to an invasion of the most fundamental of the liberties that the Founding Fathers designed the Constitution to protect.

As mentioned earlier, no constitution can protect the rights of individual citizens unless the citizens offer it support. In a time such as this, when there are threats to constitutional protections from both the populace and governmental officials, it becomes all the more necessary to stress the fragile nature of constitutions. It is important that the people themselves are alert to every invasion, deliberate or inadvertent, of personal and group liberties. This is essential if constitutional democracy as we have known it is to survive.

Suggested Readings

Bernard Bailyn, *The Ideological Origins of the American Revolution* (Cambridge: The Belknap Press of Harvard University Press, 1967)

Charles A. Beard, *An Economic Interpretation of the Constitution of the United States* (New York: Macmillan, 1956, first published in 1913)

Max Beloff, *The American Federal Government* (New York: Oxford, 1959)

Roy P. Fairfield, ed., *The Federalist Papers* (Garden City: Doubleday, 1961)

Carl J. Friedrich and Robert G. McCloskey, *From the Declaration of Independence to the Constitution* (New York: Bobbs-Merrill, 1954)*

Forrest McDonald, *We the People* (Chicago: University of Chicago Press, 1965); a massive rebuttal of the Beard thesis

* Available in paperback

C. Herman Prichett, *The American Constitution* (New York: McGraw-Hill, 2nd ed., 1968); one of the most thorough treatments of American constitutional development

Clinton Rossiter, *The Political Thought of the American Revolution* (New York: Harvest Books, 1963)*

E. E. Schattschneider, *Two Hundred Million Americans in Search of a Government* (New York: Holt, Rinehart and Winston, 1969)*

Benjamin F. Wright, *Consensus and Continuity* (Boston: Boston University Press, 1958)

* Available in paperback

3

FEDERALISM AND NATIONALISM
The Development of
the American Nation

Every state is a community of some kind, and every community is established with a view to some good.

Aristotle

But there is no perfect harmony in human nature.

Margaret Fuller

The Federal Union

When the authors of the U.S. Constitution established the outline of the American federal system, they devised a scheme that has indelibly shaped the whole of American political development and has been widely copied in other nations. In all probability, they had no clear idea of the direction that the new system would take, and they had no precedents to guide them; they were forced to innovate. How could they create a nation that would truly be a nation, without arousing the fears and jealousies of thirteen separate states, each virtually a nation in itself? Federalism was their answer.

It was obvious that there would have to be some form of geographic distribution of power. The states were political and historical entities dating back to the colonial charters granted by the English crown; neither the historical setting nor the preferences of the citizens would have permitted any move toward a unitary government. Under a unitary form of government, which Britain and France were developing, one central government has authority to govern a nation without intervening political subdivisions (variously called states, provinces, cantons, *Länder*, or republics). On the other hand, the experience under the only other form then existing, a confederacy, had been unsatisfactory. A confederacy is more a league of nearly independent units than a nation state as we think of one today. The true power lies with the subdivisions. The central authority, if any, is very weak and has no direct jurisdiction over the citizens of the subdivisions.

Because the only existing alternatives appeared to be impractical, the Founding Fathers were forced to create a new form that would, they hoped, combine the energetic central government of a unitary system with the strong subdivisions of a confederacy. The new form took the name of "federalism," which gave new meaning to an old word, previously synonymous with "confederacy." The citizen henceforth would be subject not merely to a state, as under the Articles of Confederation, and not merely to a central government, as were Englishmen, but to two governments, state and national, each "sovereign" with regard to its allotted jurisdiction. The American federal system retained strong states with powers that the national government could not abolish and added a strong national government with powers that were safe from action by the states. Each level of government had direct authority over the individual citizen and could levy taxes and enforce penalties.

The U.S. Constitution is the source of authority for all governments in the United States. It specifically "delegates" certain powers to the national government, giving it exclusive jurisdiction to perform national functions, such as coining money, declaring war, regulating interstate and foreign commerce, and conducting foreign policy. Other powers that it delegates to the national government, such as the power to tax, confer concurrent jurisdiction—that is, they are powers that both national and state governments may exercise. The Constitution forbids certain powers to the national government, others to the states, and yet others to both. Nowhere does it list the powers of the states. These are considered to be "reserved," and, under the Tenth Amendment, every power not delegated to the national government or prohibited to the states is reserved to the states or the people. Each state has its own constitution, which confers powers upon the government of the state, under the framework of the U.S. Constitution, and structures the exercise of those powers. Every state law must be consistent with that state's constitution, and all state constitutions must be consistent with the U.S. Constitution.

Each of the states has a complete government, exercising legislative, executive, and judicial powers. Although most states are divided into counties, the counties are not autonomous political subdivisions; the state creates them and could eliminate them, as some states have; the cities also are not autonomous in any way but are totally subordinate to the

FIGURE 1. Territorial Structure of Governments

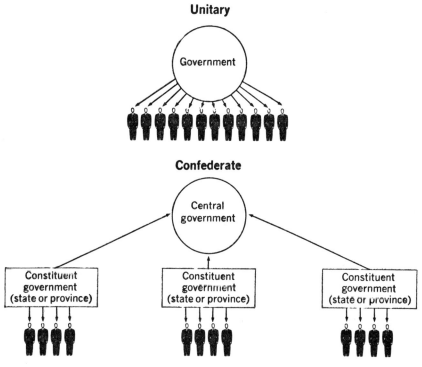

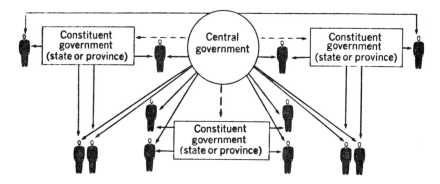

———▶ Direction of authority
— — ▶ Direction of authority when exercised within limited jurisdiction

state. In fact, a state has a miniature form of unitary government and could function quite well so far as internal politics is concerned, with no change in its governmental structure if it suddenly were to become an independent nation. Yet under the federal system, another authority, the national government, also governs the same territory that the state governs, and neither under the Constitution is permitted to infringe upon the powers of the other.

Such a highly complicated system requires some mechanism for settling disputes, not only between a state and the national government, but between neighboring states. This mechanism is the federal court system, usually the U.S. Supreme Court. So long as it stays within the limits of its powers under the Constitution, the national government is supreme. Under the terms of Article VI, federal laws and treaties are the "supreme law of the land," although they may not conflict with the Constitution as interpreted by the Supreme Court; any state law, even if otherwise within the state's power to enact, that conflicts with federal law or treaty is invalid.

There is little today that remains exclusively under the jurisdiction of the states because the interpretations of the Constitution by the Supreme Court, beginning soon after the nation's founding, have tended toward the expansion of national powers. States today set their own tax policies, exercise police powers, and establish their own educational, health, and welfare systems. Even in these traditionally state activities, there is considerable federal participation through grants-in-aid, the single largest source of revenue for every state, which require that the state functions meet federal standards. The exclusively state functions must also meet constitutional requirements, which gives the federal courts jurisdiction over them in certain situations.

This does not mean that federalism is dying or that the states are not vigorous, thriving political entities. State governments are growing at a rapid rate and, like local and national governments, constantly perform more functions.

The states today have dual identities: they are governmental entities with powers and responsibilities of their own, and they voluntarily act as administrative arms for many federal-state cooperative programs. Any person who believes that the national government ignores the states, or that it seeks to reduce their powers wherever possible, should spend some time in a federal agency in Washington. Generally, the mere hint that

FIGURE 2. Governmental Powers in the United States

State	Concurrent	National
Regulate commerce within state	Taxation	Regulation of interstate and foreign commerce
Create counties or districts for local rule	Regulate health and public safety	
Regulate political parties	Pollution control	Declaration of war
Regulation of marriage and divorce	Consumer protection	Making of treaties
Establish systems of public education	Regulation of public utilities	Coining of money
Establish electoral districts	Etc.	Etc.
Etc.		

an action might incur broad displeasure among state agencies sends federal bureaucrats scurrying for cover.

There are very few purely federal domestic programs; most require state involvement, and active state cooperation. Although generalizations are dangerous, it probably is safe to say that federal agencies, as a rule, are *too* sensitive to state desires, rather than not sensitive enough, a situation that often permits the continuation of such things as racial segregation in the public schools and discriminatory welfare practices based upon state or regional prejudice. Lack of action on the part of Congress has often allowed these and similar violations of constitutional requirements to continue until the federal courts have been forced to act. Even when Congress and the courts have acted, the timidity of the bureaucracy, or a lack of interest or even a covert hostility on the part of the administration, can delay considerably the righting of the wrongs.

The federal principle is rooted firmly in American governmental institutions. The Senate, where every state is equally represented, expresses the purest form of federalism, but other institutions of government reflect the federal principle in varying degrees. The U.S. House of Representatives, for example, was designed to represent the people, not the states, and representatives are allotted to the states on the basis of their population. Nevertheless, the fact that each state, no matter how small, is entitled to one representative means that even the "peoples' branch," the House, to some extent must reflect the existence of states. The Electoral College also is based within the states, reflecting both population size and the states as units, since each state is entitled to the same number of electors as it has members of Congress. In the event that the Electoral College fails to select a President, the selection falls to the House of Representatives, where, however, each state delegation, regardless of its size, may cast only one vote. The political parties themselves are based in the states and are considerably stronger at the state and local levels than at the national level. Therefore, although the balance of powers has shifted considerably toward the national government, there is little likelihood that federalism is on its way out.

But is this federal vitality a good thing? Has federalism outlived its usefulness? Some scholars believe that it has, and others vigorously dispute them. It is true that federalism has certain disadvantages. There may, for example, be a great divergence between the laws of one state and those of another. The drivers of interstate trucks are well aware of this, because they must be certain to meet the varying requirements of weight, height, length, and width of every state through which they will be driving, and they will be stopped in each one to be sure that they do meet them. Variations in divorce laws have also caused disputes in the past, with instances in which persons are considered to be divorced in one state but not in another. In general, however, the "full faith and credit" clause of Article IV of the Constitution insures that such inconveniences will be held to a minimum, and under normal circumstances each state must recognize the actions of other states.

The critics of federalism, though, appear to have strong arguments when they point out that the existence of states has permitted the perpetuation of injustices such as racial segregation and the infringement of various civil rights and liberties because the Bill of Rights did not limit state action. On the other hand, segregation began because the national government either was unconcerned or was sympathetic to bigotry. Under these circumstances, it could well have existed on a regional basis in a unitary state. For example, the Supreme Court decision that permitted the South and border areas to become thoroughly segregated, *Plessy* v. *Fergu-*

son (1896), occurred long after the adoption of the Fourteenth Amendment, which was designed among other things to guard against state infringement of the rights of racial minorities, and it was not until the presidency of Woodrow Wilson, well into the twentieth century, that the District of Columbia instituted formal racial segregation. The same inferences apply to state violations of other civil rights and liberties. If they, like segregation, are permitted by the Supreme Court, by the Congress, and by the President, and are approved or tolerated by the people, it would appear that the cause is not the federal structure but public attitudes.

Some dissatisfaction with federalism has come from those who see the national government of the 1960's as the leading force for justice, civil rights, and civil liberties in the American political system. This perception of the role of the national government during that period is correct, as is the recognition of the reactionary nature of many state governments throughout much of American history, especially the 1950's and 1960's. Less known and little recognized, however, is the role played by many of the state governments themselves in leading the national government in the fields of justice, civil rights, and civil liberties. The Supreme Court of the State of California, for example, is one of the most enlightened judicial bodies in the nation and has led the U.S. Supreme Court on many decisions, such as in abolishing capital punishment; even today the California court is far beyond the national Court in the judgment of many judicial scholars, who point to its recent decision that property taxes are inequitable as a means of funding the public schools. Similarly, many states such as Minnesota and Colorado had legislation establishing civil rights for racial minorities far earlier than the first truly significant federal civil rights legislation of 1964. The state of Wyoming admitted women to the vote almost thirty years before the Nineteenth Amendment. There are controversies today between the national government and state governments that wish to set certain health, safety and quality standards higher than those required by Washington. For example, the federal government is seeking, successfully, it appears, to prevent states from requiring safety provisions for nuclear power plants more rigorous than those required by the Atomic Energy Commission (whose standards some states and prominent scientists have criticized as dangerously lax); federal agencies have also moved to prevent some states from enforcing noise restrictions at airports that exceed federal standards, or from insisting that bacon and

hot dogs be of higher quality than that required by the federal government (which permits them to consist overwhelmingly of fat and water).
It is easy to identify instances of recalcitrant states being forced by federal
action to humanize their policies and to abide by the U.S. Constitution.
It is easy to overlook other instances when states have been in advance of
the federal government, which at times has even retarded the development of progressive policies within the states.

Federalism has been accused of being cumbersome and inefficient. It is
these things, but this is not necessarily a disadvantage. A government that
is too efficient may be dangerous, and, if too much inefficiency can create
tremendous social and political problems, so can too much efficiency.
Federalism is another way of separating governmental powers so that they
are not all in one hand. It is probable, as the proponents of federalism
believe, that it would make it somewhat more difficult for a political
leader who is willing to violate the constitutional restrictions upon his
power to gain dictatorial control. It is also true, as critics point out, that
federalism tends to delay many needed social programs because of disputes about who should do what.

Some adherents of federalism assert that it helps bring the administration of programs closer to the people because most federal programs
are administered by the states. This is consistent with the views of the
early democratic theorists, who believed that the people would be more
concerned with local and state governments and would be better able to
follow their activities. For some reason, however, this has not proved to be
the case. The high level of corruption in many local and state governments attests to the general lack of concern with them, as does the fact
that elections with national issues at stake, especially presidential elections,
routinely bring out a much higher voter participation than do other
elections. It is questionable whether the average citizen is any better informed about a state program than about one administered directly from
Washington.

Some of the solid advantages of federalism are that it can provide
political experience at the state and local level for future national leaders
and that it can permit states to experiment with and assess programs before they are adopted by other states or nationwide. When the national
government adopted the Social Security Act in 1935, for instance, it included a provision for Old Age Assistance to help states pay pensions to
the elderly who were in need; Wisconsin had begun such payments

decades before and had been followed by several other states, thus giving experience upon which the federal planners could rely.

The most obvious advantage of federalism is that it can help to adjust governmental requirements to local or regional conditions. This is especially true in countries that have varied ethnic, linguistic, or religious groupings concentrated by region. Generally speaking, the United States has no regionally distributed groupings of this kind, but there are substantial cultural differences between regions originally based on ethnic and other distinctions, making Texas, for example, very different from Vermont; moreover, federalism appears to offer some advantages because of the sheer size of the nation, which makes some sort of administrative subdivisions almost a necessity.

It should be evident that American federalism has evolved to such an extent that it would hardly be recognized by the Framers. This has been a long process, with only one dramatic and sudden development, the Civil War. It is to be expected that a system that was designed as an innovation, and was more or less the result of a pragmatic compromise, would change considerably, not only as the nation gained experience with it, but as the conditions of life changed through time. The Framers seemed to expect this by designing the provisions of federalism in the Constitution in very general terms, which would allow and encourage change. Although it has changed, the system nevertheless remains truly federal, that is, there are stong state governments that the national government cannot eliminate, and the states retain powers that are safe from interference by the national government; conversely, the national government cannot be eliminated by the states, nor can they infringe upon its powers. Some states originally asserted the right to "nullify" the operations of federal laws within their territory, or to "interpose" state power to shield citizens from the federal government. Such doctrines were never accepted legally and were laid to rest by the Civil War. To be sure, some southern states exhumed them after the Supreme Court outlawed school segregation, but this was mere breast beating on the part of a few state officials.

Not every nation that appears on paper to be federal meets the criteria outlined above. There are many truly federal states in the world in addition to the United States, such as Canada, Australia, Switzerland, and the German Federal Republic (West Germany). There are others that are federal in structure but not truly federal in practice. Brazil, for example, has varied, depending upon the government in power, between a federal state and one in which the national government removes most, if not all, power from the states. Nevertheless, its formal structure appears similar to that of the United States. The U.S.S.R. is another interesting case. Each constituent republic is guaranteed autonomy by the Soviet Constitution, but the Constitution permits the central government to retain such tight control that it even approves the budgets of the constituent units. Therefore, although the structure is designed to be truly federal, and many of the formal constitutional and legal provisions ostensibly preserve the federal structure, the Soviet system in many respects functions almost as if it were unitary.

The Growth of National Power

In the early years of the nation there was great controversy between those who believed that the national government's powers were limited to those clearly specified in the Constitution, and those who argued that the Constitution itself "implied" certain powers that could be inferred from those that were listed. The "strict constructionists," led by Jefferson, insisted that it would be dangerous to accept the interpretations that the "loose constructionists," led by Hamilton, continually put forth.

The argument burst forth in full bloom when Hamilton, as Secretary of the Treasury, proposed that the national government charter a national bank. In 1791, President Washington requested Jefferson, his Secretary of State, to prepare an opinion as to the proposed bank's constitutionality. Jefferson argued that nowhere in the Constitution was there authority permitting the national government to issue a charter, and that to do so would expand its powers more than the Constitution intended; the government was limited to those powers specifically *noted* in the Constitution. In rebuttal, Hamilton prepared a closely reasoned document justifying the doctrine of *implied* powers, saying that any power that the Constitution enumerated was directed toward an end, and that any means to that end, unless specifically forbidden by the Constitution, were therefore also permitted. Washington accepted Hamilton's argument and, when Congress passed the act establishing the bank, signed it into law.

Although the national government created a bank, the controversy over strict versus loose construction of the Constitution continued, despite the fact that Jefferson, after he became President, used the doctrine of implied powers to justify such things as the annexation of Louisiana in 1803 and the embargo of foreign trade in 1807. If there ever had been doubt as to the eventual outcome, the Supreme Court tipped the balance. Several decisions handed down under the influence of the great Chief Justice John Marshall strengthened the national government and encouraged the nationalizing tendencies. The classic expression of the Court's preferences came in 1819 in the case of *McCulloch* v. *Maryland*. The Chief Justice wrote that although the government is one of strictly limited powers, if the goal is constitutional, then any means to that goal, if they are consistent with the goal and are not forbidden by the Constitution, are also constitutional. This decision, which denied the State of Maryland the power to tax a branch of the Bank of the United States, has become a firm fixture in American constitutional law.

It was the Civil War that finally laid to rest most of the questions regarding national supremacy. The Constitution plainly declares, in Article VI, that treaties and federal laws, so long as they are consistent with the Constitution, are to be the "supreme law of the land" and that they also bind state judges. Before the Civil War, some had argued for the right of secession as the final recourse of a state that opposed national policy, but the Civil War settled the issue. The Fourteenth Amendment, which followed the War, provided the basis for national citizenship and strengthened the federal judiciary's power to review state actions to force compliance with national policy. For years the courts restricted their interpretations of the Fourteenth Amendment, limiting its impact on the states, but in the last few decades it has become the vehicle for national insistence upon a system of civil rights and liberties for Americans regardless of state policy.

The Great Depression of the thirties intensified national power by presenting the nation with such tremendous difficulties that only the national government could possibly be strong enough to deal with them. Following quickly upon the Depression was World War II, which required even more national power. The years that have followed this war have seen the continuation of a wartime state because of "cold war" tensions, the demands of world leadership, and the fears of many that America is ever in danger of becoming weak. No nation in modern times can fight a major war without devoting considerable time and energy to it on a national basis. The demands of war and of defense in a world that fears war are by far the greatest forces that strengthen nationalizing tendencies. Those who favor less federal government and more military forces are asking the impossible; the military is part of the government. The economic centralization brought about by the Great Depression was considerable, but that caused by the Second World War and the military policies of the postwar years, including Korea and Vietnam, make the centralizing tendencies of the Depression pale into insignificance by contrast.

There are, of course, forces other than political that have encouraged the tendencies toward centralization in this country. The automobile (with its interstate highway system) and the computer, to name only two, have revolutionized our lives and the character of the nation with no planning or forethought whatsoever; some of the most significant forces in the contemporary world are completely beyond democratic control. Developments in communications—the telephone, movies, radio, and television—similarly have strengthened centralizing tendencies by reducing regional differences.

Recently there have been calls to return some power and responsibility to the states, to curb the nation's centralizing tendencies. Until the last few years, most such concerns were thinly disguised excuses for racism or were attempts to justify attitudes based upon selfish interests. Now, however, many who earlier advocated strengthening the powers of the national government have concluded that the government sufficiently strong to accomplish their goals may also be sufficiently strong to work against them and to become repressive. Whether these fears are justified only time will tell; whether, if they are, it is too late to change direction, again only time will tell.

The Growth of Nationalism

Originally, white Americans were nothing but transplanted Europeans. They brought with them European ideals, outlooks, and practices, which they modified to make more or less consistent with the new and primitive environment. By the time of the Revolution, a change had occurred. No longer were Americans local representatives of other societies and cultures; they had instead developed a strong national consciousness and a thriving new culture of their own. It is not possible to determine at what point in history Americans became conscious of themselves as American, but many factors clearly contributed to the development of a specifically American character.

At the close of the Revolution, Crevecoeur, a French immigrant to

America, asked in his *Letters from an American Farmer* the question, "What, then, is this American, this new man?" He answered that everything here regenerated those who had been European into something new, a new man with a new psychology that differentiated the American from the European. With a vastly greater potential for movement, both socially and geographically, the American was less rooted to the soil than was his European counterpart, but he nonetheless had a greater stake in society. In a land permeated by democratic theory, he conceived of the nation and the government as his own.

Paradoxically, it is the very mobility and rootlessness of Americans, a people to some extent cut off from their ties with the past and who had carved out a new world in the Western Hemisphere, that have encouraged the development of a particular kind of nationalism. In 1893, the historian Frederick Jackson Turner read a paper entitled "The Significance of the Frontier in American History" at a meeting of historians in Chicago. Turner's "Frontier Thesis" sought to explain the development of the American character by attributing it to the existence of a frontier that continually called Americans forth from the cities to the American West. He concluded that it was the westward movement with its wilderness experience that developed the American qualities of self-reliance and democracy.

Turner's thesis is inadequate in many respects, and it ignores how Americans were, and are, connected to the rest of the world, but it is noteworthy that it immediately struck a responsive chord in the hearts of Americans, and for a time it seemed to be a complete explanation. It told Americans that historians had concluded what they had known instinctively all along, that they were unique, that they were totally separate from the old and corrupt institutions of Europe, that they could make their own way in the world. And make their own way they did. They swept across a continent, virtually exterminating the Indians as they went. They seized, purchased, or negotiated for a vast expanse of land that had been owned by others, from Florida, through the huge interior region of the Louisiana Purchase, on to the Pacific coast, taking Texas and the arid lands of the Southwest in passing. Not even the ocean stopped them, as they pressed onward to accumulate the distant lands of Alaska and Hawaii. Wherever Americans went, they carried their traditions and institutions with them, ultimately carving new states from all these territories.

This movement to acquire new land and to incorporate it into a new

American empire came to take the name "Manifest Destiny." Americans, from the highest government leaders to the everyday man in the street, believed that it was America's destiny to engulf the continent, to bring enlightenment to "inferior" peoples, to spread the benefits of American civilization, and to expand the American Union. Before the end of the nineteenth century, the United States had spread from the Atlantic to the Pacific.

Manifest Destiny, in its classic form, was ended by completion, but the thirst for expansion was not dead. The impulses that had fed it in the middle of the 1880s resurged in the 1890s to continue into the twentieth century as open imperialism. Because of its intense nationalism and its tremendous wealth and resources, the United States succeeded in annexing Hawaii, seizing the Philippines, wresting Cuba from Spain and reducing it for a time to a virtual American possession, interfering (along with other countries) with the sovereignty and internal affairs of China, and asserting the right to police the manners and morals of the Latin American nations.

Nationalism has become one of the major forces in world affairs, often overshadowing everything else including social class and economic and political considerations. It seems characteristic to the modern world that all peoples are intensely nationalistic. Marxists long assumed that the interests of the working classes, for example, would lead workers of various nations to unite against capitalists. In reality, the forces of nationalism have become so strong that there is relatively little cross-national social and political current. Even the so-called "wars of national liberation" tend to be self-consciously nationalistic movements.

Intense nationalism developed early in the United States, partly, it seems, as a reaction to the European institutions from which many of the early American settlers fled. Throughout our history, it has taken varied forms. It has led to some of the most impressive acts of international generosity in world history, such as the Marshall Plan, which helped to re-build a Europe that had been ravaged by war, just as it has upon occasion led to irrationalities, such as the excesses of the McCarthy period, the removal of Americans of Japanese ancestry to concentration camps during the Second World War, and the Palmer raids of the post-World War I era.

Americans have much to be proud of. American political thought has been an enlightening force throughout the world for two hundred years. American economic accomplishments are probably the most impressive

Copyright © 1956 by Walt Kelly. Courtesy Publishers-Hall Syndicate.

that the world has ever known. But American pride can lead to contradictions, such as that pointed out by Mark Twain and other critics of American imperialism in the Philippines early in the twentieth century. How can a democratic nation maintain democratic ideals at home and subvert them elsewhere? Can democracy stop (as politics is supposed to, but rarely does) at the water's edge?

Pride has led the nation into military excesses, such as the Vietnamese War, which is the longest war in American history, despite the fact that it was never declared. It is generally true that war is simply incompatible with constitutional democracy. Democracy stresses open discussion; war demands secrecy. Democracy thrives upon dissent and disagreement; war represses all opinion not consistent with the waging of the conflict. Democracy is based on the solution of problems by reason; war is based on solutions by force and violence—the greatest possible breakdown of law and order. Democracy places value on the individual; war subjects the individual to a rigid authoritarian hierarchy. Unfortunately, the same nationalism that is built on democratic theory and the American past, can, if unrestrained, lead into the very situations that are most destructive of the institutions that brought forth the nationalistic pride.

Two of the most prominent characteristics of the American character have been a sense of mission and a belief that nothing was beyond the power of the American nation to accomplish. World War I struck a blow at both of these. Americans had gone into the war with highly idealistic aims; they had intended to "make the world safe for democracy." Instead, there was repression at home, with a Sedition Act making it a crime to criticize the government and resulting in the jailing of almost two thousand persons, and there was greed and disillusionment abroad as the victors fought for national advantage at the expense of democratic principles. Both the high idealism and the subsequent disillusionment resulted in part from Americans' naive tendency to accept views so over-simplified that they failed to understand the significance of world happenings.

America then turned inward, with the Senate refusing to grant President Wilson's plea to join the League of Nations. The government even incorporated into law the racist doctrines that earlier had encouraged imperialism, and it adopted restrictive immigration legislation that effectively excluded those of certain races and severely restricted the immigration of others; internally, it made no move to eliminate or reduce segregation and other racist policies, and in fact as often as not appeared to encourage them.

World War II partially restored American confidence and enabled Americans to point with pride to impressive industrial and technological feats, but the subsequent development of the Cold War and America's insistence that only the United States and the Soviet Union were "world leaders" brought further disillusionment. The oversimplified viewpoint that assumed that other nations must accept the leadership of one of the two "superpowers" reflects the general lack of awareness of the strength of nationalism in nations other than the United States; it impeded awareness of the wish of other countries, especially in the so-called developing areas, to direct their own political futures independent of the major power centers. Such failures of understanding contributed greatly to the tragic developments in Southeast Asia and, to some extent, resulted from an exaggerated nationalism that caused many leaders to misinterpret situations elsewhere in the world.

Suggested Readings

Yehoshua Arieli, *Individualism and Nationalism in American Ideology* (Baltimore: Penguin Books, 1966)*

Walter II. Bennett, *American Theories of Federalism* (University: University of Alabama Press, 1964)

Valerie Earle, ed., *Federalism: Infinite Variety in Theory and Practice* (Itasca, Ill.: F. E. Peacock, 1968)*

Daniel J. Elazar, *American Federalism: A View from the States* (New York: Thomas Y. Crowell, 2nd ed., 1972)*

Roy P. Fairfield, ed., *The Federalist Papers* (Garden City: Doubleday, 1961)

Max Lerner, *America as a Civilization* (New York: Simon and Schuster, 1957)

Michael McGiffert, ed., *The Character of Americans* (Homewood, Ill.: The Dorsey Press, 1964)*

Frederick Merk, *Manifest Destiny and Mission in American History* (New York: Vintage Books, 1963)*

Michael D. Reagan, *The New Federalism* (New York: Oxford University Press, 1972)*

Alexis de Tocqueville, *Democracy in America* (New York: Vintage Books, 2 vols., 1957)*; a classic view of American democracy in the nineteenth century

M. J. C. Vile, *The Structure of American Federalism* (London: Oxford University Press, 1961)

* Available in paperback

THE LEGISLATIVE PROCESS

Congress, the People's Branch?

It could probably be shown by facts and figures that there is no distinctly American criminal class except Congress.
Mark Twain

In every society there must be some way to formulate basic rules governing relationships among the members and between each person and the group. In modern political systems this is the legislative process that culminates in the formal passage of laws by bodies designated to act as legislatures. This process not only produces those rules necessary to preserve a cohesive community but introduces some measure of collective action in deciding upon policy; in democratic nations it provides, at least in theory, a voice for the people in the governing of the state.

Although nearly all contemporary political systems incorporate some form of collective decision-making, and some "primitive" societies have even exceeded the modern level of participation, leaders throughout human history have frequently exercised the full powers of government with little if any institutional check. The development of legislatures in the Western world is largely the result of deliberate effort to prevent one-person rule. In some societies, a group or council of some sort has functioned as the interpretor of tradition and the formulator of new rules of procedure to meet changing conditions, but these rules seem to have contributed less to the growth of legislatures than did efforts by nobles to restrict the arbitrary power of kings and to have their own interests represented in decisions of state. Gradually the legislative process as we know it evolved, serving to regulate political life and theoretically to represent the people collectively.

Types of Democratic Legislatures

In the Western democratic nations, legislatures have taken two predominant forms. The majority are parliamentary; the legislature chooses the executive, and there is no separation of powers. If there is a serious disagreement between the executive and the parliament the issue is presented to the people; there are new elections to determine whether the former leadership retains power or surrenders it to another party. Typically, there will be considerable party discipline or responsibility—that is, the party will have a large measure of control over the votes of its members in parliament. The system is designed, not only to provide the people with the opportunity to participate in deciding the major direction of governmental policies, but also to give some assurance that the government will follow the broad outlines that the winning party advocated during the elections.

Parliamentary governments are an outgrowth of the principles that evolved in England over a period of centuries and resulted in the development of the English Parliament. As a rule, they split the executive into two parts, the head of state and the head of government, but there are some exceptions (such as the arrangements in certain African states) in which the two are combined. In Great Britain, the monarch is head of state; in nonmonarchical parliamentary nations the head of state usually is designated a president. The head of state exercises primarily ceremonial functions, such as conferring the honors specified by the government, receiving ambassadors and visiting dignitaries, and otherwise performing symbolic acts. The real power lies with the head of government, who usually is called the prime minister, and it is this official, along with other ministers or department heads whom the parliament selects from among its own ranks, who truly exercises the power of the executive.

The other major type of democratic legislature is found in the United States and in those countries having a presidential form of government. The primary principle distinguishing the two forms is separation of powers. The legislature is elected for a specific term, and the president is elected separately, also for a definite period of time. Major elections cannot occur irregularly, as they may in a parliamentary system, but must take place only at prescribed times in a regular cycle. The independence of the legislature and the executive means that there may be significant disagreement for a considerable period. If this happens, the system provides no way to consult the people through new elections. Many political scientists dislike separation of powers for this reason. They believe that it can lead to deadlock in government and that the parliamentary system is more efficient. Others, however, prefer the presidential arrangement because it institutionalizes stability; there cannot be a rapid succession of governments as has sometimes happened in some parliamentary systems, such as in France under the Third and Fourth Republics and in Italy. In Italy, for example, there have been some three dozen changes in leadership since the Second World War!

A rather new form of government combines the parliamentary and presidential principles, providing a strong and independent executive superimposed upon a more or less traditional parliamentary system. Variations of this hybrid form can be seen in France under the present Fifth Republic and, until recently, in the Republic of Korea. Many of the Third World nations, such as Tanzania and Zambia, have experimented with such arrangements, although most have been overthrown. In these forms of government the president seems to be similar to the most powerful of presidents in presidential systems. Outwardly the functioning of the legislatures approximates that of legislatures in parliamentary systems, but their importance tends to be considerably diminished because of the independently powerful executive.

The Legislator: Delegate or Free Agent?

Because the legislature is the body that adopts rules binding upon the whole of society, it plays a vital role in all liberal democracies. Nevertheless, there is no firm agreement regarding the proper function of the legislator, even though political theorists frequently have concentrated upon him and his role as a representative of the people. At the one extreme are those who believe that a member of a democratically elected legislature should simply reflect the wishes of those who put him in office, that he should function as a delegate from the people to the representative body. At the other extreme is the point of view set forth so well by the conservative theorist Edmund Burke after his election to the British House of Commons in 1774. Burke indicated that the voters elected him to Parliament to represent the best interests of the nation and that he would exercise his best judgment, regardless of the wishes of the people.

To some extent the question is one of constituency. Does the legislator represent his district or the entire nation? Does he represent the desires of

Copyright © 1958 by Walt Kelly. Courtesy Publishers-Hall Syndicate.

the people or their "best interest" when the two seem to diverge? Is it proper for him to follow his judgment of what is best if he knows it to be against the people's desires? Is it honest of him not to do so? The answer inevitably depends upon the definition of democracy and may be influenced by the kind of government under study. For example, one could argue that the "delegate" interpretation is less appropriate in a parliamentary system than in a presidential system, because the people at least in theory have more frequent opportunities to check their representatives and remove those from office with whom they often disagree; in a presidential system in which people are given little opportunity to express their displeasures effectively except during regularly scheduled elections, the advocates of the "delegate" system might have stronger arguments. In the United States there is little popular discussion of these issues, and many studies indicate that legislators express considerable disagreement among themselves as to what their proper function should be.

It would seem that the notion that the representative should be purely a delegate is simply too unrealistic to be taken seriously in a large modern state. Many writers have demonstrated that the people know very little about the actual effect of their representatives within a legislature, and that even those who have some familiarity with their legislator's voting record are unlikely to know whether it truly reflects his positions; he may have worked to weaken a bill for which he voted, he may have succeeded in killing a bill before it ever reached a vote, or he may have voted against a bill that in principle he would support hoping that he may thereby work for a stronger one. The possibilities are endless. The "will of the people" is probably even more difficult to ascertain. The science of polling can provide considerable information, but it is far from perfect. The legislator's mail may be a strong indication of the way the people think, but it may not reflect their thoughts adequately. In all probability, on most complex issues the people are insufficiently informed to give a meaningful opinion. If there is strong opinion, will it remain, or will it shift? Although "public opinion," in the popular sense, may exist, it is doubtful whether a legislator could follow it completely if he were to try.

On the other hand, if a legislator is able to determine existing public opinion, should he completely disregard it? If he were to do so could democracy survive? Many persons believe that the legislator should vote his conscience and that he should work to educate the public if in his view its opinion is wrong. Nevertheless, few legislators could blatantly disregard public opinion very often because of the necessity of facing re-election.

As with many questions in politics, this one can never be answered completely. The American political system is one of adjustment and compromise and is often simply a search for anything that works. Members of most contemporary legislatures operate under many guises: they do attempt to represent their constituents' interests, they do act according to their consciences, and they do respond to special interests. Sometimes they behave in one way and sometimes in another. Clearly, the voters can affect their legislators to some extent; clearly the legislators can exercise some independence; clearly the system is imperfect. Perhaps it all works out for the best. Some issues probably are better resolved by one approach, others by another. The arrangement works—often poorly—but it does work.

The Functions of American Legislatures

The Framers of the Constitution obviously intended the Congress to be the center of the political system in the United States and to be the pre-eminent branch of government. For a variety of reasons Congress during the twentieth century has lost or surrendered much of its power and influence to the President. This is not unique to the United States or to the national government. Similar tendencies are apparent in other democratic nations, and they are at work in state governments as well, although to a somewhat lesser degree because of the tight restrictions that state constitutions tend to place on the powers of governors, and the governors' lack of power in foreign affairs.

For better or worse, it is generally accepted that the prime motivating forces in American governments are generated from executive branches and that legislatures are unlikely to become significant initiators of policy. Although there may be exceptions in some state governments and even more at the local levels, where the pattern of government often differs from the traditional American bicameral legislature and separated powers, the national government gives every indication that it will continue to be dominated by the executive branch, despite the reforms that may result from the investigations into the Watergate affair.

This is not to say that the Congress will be, or has been, a rubber stamp. Like most other legislatures in democratic nations the Congress considers policies proposed by the executive, and it may reject or revise as well as adopt them. Some pressure is building for reform that would inject more energy into the Congress in its dealings with the executive branch and would somewhat increase congressional initiative in formulating policy; this is particularly true with regard to budgetary and fiscal matters. In June of 1973, for example, the Congress sent to the President an appropriation act that he had requested but included in it a prohibition against spending any money from any source on military activities in Indo-China. The President promptly vetoed the measure, and the House majority that voted to overturn the veto fell short of the required two-thirds. Congressional leaders threatened to attach the same prohibition to another appropriation act, this time one that was essential to the continued operation of some governmental offices. In this rare show of strength Congress alerted the President that it considered certain of his policies to be impermissible and that he must accept congressional restrictions upon his power or bring the government close to a halt. Eventually Congress and the

President compromised by agreeing upon a date beyond which the bombing and other military activities had to cease and enacting it into law. It is worth noting that such a vote of no confidence in executive policies in a parliamentary system would have caused the government to fall, bringing about new general elections.

Congress is asserting itself somewhat more than in the recent past, but as many recent examples illustrate, it still hesitates to push for maximum advantage in its relations with the executive. The explanation may be timidity, reverence for the presidential office or fear of its power, simple inertia, poor organization, lack of will or leadership, or any combination of these. For many reasons the presidency is likely to remain the primary source of policy initiation. The executive is more cohesive and less cumbersome than the Congress, and the President can put forth some claim to a national constituency that Congress, although it is a national legislature, cannot unless it could act with vastly more single-mindedness than it ever has. In addition, the importance of foreign affairs in contemporary national life gives maximum disadvantage to the Congress and maximum advantage to the President.

LAWMAKING.   The American legislature as a representative assembly has many functions, but the most central is the passage of laws. The range of legislation is almost unlimited; nearly any subject could be considered as the basis for legislative action. In addition, needs change as do desires and even tastes. The legislature must continually revise and reconstitute the statutory structure of the society in order to avoid stagnation and injustice. Because the legislature must adopt laws binding on all, there will inevitably be some injustice even when the laws are well designed and well administered. It is the responsibility of the legislature to keep such injustice at a minimum by insuring, among other things, that the coercive force of the laws it passes is no more than is absolutely necessary and that the rules for conduct that it prescribes are those that truly are needed, and no more.

Ideas for legislation come from constituents, parties, interest groups, the legislators themselves, and an endless variety of other sources. The primary stimulus is the executive branch, but it too responds to the ideas of others, including those of members of Congress. Many of the acts that Congress adopts have been introduced in previous sessions but for one reason or another did not succeed. Even some proposals passed with administration support have gained that support only recently, and have originated in earlier sessions of Congress. It thus is difficult if not impossible to determine the original sources of most legislation, and it may be that there is a tendency to exaggerate executive influence and underplay the role of Congress itself. Whatever the origins of legislation, it is the Congress that sifts the competing demands and arrives at the compromises that become the laws of the land. Regardless of the degree to which it initiates policies, the Congress indelibly stamps its imprint upon them.

In addition to the passage of statutes, lawmaking involves other functions. Under the Constitution, the Congress participates in the adoption of treaties; because they bind two or more nations to certain conduct and regularize relations between them they are a specialized form of law. This function is limited to the Senate, which must approve any treaty by a two-thirds vote. In this case the initiative is formally reserved to the President, who negotiates treaties and presents them to the Senate. Another form of lawmaking deals with the fundamental law, the Constitution. The Congress has the power to propose constitutional amendments by two-thirds vote of both houses.

OVERSEEING THE ADMINISTRATION.   Following closely behind the making of law in importance is the function termed, with unconscious irony, "legislative oversight." In order to assure itself that the executive branch is administering the laws in the way Congress intended, various congressional committees scrutinize the operations of the hundreds of governmental programs. Congress has many weapons at its disposal in dealing with the President and his administration, if it should choose to exercise them. It can pass new legislation, even over a presidential veto. More often, it will attempt to influence program administration by the "power of the purse."

One powerful tool is the General Accounting Office, headed by the Comptroller General; GAO reports to Congress, not to the President, and has full authority to conduct investigations into any use of funds or into the administration of any program. Special interests both in and out of the government sometimes succeed in suppressing or weakening GAO reports, but the agency's potential is limited only by the willingness of Congress to act.

Congress must appropriate all money that the government spends; if it is unhappy with a specific program, Congress may reduce or eliminate the appropriation for that program. Rarely is anything more vital to any administrator of a government agency than the agency's relations with the House and Senate appropriations subcommittees. Some members of Congress, because of their key committee appointments, exert extraordinary control over certain executive officials and their agencies. Often, because of his ability to influence the committee, even an appropriations committee staff member becomes accustomed to exercising command over certain virtually defenseless bureaucrats; if the official had the temerity to protest, his programs would suffer.

Unfortunately, congressional oversight of executive programs tends to be chaotic, uncoordinated, and frequently confused. There is no doubt that Congress has the potential to be a powerful force in promoting sound and effective administration, but it rarely does so. There are numerous instances in which Congress fails to check the most flagrant examples of mismanagement, and others in which it can lead to inefficiency in the administration of programs because of personal whims of members or staff personnel. Under its current organization, congressional oversight is erratic and often irresponsible, but the potential for beneficial and much needed checks on the administration exists. In order to realize it, Congress not only would have to improve its present structure and make better use of the GAO, but would be required to provide itself with sufficient qualified staff and research resources to be able to deal with a monstrous and technically sophisticated executive branch.

OTHER FUNCTIONS.   The Scandinavian countries have developed an office to protect the citizen against arbitrary and unfair actions of government agencies. The official holding this office is known as the Ombudsman, and it is his duty to listen to citizen complaints and to investigate to determine whether or not they are justified. This office not only aids the citizen, but serves to protect government agencies and officials from unfair complaints. In the U.S.S.R. the Procurator has some ombudsman duties. Civilian review boards exercise similar functions locally in a few American cities by reviewing citizen complaints against the police.

To a limited extent, the Congress performs an ombudsman function, but only on a hit or miss basis. The individual member of Congress, if he is so inclined, may hear citizen complaints and investigate them. The effectiveness varies, not only with the ability of the member, but with his position in Congress, the kind of complaint, and the agency against which it is directed. Many agencies will go to great lengths to avoid offending any member of Congress; others exhibit great nonchalance in the face of congressional criticism unless the critic is especially powerful or is on appropriations or another relevant committee. Also, if the citizen's cause is just but unpopular, the member of Congress may be intimidated by public pressure and refuse to give more than token assistance, if that.

Related indirectly to the ombudsman function and much more central to the duties of legislators is the offering of services to the constituents of the district, powerful factions in the district, or individual voters in the district. Whether the member truly performs this function or not, it is important for him to convince these persons and groups that he is performing it well if he is to be re-elected. Catering to these interests may result in something as significant as the introduction of legislation or something as trivial as arranging for a constituent to receive a flag that has "flown" (probably for not more than a few seconds, because attendants continually run flags up and down the Capitol flag pole to satisfy such requests) over the nation's Capitol.

Another vitally important function of the Congress is conducting investigations, debates, and otherwise contributing to public information. Congress must have adequate information if it is to legislate wisely. The investigative power can be abused so that it improperly harms individual citizens or groups and creates or contributes to a climate of fear, as was the case with the investigations of the late Senator McCarthy and those of the old House Committee on Un-American Activities, or it can be used with great discretion and complete propriety as with Senator Sam Ervin and his committee investigating the Watergate affair and other political espionage or Senator Kennedy's committee on the treatment of Indians. In any event, an investigation provides information not only to members of Congress but to the public, as do congressional debates and many other activities. In this way, the legislature in a democracy assists the ongoing democratic process by encouraging a free flow of information about the government, and to and from the government.

In our political system, wrongdoing is to be punished by the courts, but the Congress may participate in the process in cases in which public officials are involved. The House of Representatives may impeach an official by majority vote, at which point the Senate sits as a court and tries the impeached person; a two-thirds vote is required to convict, and conviction results in removal from office. This is the only way in which the

Congress can remove officials from the executive branch, and this only under extraordinary circumstances. It has been successfully invoked less than a dozen times. Similarly, since the United States does not operate under a parliamentary system, the legislature does not participate in the selection of the elected executive unless the Electoral College fails to give a majority vote to a candidate for President or Vice President; again, extraordinary circumstances.

The legislature however participates very definitely in the selection of appointive officials, both executive and judicial, although participation is limited to the Senate. Article II, Section 2, of the Constitution requires that the Senate give its "advice and consent" before the President may appoint the major officers of government. As a rule, the Senate turns down very few nominees, but this power can be potent, as is illustrated by the refusal of the Senate to confirm two of President Nixon's nominations to the Supreme Court, Clement Haynsworth and G. Harrold Carswell. President Nixon, in a letter to the Senate, charged that its refusal to confirm his nominees was a violation of the principle of separation of powers, because it denied him the power to appoint officials of his choice. The Senate found this line of reasoning to be strange, at best, and rejected it forcefully.

It is the necessity for Senate confirmation of certain other nominations that permits the practice known as "senatorial courtesy." By custom the President must consult with any senators of his party from the state in which these officials would be serving to obtain their consent before he makes the nomination. If he nominates a person to serve in a senator's state and the senator does not approve, the senator has only to announce that the nominee is "personally abhorrent" to him, and the Senate will extend "senatorial courtesy" to that senator and refuse to confirm the President's nomination. Senatorial courtesy applies only if the senator is of the President's party and only to certain offices within his state such as judges of federal district courts and U.S. marshal. An individual senator may sometimes be able to force the defeat or withdrawal of a nomination because of animosity that he feels for the nominee even when that person would not be serving within his state, but this is not senatorial courtesy and ordinarily the senator could not count on success.

Certain high ranking officials who are in the Executive Office of the President traditionally have been considered to be presidential aides and assistants rather than "Officers of the United States," as Article II, Section

2 puts it. Despite the fact that the Director of the Office of Management and Budget is one of the most powerful officials in the government, with direct authority over the budgets of the Cabinet agencies, he is not subject to Senate confirmation because the OMB (formerly the Bureau of the Budget) is in the Executive Office of the President. The same holds true for the top presidential advisors, who may hold much more power than Cabinet officials. Neither Henry Kissinger, when he was White House adviser on foreign affairs and the architect of much of the Nixon foreign policy, John Ehrlichman, who as domestic adviser to the President was one of the most powerful men in the nation, nor H. R. Haldeman, who as Nixon's chief of staff had virtually complete control over access to the President, had been confirmed by the Senate. In mid-1973 the Congress passed legislation requiring these and other policy-making officials to have Senate confirmation as the Constitution specifies for Cabinet officers and others, but the act fell victim to a Nixon veto. The Senate voted to over-ride the veto, but the House could not muster the required two-thirds vote, even in this, a clear-cut case in which the power of Congress was at stake.

The Powers of Congress

Article I, Section 8, of the Constitution sets forth a list of the formal powers of Congress. The list is extensive and includes, among other things, the power to lay and collect taxes, borrow money, regulate commerce, provide rules for naturalization and bankruptcies, coin money and fix standards for weights and measures, establish a postal system, create a judicial system, declare war, raise and support an army and navy, provide for a militia, create a federal district, and regulate copyrights and patents. Additionally, Section 8 grants Congress the power to adopt all laws "which shall be necessary and proper" in order to exercise the powers granted in this and other sections of the Constitution. This provision establishes the basis for the doctrine of implied powers, as discussed in Chapter III.

Although Congress has broad powers, they are subject to limitations. The Constitution specifies certain prohibitions, such as the First Amendment provision that Congress shall make no law abridging freedom of speech or of the press, or the clause in Article I, Section 9, that forbids Congress to pass bills of attainder and *ex post facto* laws. Moreover, the courts have insisted that Congress must adopt clear standards to guide the executive officials who are to administer the laws; too great a grant of power to the administration would be a delegation of legislative power and therefore unconstitutional.

Congressional Structure and Organization

In order to carry their beliefs in checks and balances into the national legislature itself, the Founding Fathers provided for a bicameral Congress. To a degree, this form was required by the nature of a federal system. With the states represented equally in the Senate, the federal structure was secure, and the House of Representatives could be based upon population. Just as the legislative, executive, and judicial branches can check one another, so too can one house of the Congress check the other, since the approval of both houses is required to adopt legislation. Originally, the House of Representatives was to be the democratic, or "people's" branch, and the Senate (which initially was selected solely by state legislatures, not the voters) was to dampen the presumed excesses of democracy and represent elite interests. In recent years, the situation has changed. Both the House and the Senate are essentially conservative bodies, with extraordinarily conservative traditions and institutions that make it appear virtually impossible to challenge the *status quo* successfully. Partly because of the greater influence of urban areas in the Senate, however, at present it is inclined to be more open to social programs and other innovations than is the House, which is dominated, even more than the Senate, by rural conservatives of both parties. Because the senator's constituency is an entire state, he is likely to be oriented toward urban needs if the state is predominantly urban; urban states are nevertheless likely to have substantial rural areas, and, because members of the House are elected by districts rather than at large, even predominantly urban states may have one or more representatives whose constituencies are essentially rural, thereby giving the House still more of a rural flavor than the Senate.

The two houses are presumed to be equal in power, and members of the House of Representatives often insist that the House is equal in honor and prestige to the Senate. Nevertheless, a senator has great advantages not available to the typical representative. As one of only one hundred members, even a freshman senator is likely to have some national visibility and to be a sought after guest on the Washington cocktail circuit; few persons anywhere are so anonymous as a freshman representative. Until he builds up his position by working into prominence in the House, the representative is lost among a large group of 435. Moreover, the six year term of a senator gives him considerable independence, whereas a representative's

"Senator, I just can't get over how like your image you are!"
Drawing by William Hamilton; © 1972 The New Yorker Magazine, Inc.

two-year term means that he usually must spend much of his time getting re-elected; no sooner has he taken office than another election is just around the corner. Regardless of the pretensions of many representatives, they frequently will retire from the House in order to run for the Senate if they think that they have a good chance to win; it would be unthinkable for a modern senator to resign his seat in order to run for the House.

Today most political scientists and political reformers as well seem strongly to favor unicameral legislatures. There appears to be some pressure developing in California for a switch to a unicameral legislature, partly because of resentment over the cost of operating two houses, each with extensive research staff and other duplications. The arguments for bicameralism center largely upon the desirability of checks and balances, which many no longer take for granted, and in any event there may be many checks within one house. Additionally, since bills may be introduced into either house (except for revenue bills, which the Constitution requires to originate in the House, and appropriations bills, which originate there by tradition), some argue that a bicameral arrangement permits a legislature to handle a greater volume of work than if it were unicameral; one chamber may conduct the necessary investigations and do the essential spadework on one group of bills while the other chamber performs similarly with another group, thereby saving one another considerable effort. In practice, it rarely works this way; the House and Senate are reluctant to take one another's word for anything and usually insist on going through the entire process for each bill, regardless of what the other house has done.

Most of the literature tends to favor unicameralism as being more efficient and less expensive. There is a possibility, also, that unicameralism could increase the quality of a legislature. Some have noted a tendency in the Congress for the House to pass ill-considered and unwise legislation, which the representatives know full well should not become law, depending upon the Senate to kill it; frivolous conduct such as this would be too serious to exist in a unicameral body. It is difficult to determine accurately which form is better because there is so little experience with unicameral legislatures in the American setting. To be sure, virtually all city councils in the United States are unicameral, but the governance of cities is so different from the governance of states and nations that the experience is not directly comparable. Except for the state legislature of Nebraska, all American legislatures at the state level or higher are bicameral. Nebraska's experience seems to indicate that neither the high expectations of the reformers nor the dire predictions of traditionalists were justified. There are differences in the performance of bicameral and unicameral legislatures, but each can work reasonably well.

CONGRESSIONAL ORGANIZATION.   The life of a Congress is two years, beginning in January under the terms of the Twentieth Amendment. Article I, Section 4, of the Constitution requires Congress to assemble at least once each year, and the President is empowered by Article II, Section 3, to convene Congress on "extraordinary occasions" when he deems it necessary. The only time that a President may adjourn Congress would be if the two houses could not agree on a date of adjournment, but this has never occurred. A bill lasts as long as a Congress; if it is introduced into the first session, it may be considered in the second, but if it is not acted upon in the second, it has to be reintroduced to be considered by a future Congress. According to the Legislative Reorganization Act of 1946, Congress is supposed to adjourn each yearly session by July 31, but the pressure of work is such that the sessions continue for most of the year.

Each new Congress assembles in January of odd-numbered years, and organizes itself. Because the six-year terms of senators are staggered so that only approximately one-third face the voters during any given election the Senate is considered to be a continuing body with the majority of its members carrying over from one Congress to the next. This means that Senate rules continue through succeeding Congresses, preventing the Senate from adopting new rules every two years. Frequently, at the opening sessions of new Congresses, non-southern liberals from both parties put forth the claim that the Senate is not a continuing body and can adopt new rules at the beginning of any new Congress by a simple majority vote. So far these efforts have failed. The argument is about Rule XXII, which permits senators unlimited debate unless halted by a "cloture" motion that requires a two-thirds majority of those present and voting. This freedom for unlimited debate permits the practice known as filibuster, in which one senator, sometimes in cooperation with others, continues debate for a prolonged period with the intention of defeating a bill by so tying up the senate's business that its backers will surrender it in order to proceed. Although liberals generally work to eliminate the filibuster or to reduce the vote required for cloture on grounds that it is undemocratic to permit a small minority to prevent the Senate from acting, and it is true that the most notable use of the filibuster has been to defeat civil rights bills, it should be noted that liberals, too, resort to the filibuster when it is to their advantage to do so.

In the House of Representatives, on the other hand, every member is subject to election every biennium; the House accordingly is not considered to be a continuing body, even though most of the members are returned every election, and it adopts its rules at the beginning of each Congress. The new rules are generally the same as those in force in preceding Congresses. Because of the size of the House (set by law at 435 representatives distributed among the states on the basis of population), there is no freedom for unlimited debate as there is in the Senate, and there is correspondingly less controversy over the rules.

Both the House and the Senate go through the ritual of selecting their leaders in each new Congress. Although there is very little discipline in either party, this vote to organize each house is the one time at which all members can be expected to vote the straight party line. The majority party of the House will put forth its candidates for Speaker, who will routinely be elected. The Speaker of the House is not only the chief of his party in that chamber but also the presiding officer; he retains the right to vote. He will be a representative with prestige and seniority, but many factors enter into his selection; the Speaker is never chosen on seniority alone. His powers are great and may be enhanced by personal skills. In a body such as the House, with rigid limitations on debate, his power to recognize those wishing to speak is highly significant. He also interprets the rules, appoints members to conference and select committees, and refers bills to committees with the advice of the Parliamentarian.

In the Senate, the presiding officer is the Vice President of the United States, who also has the title of President of the Senate. Since he is imposed upon the Senate from the outside and may even be a member of the minority party, he has little power or influence within that body. He cannot vote except in case of a tie. His power to preside is of little consequence because of the unlimited debate that the Senate permits. The Senate does elect a President *Pro Tempore*, who has the right to preside whenever the Vice President is absent and who is chosen, as is the Speaker of the House, by a straight party vote. The President *Pro Tem*, however, is the member of the majority party with the greatest seniority; his position is almost entirely honorary. The power to preside is so nearly meaningless in the Senate, in fact, that freshmen senators often occupy the chair temporarily in order to gain experience, and the President *Pro Tem* rarely presides despite the numerous absences of vice presidents.

The party offices are similar in both houses. There are majority and minority leaders, and majority and minority "whips," a term taken from the British legislature. The whips are assistants to the leaders. As with the selection of the Speaker, seniority is important in the selection of these officials but is not determining.

from Straight Herblock (*Simon & Schuster, 1964*)

"YOU SEE—FIRST WOMEN, THEN NEGROES, NOW CONGRESSMEN AND SENATORS."

THE COMMITTEE SYSTEM. One factor of congressional organization whose importance can hardly be exaggerated is the committee system. Although not mentioned in the Constitution, the committee structure has evolved to the point where it is fundamental in the functioning of the political system. In order to achieve greater efficiency in handling the overwhelming number of bills, Congress has provided for committees to divide up the labor and permit a certain degree of specialization. There are four kinds of committee: select, joint, conference, and standing. Select committees are *ad hoc* bodies created for a specific purpose and for a specific length of time; when their function is completed, they are eliminated, although if they appear to be of permanent value they can be transformed into standing committees.

Joint committees are those composed of members of both houses; standing joint committees are not widely used by Congress, nor do they generally have the prestige of the standing committees within each house. The Joint Committee on Atomic Energy is the only one that considers legislation. As a rule, joint committees are used to coordinate policy between the House and Senate on relatively routine matters. Examples are the Joint Committee on Printing and the Joint Committee on the Library. Greater use of joint standing committees could well lead to greater efficiency in a bicameral legislature by eliminating the duplication of function that occurs when committees in each house separately consider a proposed piece of legislation. Joint select committees, on the other hand, are more extensively used, largely in the form of conference committees.

Congress uses conference committees to settle differences between the two houses whenever one house passes a bill that is not identical in all respects to the same bill passed by the other house. This happens in a majority of nonroutine cases. Unless both chambers pass a bill in exactly the same form, it cannot be forwarded to the executive for action. Each house appoints from three to nine members who serve as conferees. The conference committee may adopt the House version of the bill, the Senate version of the bill, or a compromise version. Although theoretically they are not supposed to do so, a conference committee may upon occasion completely re-write a bill, especially if the original House and Senate versions were radically different. In order to issue a report, a majority of the conferees from each house must agree. If they cannot agree, the bill fails even though it has passed both houses. The conference committee report goes back to the two houses for adoption without amendment, after which it is sent to the President for his action. Usually each house will accept a conference committee report routinely, but if either house refuses to do so, the measure dies.

The standing committees are the heart of the committee system. They are permanent units that each house establishes within its rules, and theirs is the task of considering proposed legislation and recommending action. Generally, standing committees are established on the basis of subject matter, with each committee having certain subjects under its jurisdiction. As a rule, the committee's action is the major factor in determining the future of a bill. When a committee reports a bill favorably to the House or the Senate, the chances are good that it will be adopted, especially if the committee has been strong in its endorsement and it has acted by a large majority. It is extraordinarily rare for a bill to succeed without committee approval.

The majority party in either house always selects all committee chairmen, and always has a majority on all committees in the chamber. It is in the selection of chairmen that the famous, or infamous, seniority system comes into play. This system guarantees that the member of the majority party with the greatest seniority on a committee, the most consecutive years of service, becomes its chairman unless he elects to step aside. It guards against bitter intraparty struggles in selecting chairmen and also insures that chairmen will be persons of experience, if not necessarily of competence; it guarantees that there will be no discrimination on the basis of race, religion, sex, or ability. The bulk of attacks on the seniority system come from liberals, usually younger liberals. As members grow in seniority and work into positions of power, they frequently come to be supporters of the system be they liberal or conservative. Liberal supporters of the system tend to be persons of somewhat lengthy tenure in Congress who may be embarrassed by their position and therefore admit that selection by seniority has disadvantages but maintain that it has sufficient advantages to compensate.

It may be easy to exaggerate the shortcomings of the seniority system, and its supporters point out that it does work and that it could be dangerous to tamper with any of the basic institutions of Congress. Nevertheless, the seniority system is relatively new as a congressional institution, and some of its flaws are obvious. In addition to ignoring competence, the seniority system offends many advocates of strong party organization and leadership. A person need not be a party supporter to obtain a committee chairmanship, and only in the most flagrant cases is a member stripped of seniority for his actions. When Representative John Bell Williams of Mississippi broke with the Democratic party to support Senator Goldwater's presidential bid in 1964, the Democrats did take action, but this was highly unusual. In most circumstances, even this would not be sufficient to result in such sanctions. To those who advocate more democracy within the houses of Congress, the system also is abhorrent. As a rule it is liberals who are most unhappy with it for the simple reason that it tends to work to the advantage of conservatives. Rural conservative states and districts are more likely to be politically "safe" for the incumbent, that is to present him with little challenge at elections, than are the districts and states that are more urban and therefore likely to be more liberal. An incumbent from a safe district is of course likely to build seniority, hence, power. Until recently, the majority of committee chairmen in both houses came from the South, and generally from the most rural districts. This tendency has lessened somewhat in recent years, but because it contains so many safe districts the South always has considerably more power in both houses than its relative size would warrant on a basis of strict equality, as have rural areas in general. The seniority system thus tends to give a great deal of power to a fairly small number of states with very similar, and often sectional, interests.

These shortcomings would be less important if committee chairmen were less powerful. The chairman may call or refuse to call meetings or hold hearings, he may reward committee members with choice subcommittee assignments or deny them, and his power over committee procedure tends to be so great that in many cases he has the power of death over any bill that he fails to favor. Partly this is a function of the American congressional committee system itself; if the committees were less powerful, the issue of seniority and the power of chairmen would be less critical. Most legislatures elsewhere, although they make use of committees, have nothing resembling the powerful American committees with their virtual life and death power over legislation and instead do what is considered here to be impossible; that is, they handle most legislative detail in the full chamber. Encouraged by weak party discipline and no executive control over the legislative schedule, the American committee system was a natural, but not an inevitable, development.

The way to become a chairman is to be assigned to a committee, continue to be elected, and outlast the other members. All members are assigned to committees, but only a select few manage to land choice spots

"I take it, Senator, you approve of the present seniority system."

such as those on the Appropriations, Ways and Means, or Rules committees in the House or the committees on Appropriations, Finance, or Foreign Relations in the Senate. For a time, representatives held positions on only one committee, and senators on two, although there were exceptions. The tendency now is for representatives to serve on two, except those who are assigned to certain committees, such as Appropriations, Agriculture, Ways and Means, Rules, and Armed Services, for which single assignments are customary.

The party leadership in each house determines committee assignments. The House Democrats make the assignments by a Committee on Committees, composed of the Democratic members of the Ways and Means Committee (who themselves were selected initially by party caucus—consisting of all party members in the chamber), the floor leader, and the Speaker, when he is a Democrat. The House Republicans employ a Committee on Committees composed of one representative from each state that has a Republican representative. Each member can cast as many votes as there are Republican representatives from his state. In the Senate, the Democratic floor leader selects a Steering Committee to make the assignments, and the Chairman of the Republican Conference appoints a Committee on Committees for the same purpose. All of these methods provide for almost complete domination by the senior members, who are unlikely to reflect changes in the general electorate. (Here, as elsewhere in Congress, the emphasis is strongly upon the *status quo*; those who get the key assignments tend to be those whom the leaders believe will not rock the boat.)

The proposals for reform usually center upon permitting the members of the majority party on a committee to elect the chairman, or upon giving to the party's members in the chamber the power to select all chairmen. In the early 1970's this latter arrangement became the formal procedure in the House, where Republicans led the way in 1971 and Democrats followed in 1973, probably as a result of pressure from such citizens' groups as Common Cause. It does provide a way to remove a chairman under ordinary procedures, but the members have never gone against their leaders' wishes, and the leaders have supported the same committee chairmen chosen under the seniority system. A selection of chairmen by lot would avoid struggle and would be no less likely to produce chairmen of competence than the present system, but that has not been considered. In any case, even the reformers almost never suggest changes in the basic system; they want only new methods of selecting the leaders of the established mechanism. Certainly, members of Congress could change the institutions if they wished. At present, the entire structure in both houses of Congress is strongly biased against reform. As the illustration above indicates, the occasional reform that is adopted may make little if any difference; this is typical of congressional reforms. There is little doubt that things remain as they are because this is the way that most members wish them to be.

Congressional Procedures: The Rocky Road to Legislation

The view of the House or the Senate as typified by open debate and action on the floor, even though reflected in the pages of the *Congressional Record*, is an illusion. In fact, most of the business of Congress takes place in committee; in fact, also, much of the action exhibited by the *Congressional Record* borders on fiction. The Constitution requires each house to keep a journal of its proceedings, but the proceedings within the committees, which are vitally important, are not included. A member of Congress may insert material in the *Record*, perhaps making it appear that there has been vigorous debate and that he has participated extensively when in reality he has said little if anything on the floor. This occurs when the member asks unanimous consent (which is always granted) to "revise and extend" his remarks. Members may also insert virtually any material that they please in the rear section of the *Record* labeled "Extensions of Remarks." Debate does occur, and sometimes (though too rarely) at a high level, but the pages of the *Record* are not a perfect reflection of what happened. The member receives copies of his remarks on the floor, which he may edit to remove illiteracies or otherwise revise before they appear in the *Record*. This means that each member will appear in the pages of the *Record* to maximum advantage as he sees it. If the member has failed to edit his copy and get it back in time to make the printing deadline, his portion will be deleted, and it will be noted that so-and-so's remarks will appear hereafter in Extensions of Remarks. Despite these shortcomings, the *Record* is still the best picture of congressional proceedings that exists for those who wish to follow the day to day workings of Congress; it is a valuable resource and one of the publishing marvels of the world, routinely appearing the day after a session, day after day, under conditions of pressure that make it remarkable that it is printed at all.

Another illusion is the stereotyped view that members of Congress sit in Washington, passing laws right and left, throwing away "the taxpayers' money." In order to appreciate the difficulty of enacting legislation, let us trace the path of a bill from its introduction until it becomes law.

Only a representative or a senator may introduce a bill. Except for revenue bills, which the Constitution requires to originate in the House, a bill may begin in either the House or the Senate or simultaneously in each. By tradition, appropriations bills also originate in the House, but this is not a legal requirement. For our illustration, let us follow a bill, originating in the House, to establish a program of tuition subsidies to college students for which the introducing representative designed to authorize a total appropriation of $200 million. Because he is not likely to be able to draft so technical a bill without assistance beyond that avail-

FIGURE 3. Typical Path from Bill to Law for Major Bill Originating in House

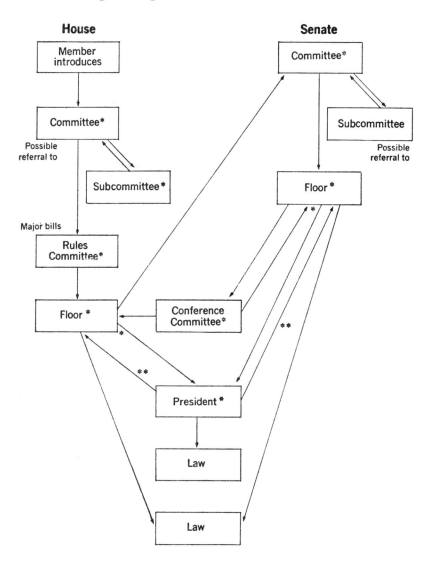

Note: Bill may originate in either House or Senate, except for revenue bills which must originate in House, or appropriations bills which originate there by custom

* Points at which bill may die

** If vetoed while Congress is in session

Standing Committees of Congress As of January 1973

HOUSE COMMITTEE	SUB-COMMIT-TEES	CHAIRMAN	STATE
Agriculture	10	W. R. Poage	Texas
Appropriations	13	George H. Mahon	Texas
Armed Services	8	F. Edward Hébert	Louisiana
Banking and Currency	8	Wright Patman	Texas
District of Columbia	6	Charles C. Diggs	Michigan
Education and Labor	8	Carl D. Perkins	Kentucky
Foreign Affairs	10	Thomas E. Morgan	Pennsylvania
Government Operations	7	Chet Holifield	California
House Administration	8	Wayne L. Hays	Ohio
Interior and Insular Affairs	7	James A. Haley	Florida
Internal Security	0	Richard Ichord	Missouri
Interstate and Foreign Commerce	5	Harley O. Staggers	West Virginia
Judiciary	7	Peter W. Rodino	New Jersey
Merchant Marine and Fisheries	5	Leonor K. Sullivan	Missouri
Post Office and Civil Service	6	Thaddeus J. Dulski	New York
Public Works	6	John A. Blatnik	Minnesota
Rules	0	Ray J. Madden	Indiana
Science and Astronautics	6	Olin E. Teague	Texas
Standards of Official Conduct	0	Melvin Price	Illinois
Veterans Affairs	5	William Dorn	South Carolina
Ways and Means	0	Wilbur D. Mills	Arkansas

able on his staff, the member of Congress probably would supply the outlines of his proposal to specialists in the U.S. Office of Education, who, as a matter of courtesy, would prepare the draft regardless of their opinions of the program. This procedure, of course, permits the executive to have some influence on the proposed bill, even in its initial stages.

After introduction in the House, the bill is referred to the appropriate committee, which for this bill would be the Committee on Education and Labor. The committee then refers the bill to the subcommittee having jurisdiction over the subject matter involved. The subcommittee will ex-

Standing Committees of Congress As of January 1973

SENATE COMMITTEE	SUB-COMMIT-TEES	CHAIRMAN	STATE
Aeronautical and Space Sciences	0	Frank E. Moss	Utah
Agriculture and Forestry	6	Herman E. Talmadge	Georgia
Appropriations	14	John L. McClellan	Arkansas
Armed Services	12	John C. Stennis	Mississippi
Banking, Housing, and Urban Affairs	7	John J. Sparkman	Alabama
Commerce	8	Warren G. Magnuson	Washington
District of Columbia	3	Thomas F. Eagleton	Missouri
Finance	6	Russell B. Long	Louisiana
Foreign Relations	10	William Fulbright	Arkansas
Government Operations	6	Sam J. Ervin, Jr.	North Carolina
Interior and Insular Affairs	7	Henry M. Jackson	Washington
Judiciary	15	James O. Eastland	Mississippi
Labor and Public Welfare	12	Harrison A. Williams	New Jersey
Post Office and Civil Service	3	Gale W. McGee	Wyoming
Public Works	6	Jennings Randolph	West Virginia
Rules and Administration	7	Howard W. Cannon	Nevada
Veterans' Affairs	4	Vance Hartke	Indiana

amine the bill, perhaps will hold hearings and invite witnesses to testify to its virtues and shortcomings, and will make recommendations to the committee. If the subcommittee recommends against a bill, or if it fails to act, the bill usually dies. If it recommends the bill favorably, the committee may report it favorably; if, for whatever reason, the committee fails to report a bill favorably, it usually is dead. The committee may add amendments of its own, or it may completely rewrite the bill so that what comes out bears no resemblance to what went in. In our hypothetical example, the Education and Labor Committee clears the bill and reports it favorably but has amended it to provide a program of only $100 million.

Having survived thus far, the bill will be placed on a calendar and must be cleared through the Rules Committee, which controls much of the traffic on the floor of the House. The Rules Committee does not control all matters reported from the other committees because much of the action in any session is noncontroversial and is handled in routine fashion, and certain other matters are "privileged," such as those reported from the Committees on Ways and Means or Appropriations. Generally, however, most controversial measures must receive clearance by the Rules Committee before the House can act. If the Rules Committee bottles up the measure or fails to act, the bill usually dies. It is possible to force a bill out of a reluctant Rules Committee, but it is very difficult, and effort in this direction is usually futile.

In our example, however, the Rules Committee acts favorably, and the measure goes before the full House—that is, it goes to the floor. At this point there will be debate and parliamentary maneuvering; there may be efforts to table the bill or to send it back to committee which, if successful, would almost assuredly kill it. If the House votes down the bill, it is dead. Our bill survives these hurdles, and receives a favorable vote from the House, which sends it on to the Senate.

In the Senate the bill will go to the Labor and Public Welfare Committee, which has jurisdiction over educational matters. Here, everything begins again; the committee will process the bill as did its counterpart in the House. As in the House, the committee can revise or rewrite the bill, and a favorable committee report is a virtual requirement for final Senate passage. Let us assume that the committee restores the original amount of $200 million and reports the bill favorably. It then can be taken up on the floor of the Senate. Note that there is no counterpart in the Senate to the House Rules Committee (there is a Senate Committee on Rules and Administration, but this is more or less the counterpart of the House Administration Committee, not the Rules Committee). Since passage by both the House and the Senate is required for all legislation, a negative vote by the Senate would kill the bill, as would Senate inaction. As in the House, a successful motion to table or to refer it back to committee would likely spell its doom. In our example, the Senate votes favorably. Although both houses have approved it, it still is not an act of Congress because the two houses did not pass it in identical form. If there is the slightest difference between the House and Senate versions of a bill, it must go to a conference committee. Here, the House passed a bill calling for a $100 million program, but the Senate's bill called for $200 million, so it goes to conference.

The purpose of a conference committee, as discussed above, is to smooth out differences between the two houses. If a majority of the House conferees and a majority of the Senate conferees fail to agree, the bill dies even though each house had previously acted favorably. For purposes of illustration, let us assume that the conference committee approves our bill, and agrees upon a compromise figure of $150 million. The conference committee report then goes back to the two houses for final action. Usually they will accept the report, but in case either does not, the bill dies. In our illustration they adopt the report by favorable vote on the floor of each house, and it becomes an act of Congress and goes to the President.

The President receives the new act and has to decide whether to sign it into law or to veto it. If he should veto it while Congress is still in session, it goes back to Congress for reconsideration, and it dies unless each house can manage to repass it by a two-thirds vote. If Congress has adjourned, a veto will kill the act with no possibility of overriding the President's action. In the event that the President should do nothing, the act becomes law in ten days unless Congress has adjourned in the meantime, in which case the act is dead (the so-called "pocket veto"). In the case of our hypothetical program, the President signs it into law.

It is obvious that there are many pitfalls along the way, and it is no wonder that few bills that are introduced make it through to final passage and signing. In this illustration, as complicated as the procedure has been to this point, it still is only half completed! The law merely *authorizes* the appropriation of money; it does not actually provide it. In order for the program to get underway there must be another act, an appropriations act, that goes through the entire procedure all over again. One difference is that instead of going through the legislative committees that handled the original measure, this bill must go through the appropriations committees in each house, adding other points of possible hostility.

Only in cases in which Congress is of almost a single mind on an issue can it act with dispatch, and these cases are rare. In the mid-1960's, Congress made it a federal crime to burn a draft card, and President Johnson signed it into law in only a few days in what must have been record time, but it took Medicare more than twenty-five years to gain passage, and it took almost one hundred years for the adoption of anything resembling an effective civil rights program.

The Future of Congress

Until recently, the numerous inadequacies of Congress as a representative institution have encouraged reformers to suggest measures that would make it more amenable to executive leadership and direction. In the 1970's the manifest dangers of runaway executive power are encouraging many to change their minds and to suggest reforms that would enable Congress to reassert its own power in opposition to an increasingly powerful and decreasingly controlled executive. Very likely there will be some changes. The basic structure of Congress, of course, is such that changes generally come grudgingly, if at all. Nevertheless some of the most stodgy institutions in the world have changed dramatically in the last twenty years, and it is conceivable that Congress could follow their lead; not probable, but possible.

Suggested Readings

Stephen K. Bailey, *Congress Makes a Law* (New York: Columbia University Press, 1950); one of the earliest, and still one of the best, of the legislative studies

————, *Congress in the Seventies* (New York: St. Martin's Press, 2nd ed., 1970)*

Richard Bolling, *Power in the House* (New York: E. P. Dutton, 1968); a critical treatment by a member of the House

Joseph S. Clark, *Congress: The Sapless Branch* (New York: Harper & Row, 1964); a critical treatment of the Senate by the former senator from Pennsylvania

————, *Congressional Reform: Problems and Prospects* (New York: Thomas Y. Crowell, 1965); a former senator's suggestions for reform

Lewis A. Dexter, *The Sociology and Politics of Congress* (Chicago: Rand McNally, 1969)*; excellent analysis of Congress as an institution

Richard F. Fenno, Jr., *The Power of the Purse: Appropriations Politics in Congress* (Boston: Little, Brown and Co., 1966)*

Lewis A. Froman, Jr., *The Congressional Process: Strategies, Rules, and Procedures* (Boston: Little, Brown and Co., 1967)*

Mark J. Green, James M. Fallows, and David R. Zwick, *Who Runs Congress?* Ralph Nader Congress Project (New York: Bantam Books, 1972)*; one of the most revealing studies of Congress

Donald R. Matthews, *U.S. Senators and Their World* (Chapel Hill: University of North Carolina Press, 1960); a classic study

Clem Miller, *Member of the House: Letters of a Congressman*, John W. Baker, ed. (New York: Charles Scribner's Sons, 1962)*

* Available in paperback

Donald Riegle, *O Congress* (New York: Popular Library, 1972)*; reflections of a young representative

Alan Rosenthal, "The Effectiveness of Congress," in *The Performance of American Government*, Gerald Pomper, ed. (New York: The Free Press, 1972

Arthur Schlesinger, Jr., "Presidential War: See If You Can Fix Any Limit to His Power," New York *Times* Magazine, January 7, 1973.

Frank Sorauf, *Party and Representation* (New York: Atherton, 1963)

John Wahlke, Heinz Eulau, William Buchanan, and Leroy Ferguson, *The Legislative System: Exploration in Legislative Behavior* (New York: John Wiley & Sons, 1962)

5

THE EXECUTIVE

Master or Equal?

Study to see if you can fix any limit to his power.
Abraham Lincoln

The executive as an institution, a position, and a function has been dominant throughout history and across cultures. Many political systems have been governed by one man or group of men combining all the powers of government, ranging from the simple head of the family to the dictator, sun king, divine ruler, or emperor. Although a separate legislative body or judiciary might have existed, it was subject to the will of the executive. By contrast, there are few terms or forms for legislatures; if the number of words for an institution is indicative of importance in culture and history, legislatures and judiciaries rank far behind executives. Systems in which the legislature has the predominant power, the parliamentary systems, are in a minority. Even in these the power has shifted in the twentieth century to the executive; most of the colonial offshoots have followed suit. The American Constitution, while based on the ideas of separation of powers and the checking of each branch's powers by other branches, does give pre-eminence to the legislature. As we approach the third century of the Constitution, however, the executive has stepped to the center of the stage, rising partly on the discarded or delegated powers of the Congress.

In one original draft of the Constitution, the American executive was to have been elected by the Congress. In another, the President was to be elected by the people. Eventually both of these plans were rejected and a compromise devised; the President would not be merely a tool for realizing the will of the legislature, nor would he be a direct instrument of the people. The state legislatures would choose as many presidential electors as they were assigned members in Congress. This Electoral College would then pick the best two men from the citizens to be the President and Vice President. With the development of the party system it became the custom over the years, although not required by the Constitution or federal law, that the electors simply cast all of their votes for the candidate of the party winning the majority of popular votes in the state. Thus the American presidency has moved closer to the popularly elected office proposed at the convention by Gouverneur Morris as a bulwark against legislative tyranny.

The Constitutional Convention established the basis of modern executive power. The presidency was to be a single office, the Vice President having essentially no powers of his own; the executive was to be independent of the Congress and based on a national constituency, filtered through the state-based Electoral College. Powers were allocated to the President in military and foreign affairs and, somewhat more vaguely, were implied in domestic affairs; together these specifications created a new kind of executive role.

Many of the following comments upon the national executive apply as well to those in the states. The office of governor strongly resembles that of a miniature presidency, with some important exceptions. The typical governor is hemmed in by greater constitutional restrictions than is the President and must share his executive authority with other elected officials (such as auditor, attorney general, and secretary of state) over whom he has no effective control. Most states thus have weaker executives than has the nation, but even at the state level the shift of power toward the executive is discernible, and the office of governor has tended to gain in strength at the expense of the legislature throughout American history. Many governors do possess the item veto, permitting them to reject portions of certain legislative acts without sacrificing the entire act, but this generally fails to compensate for other weaknesses when their executive powers are compared to those of the President. Additionally, the restricted power of state governments themselves is a factor limiting the powers of governors. Nevertheless, the similarity of the executives at the state and national levels is an obvious reflection of the degree to which relatively uniform ideas regarding political practice permeate the system.

The Growth of Executive Power

There have been powerful men in the presidency from the beginning. Jefferson, for instance, used the presidency as an active part of government, and he dominated the federal government of the time. The office itself, however, has grown in strength since Jefferson's day. After Jefferson's terms, in fact, the Congress came into its own; for most of the nineteenth century attention focused on the men and activities of Congress. Only the strong presidents stand out in this period: Jackson and Lincoln. Lincoln in particular seized powers usually held by Congress, sometimes ignoring the Constitution in his struggle to hold the Union together. In the eyes of many historians and political scientists, Lincoln achieved the most powerful presidency in American history, lacking only modern technology. After Lincoln came another series of men less powerful and less well known than many members of Congress. As the twentieth century opened, the balance slowly began to shift. In the first three decades of the new century the presidencies of Roosevelt and Wilson were matched by the passive years of Taft, Harding, Coolidge, and Hoover, but with the coming of the New Deal the presidency passed to an almost unbroken line of men who believed that the office could be, and should be, expanded. At the same time the circumstances of history were producing demands from the public and from other parts of the political system that virtually forced expansion upon the presidency, certainly upon a man such as Eisenhower who had not wanted greater powers. Today, even such a president as Mr. Nixon, who presumably supports the restriction of federal powers and the restoration of state powers, is prepared to assume an executive role as great as any of his predecessors, perhaps even the most extensive in history, in order to implement his views of a good society.

It is significant that Lincoln, the most powerful President of the nineteenth century, was chief executive during the cruelest and most exhausting war ever fought by the United States. Other nineteenth-century Presidents who made their mark tended also to do so in military or in foreign affairs: the war against Mexico, the Indian wars, the purchase of Louisiana. Only Jackson in the years after Jefferson can be said to have left a hallmark on the domestic society and political system, as he presided over the extension of influence to the frontier elite. The tendencies that brought forth the most powerful Presidents in the nineteenth century have accelerated in the twentieth and have been supplemented by others. The reasons for the growth of presidential power are four-fold. First, there has been the increasing involvement of the United States during the twentieth century in world politics and in the wars endemic to those politics.

Second, the increase in the power of the presidency has been related to the growth in size and power of the entire executive branch. The Constitution itself barely mentioned the executive departments and made no statement on their role. The executive bureaucracy of the federal government has grown into an enormous elite, served by a great mass of clerks. Today it totals nearly 3 million persons and spends 21–22 percent of the gross national product. The President's control over this bureaucracy gives him an enormous advantage in comparison to the few thousand employees of Congress and the tiny legislative branch budget. In particular the control that Congress itself vested in the President in 1921, control of the budget of the executive branch (which is, in effect, the national budget) gives the President control of national policy so far as money shapes it.

Third, the developments in technology and the changes in society in the twentieth century have made the President the most visible political figure. The public identifies him as the head of the political system and of the country; few can identify all, or even some, of their congressmen, state and local representatives, and judges. Nearly everyone can name the President. The President is able to command television appearances and set their conditions; his activities are usually accorded a prominence in the news that no single congressman, and perhaps not the Congress itself, can match.

Finally, the type of political campaigning and the political history of the United States since 1932 have weeded out the passively oriented presidential candidates. Most of the men who have competed for the office in the past forty years have been strong personalities, clearly oriented towards an expanding presidency, regardless of their personal political philosophies on the role of the federal government or the role of the government in general.

The Structure and Powers of the Executive

The federal executive may be divided into two parts: first are the elected leader and his policy subordinates, some two thousand appointive offices under the direct control of the President, which constitute the policy head of the executive branch; second are the bureaucracies, controlled today by civil service hiring on the basis of merit rather than on the basis of patronage or class considerations, which total almost 3 million persons. An additional group that can be classed with the executive is the independent agencies, or regulatory bodies set up by Congress beginning in 1887. Although these agencies are ostensibly free of executive direction, they have become increasingly subject to presidential management in the last few decades. The power of appointment to these agencies, however limited by the fixed terms served by the commissioners, gives the President some access to these agencies if he is skillful in his selections.

Although the public may think of the President when the executive is mentioned, the bureaucracy is the only part of the system with which most persons will have any personal contact; the internal revenue agent, the draft board, the post office clerk, the license plate clerk, social security personnel, and the policeman, all working for federal or state executive agencies, are the arms and legs of the government. The laws are made only once; they must be applied daily in many thousands of individual circumstances. Few citizens will write to their congressman or even go to court compared with the millions who have dealings with the bureaucracies.

The President

The President is the official with which the Constitution primarily concerns itself. It is his powers and responsibilities that are defined in Article II, following the blunt statement that "the executive power shall be vested in a President of the United States of America." The Vice President is basically only a safeguard against vacancies in the office of President. The office of Vice President has only one power of itself, that of presiding over the Senate and casting a vote in the event of a tie. Even that power is not described under the article dealing with the executive. The first Vice-President called it the "most insignificant office ever conceived," and John Nance Garner, one of FDR's vice-presidents, said that the job was "not worth a pitcher of warm spit."

As a stepping stone to higher office, the vice presidency has provided a number of presidents. Eleven vice presidents have succeeded to the presidency. Three of the eleven were elected on their own and three were elected after they gained office through the death of the President; five filled out the term of a dead President but had none of their own. Only in recent decades, however, has the office become an important newsmaker. Nixon, Johnson, Humphrey, and Agnew were all personally energetic and ambitious men, and they created interest in themselves,

DOMESTIC POWER/ROLE:	SOURCE	CHECK
Appointment and removal of major policymakers	Constitution for appointment; removal by tradition. Article II, Section 2	Confirmation by Senate if the Congress so determines. Article II, Section 2
Head of the executive; chief administrator	Implied in Article II, Sections 2 and 3	Subject to congressional approval of the number and structure of departments, etc. Article I, Section 8
Executor of the laws	Constitution, Article II, Section 3	Congress alone may make law. Article I, Section 1
Budget preparation	Budget and Accounting Act of 1921	Congress alone may appropriate funds. Article I, Section 9
Impoundment/transfer of funds	Tradition; possibly statute	????
Initiator of legislation	Constitution, Article II, Section 3, implied	Congress alone may make law. Article I, Section 1
Veto	Constitution, Article II, Section 7	Excepting ten days or less before adjournment, Congress may repass. Article II, Section 7
Convene special sessions and adjourn Congress if the houses disagree on the time	Constitution, Article II, Section 3	Congress determines all other procedural matters; Article I, Section 5
Executive order	Tradition	????
Executive privilege	Tradition	????

with the help of the President. The President still controls the circumstances of the Vice President; he can give him a great deal of responsibility and visibility, grooming him as a successor, or he can keep him in the White House closet.

Most eyes focus on the President; his hands alone hold the reins. His powers are a combination of constitutional grants, statutory additions by the Congress, additions grafted on by custom and accident, and his

FOREIGN POWER/ROLE:	SOURCE	CHECK
Making of treaties	Constitution, Article II, Section 2	Ratification by two thirds of voting Senators. Same
Appointment of ambassadors and other officers	Constitution, Article II, Section 2	Confirmation by the Senate. Same
Recognition of other nations and receiving ambassadors	Constitution, Article II, Section 3, recognition implied	????
Commander in chief and initiator of war	Constitution, Article II, Section 2, and implied	Declaration of war and military funds only by Congress. Article I, Section 8

personal attributes and abilities. A good deal will always depend upon the President's personal ability to persuade others, to keep on top of the situation, to make the best of his political status and authority without pushing his powers against the limits of others' endurance and causing a confrontation. He is faced with demands from many different constituencies. A careful use of these demands can increase his political stature, while mistakes may compound each other and drag him down under the burden. He has to deal with the enormous bureaucracy and keep it from subverting his policies; he must keep his major advisers and executive heads from becoming too independent, too important in their own right, perhaps with an eye to higher office themselves. He must deal with Congress as an institution; his party's members in Congress will make additional demands. Members of his party outside Congress will expect his support and help as the unofficial leader of the party; his personal supporters may have conflicting needs. The nation as a whole is his constituency as head of state; the world outside also will make demands on him in this role. He and his office will be the target of pressures from most of the interest groups in the nation. A major mistake in any one of these areas can tarnish a shining performance in the rest.

DOMESTIC AFFAIRS.   In this century the nominations of executive officers and (despite the notable Haynsworth and Carswell rejections) federal judges offered by the President have rarely failed to be confirmed; during the nineteenth century Congress refused to grant consent far more frequently, rejecting a quarter of the judicial appointments alone. Today the confirmation hearings may be used to publicize congressional disagreement with policy in the office under consideration; at the end, following the tradition that the President is entitled to have the men he wants, the Senate usually confirms. This also extends to the personal advisers of the President, discussed below, whom Congress does not require to be ratified. These appointments are to some extent a source of patronage for the President; as head of his party he will generally choose nominees from that party.

As head of the executive branch, the President is the head of the entire federal bureaucracy, although many of the employees are under civil service, including many of the major subordinates of his policy-makers. He and his executive heads may issue orders changing the regulations and practices of various agencies. He may reorganize the Executive Office, which includes his advisory agencies and his personal White House staff, as he sees fit unless Congress objects within sixty days. Reorganization of the executive departments or creation of new ones requires action by Congress. A President may attempt to avoid this by reorganizing his own staff along the lines he prefers and then requiring the executive departments to go through this staff in order to consult with him.

As executor of the laws, the President is effectively free to determine how much attention will be devoted to various areas; if he is confident of public support, he may even openly refuse to implement a policy approved by Congress. Even though the Constitution requires the President to "faithfully execute" the laws, presidents have argued that this does not bind them to execute laws that they believe are intrusions into executive powers. Congress cannot force the President to take action except by using its monetary powers to deny him funds for some other project. Executive discretion has become a necessity as the amount of federal legislation mushrooms; yet at the same time it gives the President great power in shaping policy. The Constitution has no remedy. There was one attempt by Congress to utilize impeachment proceedings as a means of attacking a President whose policy it found offensive, against Andrew Johnson, which came within one vote of success. Other efforts to impeach were directed at Tyler and Coolidge but failed completely. As of early 1974 impeachment resolutions against Nixon were pending. In general, however, the only effective remedy remains in the hands of the people, if the President asks for re-election.

Congress created the budget powers of the President in 1921 and extended them in 1939 by putting the budget agency in the executive office, where the President could easily control it. Prior to that the executive departments submitted their requests to Congress separately, and it was up to Congress to determine the priorities. In the present arrangement the President, assisted by the budget agency (now called the Office of Management and Budget), presides over the determination of priorities. Departments submit requests to the OMB, which can reshape them as it wishes; no requests are submitted directly to Congress, although some powerful agencies with close ties to a congressional committee may in fact do so informally.

In the 1940s there were some brief efforts to create a "legislative budget" as a means of enabling Congress to establish its own set of priorities as a check on the executive determination, but the attempt failed. Many present-day critics believe that the time has come, and Congress is moving toward the formation of a joint committee on the budget. The argument is that unless Congress does this it will have lost its monetary powers forever and will be relegated to the role of check writer. The difficulty of a reassertion of powers is compounded by the practices Congress has allowed to develop of impounding and transferring funds. Funds may be shifted about within a department; funds that the President does not wish to spend may be impounded, or frozen. The legality of this is uncertain. Congress has given the President authority to effect savings in administering programs; it has never given him the right to refuse to spend funds for some purpose *in toto*. Yet since the Second World War Congress has given at least implied consent by allowing the ever increasing use of impounding, often without even a protest. The total of impounded funds has risen to nearly $15 billion today. Considerable reaction against this is appearing in Congress; bills are pending that would require the Congress to be notified of impounded funds and either require approval within a certain period or allow a certain period for a vote of disapproval. If one of these bills is passed into law, perhaps over the President's veto, and impoundment should continue it would probably precipitate a Supreme Court test.

A second major legislative role of the President is based upon his power to suggest legislation to the Congress. Through the State of the Union message, in which he yearly lays down the outline of his administration's programs, and the periodic suggestion of legislation that he thinks "necessary and expedient," in the Constitution's phrase, the President and the executive branch have become the source of the majority of national legislation. Since the Second World War, the process has been accelerated. Perhaps two-thirds of all legislation originates in the executive branch; if the minor bills are excepted, executive inspiration accounts for nearly four-fifths of the major proposals passed by Congress in the years since the war. Today it is expected that the White House will draw up legislation and present it to Congress as part of an overall administration program. The congressional leadership, whether of the President's party or not, has failed to respond with a program of its own; instead, it merely reacts to White House proposals. Various congressmen, particularly senators, may introduce legislation, and some few will draw up major bills, often with the help of interested organizations. A major proposal on the health-care system, for instance, may have the backing and assistance of the American Hospital Association or the Committee of 100, a labor-union backed coalition. The resources of the executive branch, however, and the political purpose and will of its single head, are far greater than those of Congress, which are divided among its elected leaders and its committee heads and additionally split by party lines. The executive has assumed a great deal of the legislative power, through both presidential initiative and congressional default.

If the White House proposals are mutilated by Congress, or if it passes other legislation not acceptable to the President, he may use the veto, having ten days to do so. Congress may then repass the bill over the veto, unless it has adjourned within the ten-day period, but this requires a two-thirds vote of each house. (There is currently pending in the federal courts a suit brought by Senator Kennedy challenging a recent executive practice of treating a brief recess of Congress as an adjournment and refusing to return a bill for reconsideration.) The possibility that Congress may repass a bill makes the veto much less useful to a President than a final veto. Additionally, the veto is a general veto rather than the item veto possessed by some of the state executives; the President may not veto only part of a bill but must accept it or reject it in its entirety. Thus, if an unrelated item is added in a "rider," he must reject the entire bill in order to reject the rider; some legislation that the President does not like may be forced upon him by attaching it to material he is intent upon having.

The final legislative power of the President, that of convening special sessions of Congress, is essentially an emergency power; if a crisis of some kind occurs when Congress is not in session, the President may summon it to meet. Of course, there is no assurance that Congress, once convened, will act favorably on the President's request. Special sessions have become rare in the twentieth century, as the regular sessions of Congress now consume most of the year.

Through the executive order and executive privilege, the President's actions may escape scrutiny by the Congress. These two powers have evolved from historical necessity and exist only by implication, if at all, in the Constitution. Executive privilege originally meant that the President himself could not be called upon to testify before Congress; this was held to be necessary under the separation of powers. By extension, his few personal assistants were also free from testifying. This right of refusal underlines the difference between the President and a prime minister in parliamentary government; the prime minister, during "question time" may be ruthlessly interrogated by any and all members of the legislature, a probing that cannot be escaped by refusal to appear.

The contrast has grown sharper in the post World War II years, as presidents have gradually extended the privilege to more and more of their ever more important advisers. Men such as the Assistant for National Security and the Assistant for Domestic Affairs, not subject to Senate confirmation, have also not been subject to congressional questioning. In 1973 the Nixon Administration expanded the interpretation of the privilege, ruling that no members of the executive office would appear before Congress even after they left office, although it subsequently retreated from this position and did permit them to testify. Critics in and out of Congress have noted that the effect of executive privilege has been to diminish sharply the congressional ability to share in policy-making. If Congress cannot question the men who are the effective determiners of policy in the executive branch, its ability to analyze those policies and suggest changes or alternatives is considerably reduced.

An executive order is a directive issued under the authority of the President, either by him personally or by one of the executive departments. Congress could not conceivably consider and pass as law every minute change that needs to be made in the bureaucracy as circumstances change, and so it has allowed this quasi-legislative activity. Executive orders usually involve a change in the regulations of an agency or an action that must be taken to implement legislation or enforce a provision of a treaty or of the Constitution as the courts interpret it. Most of these are not controversial; but some postwar executive orders have generated disputes, and a number of recent orders have actually involved major policy changes. In the Kennedy Administration, for instance, military bases were desegregated by executive action; the Nixon Administration has made major changes in matters such as tax structure and day-care eligibility by changing regulations. Thus an executive order may involve a change in policy no less significant than many of the changes submitted to Congress for approval. There have been challenges to some of these orders; a suit was brought against the changes in the Treasury Department regulations, for example, but with no success. General criticism of the expansion of executive orders has pointed out that they mark another intrusion of the President into legislative territory, adding to the imbalance between President and Congress in the twentieth century.

Devising a means to control the executive order without crippling governmental efficiency is difficult. Perhaps, after the publication of the order, Congress could be given a period of time in which to examine the order, which would then take effect unless Congress disapproved it. The burden of examining the mass of executive orders would be substantial, but the members of Congress have the power to provide themselves with the staff necessary to do this, just as they have the power to give the executive the authority and staff necessary to issue executive orders.

FOREIGN AFFAIRS.   The major foreign policy powers given to the President in the Constitution are his role as Commander in Chief of the armed services, with the implied right to initiate hostilities, and his treaty-making power. In the early days of the republic, when the armed services numbered only one or two thousand and the United States shunned the entanglements of the old world as Washington advised, these powers seemed insignificant. As the armed strength of the United States rose in the nineteenth century, the power of the President increased; when the United States assumed a major, and for a time the dominant, role in world affairs, the President accordingly became a world leader. The weapons technology of the twentieth century, spurred by the Cold War and culminating in the nuclear age, gave the President enormous powers, which were inevitably reflected in increases in domestic might. The exercise of these powers parallels that of much of the domestic powers: The President takes the initiative, and Congress reacts. The active role belongs to the President.

The Constitution provided checks both to the President's treaty-making powers and to his powers as Commander in Chief. Only the Congress can declare war, and presumably it need not wait to be asked to do so by the President; Congress alone can raise and equip an army, and the Constitution limits appropriations for that purpose to two-year periods, unlike any other appropriations. Treaties must be submitted to the Senate and ratified by approval of two-thirds of those voting before they are legally binding on the United States. (This process has been puzzling to some nations, which have regarded the signature of the American representative as constituting a commitment which is not erased by Senate rejection of the agreement.)

In the two centuries since the framing of the Constitution the checks have gradually lost most of their effectiveness. Congress has declared war on only five occasions, but many dozens of military actions have been undertaken and continued by the executive without benefit of a formal declaration. Many of these initiatives did not result in any major fighting; e.g., the landing of the troops in Lebanon. Other "undeclared wars" have assumed outsized dimensions; the Mexican War in the nineteenth century and the Vietnam War in this century were the subject of bitter criticism by part of the public and by some congressmen, leading to suggestions that the war-making powers of the President be curtailed. After a long series of proposals by some members, including many conservatives, that would require the President to obtain congressional approval for his military actions within a set period of time, the Congress in late 1973 enacted such a proposal. As expected the President promptly vetoed it, but the Congress at last had been aroused, and the required two-thirds majority in each house voted to overturn the veto. The new law requires the President to notify Congress within forty-eight hours if he sends troops into another nation, and to withdraw them after sixty days unless Congress approves the action. The law provides further that Congress may force troop withdrawal during the sixty-day period by a majority vote that is not subject to veto. There are practical difficulties with this law, including the possibility that presidents could be tempted to direct short but exceedingly destructive actions in order to accomplish their purpose before end of the sixty days. Despite the inherent difficulties, however, Congress felt that some such action was necessary; otherwise its power to declare war would remain a dead letter, and the war-making powers would remain almost completely in the President's hands.

Similarly, the check exercised by the Senate over relations with other countries in treaties has declined in significance in the twentieth century as the use of treaties has declined. Instead, the executive has turned to the executive agreement. In its original form, the executive agreement was simply a compact with another national head or delegate, not requiring Senate concurrence; the subject matter might be the details consequent to a treaty, or administrative problems, generally not serious enough to require a treaty. As the years passed, however, executive agreements have been used increasingly to deal with major problems without submitting the action to the Senate; executive agreements outnumber treaties in the twentieth century. The President thus has further increased his control over foreign affairs. In addition many of these agreements were concluded with no notice of their existence being given even to the Senate, much less to the public. Although executive agreements are not binding on successive administrations unless those administrations consent, they do commit the United States in the eyes of the other nation in many cases, and dozens of agreements are still in force from past administrations by consent. The recent discovery by the Senate Foreign Relations Committee of a number of secret agreements involving military support of nations such as Ethiopia, Laos, and Spain led to consideration and passage of legislation requiring all agreements to be submitted to Congress at least for its own information, although no right of congressional veto was established. A similar bill was considered in the 1950's without success. The executive agreement, and its control by Congress, poses problems paralleling those in controlling the executive order. Executive agreements developed as a necessary means of conducting the minor details of American interaction with nearly two hundred nations; to forbid them or to require that all agreements be treated as formal treaties, as the "Bricker Amendment," sponsored by the conservative Ohio senator in the 1950's would have done, would cripple conduct of our foreign relations. Yet if Congress does not find some way to bring the substantive executive agreement under control, its treaty powers will continue to wither, and its present minor role in foreign policy to dwindle.

Through his appointment of ambassadors to other nations, subject to Senate confirmation, and his power to receive ambassadors, not subject to Senate approval, which carries with it the power to recognize those nations, the President acts as the head of state. He is the determiner of which nations we will have relations with, and on what basis. There is no way that Congress can force the President to recognize or to refuse recognition to any nation, although it may attempt to do so by refusing to allocate any funds necessary to establish relations. There have been some occasions when confirmation of an ambassadorial nominee would be held up while the Senate expressed its disapproval of the policy in regard to the nation that would receive the ambassador (most recently in the case of the ambassador to Greece), but this is not much more than a symbolic gesture. Since the beginning of the republic, it has been generally regarded as the rightful role of the President to take the lead in foreign affairs. Even when this means slighting or ignoring congressional directives, there has rarely been protest. For instance, Congress passed a law in the forties requiring congressional action to revalue the dollar. In recent years the President has unilaterally directed reevaluation of the currency and Congress has lodged no complaint, on the grounds that foreign speculators would benefit from the advance knowledge of a devaluation, to the economic disadvantage of the United States, if the President sought consent.

THE LIMITS OF PRESIDENTIAL POWER.   The first limit on any President's power is his own personality and capabilities. Each man has his own strengths and weaknesses, which help to shape the results of his action. Presidents can choose White House and Executive Office staffs to help compensate for this; a man who is not a good administrator of personnel can partly overcome this lack by choosing an assistant who is and giving him the job of supervising the choice of executive appointments. Similarly, the President can supplement his strengths, choosing other advisers whose strong points reflect the President's own. Skillful selection of staff can reduce the limits imposed by the President's capabilities but never eliminate them; the decisions must ultimately be made by the one man, and his intellect, judgment, and personality are critical.

The President is subject to many other limitations, some traditional, some laid down in the Constitution, some determined by circumstances. Although he can try to stretch his powers through reinterpreting the Constitution, the survival of constitutional democracy obliges him to abide by it, and by decisions of the courts. When Truman interpreted his powers as Commander in Chief to allow him to seize the steel mills during a strike in the Korean War, his opponents quickly obtained a Supreme Court ruling to the contrary, and he was forced to back down. Moreover, even when there is no constitutional or legal bar, action is limited by the degree to which other powerful persons accept it: Congressional leaders, the President's own advisers and executive heads, the bureaucracy itself, leaders of other nations, pressure group interests, and, in some cases, the general public may all be able to thwart presidential plans. A President's resources are great, but they are limited; even allocated carefully and thriftily, they will probably not cover all of his goals. The past restrains him; commitments in foreign policy, for instance, are not easily reversed. The costs of attempting to reverse them may hamper him in some other policy. Domestic programs build up powerful constituencies that will resist change. Finally, the acceleration of problems in the mid-twentieth century makes many of the President's routine chores today equal to emergency conditions in the White House of the past. This imposes limits of time and information. There are deadlines that must be met, vast amounts of information that the President must sift through, and the greater problem of getting enough information. There must be decisions on a vast array of domestic and foreign issues, some of which are new in this century and impose staggering burdens, such as nuclear weapons, biological warfare, control of international corporations, and the military uses of space. And, in the end, it may all be undone by some chance event somewhere, by mob action in Birmingham, a U-2 in Russia, or a bullet in Dallas.

THE FUTURE.   In general, the balance of powers set up between the Congress and the President in both foreign and domestic affairs has shifted dramatically over the years. The executives of the twentieth century, and some of their predecessors, have acted aggressively to make the presidency into a powerful central office. They acted from a combination of personal enjoyment of power and a desire to see their own vision of the social good become reality. A good deal of the executive expansion involved seizing powers from Congress, which sometimes meant nothing more than taking what was offered on a silver platter. Congress delegated many of its powers to the President over the years, while no President in the twentieth century has delegated any power to Congress, as a few did in the Congressional heyday of the nineteenth century.

The central role played by the President in the political system is not likely to change, even if the legislature should reassert some of its authority. In the nuclear age the central position of the President in war-making is unlikely to be displaced, and the general control of the executive over foreign affairs is underpinned by the Constitution itself. At best Congress can hope for a greater share of the responsibility of setting the limits of American action; it will make little policy. In domestic affairs Congress originally had the major role, and the need to restore its rightful share of power is more pressing. The shift to executive dominance is already a *fait accompli* in many areas, however, and the role of executive leadership in the progress of American society is accepted and celebrated by much of the public and by many intellectuals, although some recently have come to have second thoughts. Recapturing powers lost or given away is always much more difficult than their forfeiture. For those powers specified in the Constitution, a check is also specified; Congress must find some way to reassert that check. Those powers that have been developed by the executive "from scratch," such as executive privilege, are much more difficult to control; new checks must be devised. Outside groups that are affected may become part of the control process by challenging executive action in the courts; the public itself can assist by indicating to the President and the Congress the public reaction to executive action. In turn the press bears a large responsibility in making knowledge of executive actions and their implications available to the public. In the end the President will still have the great power to act first, to seize the initiative.

The Bureaucracy: Arms and Legs of the Executive Body

The federal bureaucracies, and their state and local counterparts, bear a closer resemblance to the bureaucracies of other nations than do other parts of the political system to their foreign counterparts. Bureaucracies tend to have the same characteristics whether they are located in Washington, Paris, or Moscow. As they grow in size and responsibilities, bureaucracies have assumed leading roles in various governmental functions and may even eventually dominate some of them. The American bureaucracy is no exception. In their day-to-day administrative actions, the federal (and other) bureaucracies carry out quasi-legislative and quasi-judicial functions as well as executive ones. Since their size and cost escalated with the beginning of the New Deal, the bureaucracies have become some of the nation's most powerful interest groups; in turn, many of the major private interest groups have found a home in the recesses of the bureaucracy. The bureaucracy itself has become a major policy-maker.

The Constitution does not discuss the federal bureaucracy except as an aid to the President. The electoral base of the President, who heads the

Reproduced by permission of Johnny Hart and Field Enterprises, Inc.

bureaucracy, constitutes the political control of the bureaucracy. At the outset of the republic, there were only the departments of State, Treasury, and War, headed by secretaries, and an Attorney General and Postmaster General. Federal employees numbered less than a thousand.

Today there are eleven departments whose heads constitute the Cabinet, with the postal service and Postmaster General having been removed. In addition to the thousands of divisions in these departments, there are some 3,000 other advisory committees, boards, commissions, councils, conferences, panels, task forces, and the like; not even the government itself knows how many there are. Whatever the exact figure, it is many times the number of employees in 1789. A third group in the bureaucracy is the independent agencies, with administrative, regulatory, or corporate character; examples are the Federal Reserve System Board of Governors, the Federal Trade Commission, and the Tennessee Valley Authority, respectively. These are bodies created by Congress, with executive heads appointed by the President for fixed and staggered terms. Their responsibilities lie primarily in the economy, particularly in regulating some aspect of the economy such as the production and distribution of energy resources. Ostensibly these agencies are independent of the executive, but the President can and does attempt to control them through his appointments and through his budget control over them. Many critics of the independent agencies have suggested that they have become supporters of the industries that they are supposed to regulate and no longer fulfill their purpose; in addition their increasing subservience to the President in some instances increases the President's power in the economy. Some students of these agencies have suggested that they should simply be abolished.

Much of the growth of the bureaucracy in this century is the direct result of the expansion of the renamed Department of War, the Defense Department. It has approximately half of all civilian federal employees, in addition to the several million men under arms. The second largest department, now an independent agency, is the postal service. Far behind these two is the Department of Health, Education, and Welfare, with less than a tenth of the Defense Department roster.

The distribution of the budget also determines to a large extent the influence of the various departments in the government policy-making process. Again the Department of Defense leads, with the largest single departmental allocation, roughly a third of the budget. Additional military-related expenditures, such as veterans affairs, military aspects of foreign aid and the Food for Peace program, the space program, military work of the Atomic Energy Commission, interest on the national debt resulting from past wars, and the like increase the defense share. The highest estimate is that defense spending accounts for two-thirds of the budget. Regardless of which estimate one accepts, defense spending represents an enormous factor in the economy; some 20 to 25 percent of the economy is dependent in some way on military expenditures. Few congressional districts are without a military installation or contractor. The interrelationship between the upper levels of the Pentagon staff and the upper levels of military industries is strong; hundreds of retired military leaders and heads of civilian agencies have found work in defense industries, while a smaller contingent of men leave the industries and join the Pentagon or the White House staff. This combined economic strength and enormous staff size make the Defense Department more equal than its peers, the other departments. Any change in federal spending priorities must of necessity involve the Pentagon.

POLITICAL PROBLEMS OF THE BUREAUCRACY.   The impact of the Pentagon on the shape of government policy is one major problem. The growth of the bureaucracy in general, related to the growth of the Defense Department, is another. Control of this vast apparatus is difficult. Lower level employees may fail to implement policies made by the department heads, either through inertia or malice, and the policy-makers may not be able to discover the source of the trouble. Civil service employment makes it difficult, although not impossible, to eliminate troublesome or sluggish employees. The public and other elements of the government may have to toil patiently to extract any information from the mass of departments. Despite the passage of the Freedom of Information Act of 1967, the flow of information has not quickened. The new law allowed the agencies only nine specific reasons for withholding information, but most have apparently been able to fit any information that they wished to keep private into one of these categories. Finally, pinning down responsibility in a huge organization is difficult for the public and even for political figures; government by bureaucracy is essentially government by nobody.

A third problem, parallel to a problem in private organizations, is the kind and amount of information collected by these agencies in the discharge of their duties and the supervision of these masses of data. This is the opposite side of the information coin; how much control can there be over the distribution of information that ought to remain private? As

Major Executive Agencies

THE CABINET	THE WHITE HOUSE	INDEPENDENT OFFICES
State (original)	White House Office	Atomic Energy Commission
Defense (original)	Office of Management and Budget	Federal Reserve System
Treasury (original)	Council of Economic Advisors	General Services Administration
Justice (1870)	National Security Council (CIA)	National Aeronautics and Space Administration
Interior (1849)	Domestic Council	Civil Service Commission
Agriculture (1862)	Council on Environmental Quality	Veterans Administration
Commerce (1903)	* Office of Economic Opportunity	Civil Aeronautics Board
Labor (1913)	* Office of Science and Technology	Federal Communications Commission
Health, Education and Welfare (1953)	* Office of Emergency Preparedness	Federal Power Commission
Housing and Urban Development (1965)		Federal Trade Commission
Transportation (1967)		Interstate Commerce Commission
		National Labor Relations Board
		Securities and Exchange Commission

Dates are those of establishment.
* Scheduled for elimination by the Nixon Administration.

the computer has come into wide use (there are some 60,000 in the federal executive branch), the problem of the invasion of privacy grows. Every smidgen of information ever collected can be easily stored, collated, and retrieved. The problem is compounded by illegitimate collection of information, but even the massing of legitimate information poses a problem. Relatively few persons came under the illegitimate political scrutiny of the army intelligence service, but almost every adult in America is the subject of one or more government dossiers. (Adding private forms such as credit data, the average adult is documented in some ten records.) The list of the different kinds of forms on which the federal government collects information is itself nearly 400 pages long!

In a profound sense, government by bureaucracy is incompatible with democracy. Bureaucracy by definition is a form of organization based upon routine and efficiency; individual considerations and exceptions are inconsistent with the regulations. A government concerned with individual problems may occasionally be inconsistent and inefficient; a democracy can hardly escape individual problems. The ability of the bureaucracy to escape executive supervision additionally means that it is not a subject to popular control, a major criterion of democracy. But bureaucracy seems inevitable, so ways must be found to limit its worst tendencies. The answer lies in developing more effective political leadership of the bureaucracies. This does not necessarily mean greater control by the President, although substantial presidential supervision is needed if the executive is going to be able to implement his policies. Congress can also play a major role. It already has an effective investigatory arm in the General Accounting Office; if this body were given increased staff and authority, and the support of the Congress when it trod upon tender toes, the Congress would be able to play a greater policy-making role. And the development of two sources of control, both accountable to the public, would bring the bureaucracy into at least indirect accountability to the public, a necessity for democracy.

Suggested Readings
James D. Barber, "Passive-Positive to Active-Negative: The Style and Character of Presidents," *Washington Monthly*, 1:9 (October, 1969)
Edward F. Cox, *et al, Nader's Raiders Report on the Federal Trade Commission* (New York: Grove Press, 1969)*
Thomas E. Cronin, "Superman: Our Textbook President," *Washington Monthly*, 2:8 (October, 1970)
Roy P. Fairfield, ed., *The Federalist Papers* (Garden City: Doubleday, 1961)
Robert Fellmeth, *The Interstate Commerce Commission: The Public Interest and the ICC* (New York: Grossman, 1970)*
Louis Koenig, *The Chief Executive* (New York: Harcourt, Brace Jovanovich, 1968)*
Louis M. Kohlmeier, Jr., "The Regulatory Agencies: What Should Be Done?" *Washington Monthly*, 1:7 (August, 1969)
Arthur Miller, *The Invasion of Privacy* (Ann Arbor: University of Michigan, 1971)
Richard Neustadt, *Presidential Power* (New York: Signet Books, 1964)*
Peter Woll, *American Bureaucracy* (New York: Norton, 1963)*

* Available in paperback

6

THE JUDICIAL PROCESS

Justice in America?

The dispensing of injustice is always in the right hands.
Stanislaus Lec

Ethologists—students of animal behavior—have pointed out in recent years that one reason why many species of animals seem so much less violent than man is that these species have by instinct a ritual behavior of some kind that limits aggression. Much of man's political history may be summarized as a struggle to develop alternatives to violence in human society, first between individuals and then between groups and the larger groups called nations. The judicial process in its many forms is the human cultural answer to the ritual of instinct. Institutionally, the judicial process is in a sense the heart of the political system. In the most simply organized societies, with few specialized roles, the role of the leader in the settling of disputes is often his most important, most frequently seen face. As the organization of society becomes more complex this basic role is still important, even though the leadership assumes other roles as well. Eventually if the level of organization becomes complex enough, and the society has the economic resources to afford the luxury, a specialized judiciary may be created. Regardless of what form the judicial system takes, its basic political role is the same: the creation and maintenance of forms of dispute settlement that enable the society to control its conflicts. The system may employ violence or the threat of violence to support its decisions, but only as a last resort; if compliance is not forthcoming on most decisions, then the judicial system is not functioning well. If public acceptance of judicial actions continues to decline, then the society may slip

105

back into violence, as individuals turn to their personal solutions, a kind of chaotic self-help that rests ultimately on force; alternatively a powerful government may force compliance, as least for a time, again basing the society on force.

The American System

The judicial systems that developed in the colonies drew upon English law and institutions, and a number of other legal systems, which the pressure of colonial circumstances and needs shaped into very different law and courts. In particular, the political character of the American judicial systems that emerged from colonial history was unique. In the colonies, judicial functions had been closely intertwined with the legislative and executive branches; the highest court in a colony was often the royal council, which was also the upper house of the legislature. The colonists rejected this fusion of powers after the Revolution; in the states, and in the new federal system, they created a separate set of courts, headed by independent judges. At the top of the national judicial system would be the Supreme Court created by the federal Constitution; the other federal courts were left to the Congress to arrange. State courts, under the federal system, were part of the powers of the individual states. All of these courts heard cases based on controversies only; they would not rule on hypothetical questions. The colonial and post-revolutionary growth of American law has provided four basic sources of law, rules that guide the courts in the resolution of these disputes.

The Ground of the Law

All courts in the United States are to uphold the Constitution and may try cases arising under it within their jurisdiction. The Supreme Court has the power of final resolution, at least within the judicial system, of constitutional questions through its power to hear cases under the U.S. Constitution and determine any conflicts in lower court decisions on the Constitution. The federal Constitution takes precedence over the other political charters of the nation; state constitutions must contain no provisions forbidden by the federal Constitution; city and county charters must be consistent with the constitution of the state where they are located and with the national Constitution. The judges of state and local courts have the power to rule on cases concerning interpretation of the lower constitutions, and the high court of the state has the final say.

This power to hold unconstitutional the laws and other actions of public officials is known as *judicial review*; it is the basis of the political power of courts in the United States. First, the courts, headed by the Supreme Court, become the final interpretor of the Constitution itself; the continued longevity of the Constitution depends in part upon the judiciary. Using the Constitution as a measure, the courts may weigh the acts and laws of all public officials and the decisions of lower courts. Even co-equal branches may be judged; the Supreme Court may thus scrutinize the acts of Congress and the President. By measuring politics against the Constitution, particularly the Bill of Rights, the courts become, even against their will, the conscience of the nation; they must keep the values they see in the Constitution and remind the public of them from time to time. Other nations rarely have given their courts such power, allowing them to interpret laws but not constitutions. Judicial review is found in other federal systems, and to some extent in the new nations which modeled themselves partly upon the American example, but it is comparatively rare.

The courts must also enforce *treaty obligations*. A treaty may not be enforced if it requires acts that are inconsistent with the Constitution, and any federal or state legislation that is inconsistent with a valid treaty is void. For example, if a treaty is signed regulating the hunting of migratory song birds, any state laws that allow a conflicting practice may not be enforced; a treaty with an Indian nation granting them fishing rights in perpetuity takes precedence over state fishing regulations.

The bulk of the judicial system's work is based upon the third and fourth elements of law, the *statutory and common law*, rather than on constitutions and treaties. The American system is part of a great legal tradition, the common law tradition, which spread from England to her colonies in the New World, in Africa, and Asia; in England it had its beginnings a thousand years ago in the creation of a legal system by the early nobles and kings. Essentially the common law is based upon the idea of decision grounded in community norms and history. Judges may rule on the basis of these communal patterns as well as specific statutes or rules. Thus the California Supreme Court ruled against capital punishment in part because it found that the consensus of the community was against the penalty. Judges also may base their decisions upon the precedents set in other cases, and they may choose to overthrow those precedents, even their own. This emphasis on the judge's interpretations of community beliefs, other cases, and changing circumstances gives the common law tradition another name, "judge made" or "bench made" law. The judge has great flexibility, and his personality and background become correspondingly important. How he sees the law and interprets the traditions of the community and the meaning of statutes will be greatly affected by his personal experience. The long hand of tradition restrains the judge, yet he is free to take account of historical changes in society, to find another precedent or to interpret a statute—in short, to keep the law a living thing. This makes the common law tradition a conservative legal system that is at the same time capable of encompassing vast social and political changes if the judges are able to understand those changes. (The other major Western legal tradition, *civil law*, has its roots in Roman law and is based on statutes and codes, with little judicial interpretation; it is represented in the United States in the legal system of Louisiana, a heritage of the state's French background. Other states of the union that had civil law traditions as French, Spanish, or Mexican ruled territories have since become common law systems. It is interesting to note that Louisiana leads the list of states in the number of times the Supreme Court has declared its enactments invalid.)

At present, the growing body of statutes outweighs the common law as a basis of decision, a process that began in the second quarter of the nineteenth century; today there are well over a million statutes on the books. This maze of laws, regulations, and ordinances gives the judges new sources of decisions. It confronts the citizen with a vast array of responsibilities and obligations as well as rights, providing ever growing numbers of controversies and so increasing the level of judicial activity. The entire body of laws enacted in American history, including statutes in force in the states before the ratification of the Constitution, may be called upon by litigants and judges to settle disputes or create legal obligations. Even though a law has not been enforced for decades, it is not thereby invalid, although its subsequent application may be challenged on that ground as discriminatory. Unless a statute contains an expiration date, it remains in force until a legislature purges it from the statute books or a judge voids it. Thus the federal law of 1870 on housing discrimination remains valid for the 1970's even though it lay dormant for nearly a hundred years. The legislatures rarely purge the laws, and judicial invalidation proceeds one law at a time. As the number of laws rises, prosecutors are forced to use discretion in which laws they apply, and to what acts. The statute books contain an incredible array of prohibitions. Recently discovered laws forbid persons who have a "disgusting" appearance to expose themselves to public view; kite-flying; taking a lion to the theatre; going unshaven; keeping a mule in the bathtub; scowling; male topless bathing suits; sneezing on a train; and wearing roller skates in a restroom. Most of these laws are never enforced, and no one expects them to be. However, from the vast array of laws, some serious, some silly, the state can find a way to prosecute almost anyone—which could have political overtones. Did the government prosecute kiteflyers in Washington because it objected to kite-flying or because it objected to their participation in an anti-war demonstration a few minutes before? Was the gambler prosecuted for possessing 563 game birds, 539 over the limit, because of government zeal in protecting game birds or because the gambler was suspected of taking part in organized crime? As long as the statutes are so numerous, discretion in prosecution—the power to determine whether or not to prosecute—remains a necessity; in those cases where the defendant is in some way an opponent of the government, discretion in prosecution results in a political trial, a trial in which the judicial system has become the background to a struggle over the possession and maintenance of political power.

A basic distinction is made in this system, as in most Western systems, between various types of law. Law may be divided into *public* and *private* law; the latter is that governing relations between private persons, such as marriage, while the former covers the operations of the state and is subdivided into *administrative* and *constitutional* law. Administrative law applies to the operations of the various agencies of government; constitutional law, as we have seen, is the application of the provisions of a constitution to the acts of public officers. Finally, there is the distinction in both common law and civil law systems between *civil* and *criminal* law. Most civil law is private law, although the government may be a plaintiff or defendant in a civil case. In those instances its role is different from its role under criminal law, in which the government acts as the prosecutor in the name of the community as a whole. A criminal offense, in other words, may be thought of as an offense against the society, an offense against the public order. In a murder, for instance, the family of the victim does not sue the accused; society, in the person of government, accuses and tries the offender, and the prosecution side is spoken of interchangeably as The People, or The State.

Any one of these kinds of law may become the basis for a political trial, the means by which the state and its opponents challenge each other. Most frequently, however, constitutional law and criminal law are the sources. Any constitutional question involves the political system; frequently dramatic shifts in the distribution of power may result from a constitutional case, such as the reapportionment of legislative districts. Criminal law includes a number of acts that are specifically political in nature, offenses connected with the conduct of campaigns and elections, for example, or treason, sedition, malfeasance in public office, and assassination. Ordinary criminal offenses may also take on a political coloration; the defendant may be in the dock as a result of his political activities. Even if the accused is actually guilty of the crime, the political overtones of the case may have an effect on its conduct. A recent example of a criminal charge lodged against a political opponent of the government, which generated world wide excitement, was the trial of Angela Davis as a conspirator and accomplice to murder. Both ordinary and political crimes were at issue in the Pentagon Papers trials. Much recent political history in the United States, and in the rest of the world, is written in trial records, shaped by courts and judges.

The Courts

Laws are merely statements of intention; some agency must interpret them and apply them to specific problems. American courts deal only with actual cases, or controversies; they do not issue advisory opinions on hypothetical legislation or events. The parties involved must have standing to sue—in other words, each must be personally affected. A suit cannot be brought against a law or an act that does not affect the plaintiff but which he simply does not like or thinks is wrong. In some instances suits are permitted by courts in which the litigant has a minor personal interest but is acting for all persons in his situation. An example of this *class action* suit is an action against a polluting factory by one or two persons whose property or persons are affected, for all such persons. At the federal level the Supreme Court has, however, recently placed some restrictions upon these suits (see *Zahn* v. *International Paper Co.*, 1973). In some categories the state or federal legislature may establish the right to class action suits by statute; many environmental issues are now covered by legislation.

In most of their actions, the courts are simply carrying out the basic judicial function, resolving a dispute over a norm in a specific case: Did

A's dog dig up B's flowers, and if so what is the appropriate remedy? The total pattern of decisions in these cases has policy implications. What are the courts saying about the nature and seriousness of the responsibilities of neighbors to each other? In some instances, a single case has policy consequences: Should the city of A be allowed to close its swimming pools rather than integrate them? Should Company B be required to pay back wages to women employees who were not promoted as rapidly as men doing the same work? Here, by establishing a new norm or reaffirming an old one, the work of the courts takes on the character of legislation. This quasi-legislative activity, whether by single decisions or in the mass of decisions over time, is not a judicial usurping of the legislative function; it is implicit in the nature of judicial activity itself. As a political challenge to the other branches of government, the activity of the courts is both powerful and weak. The courts have few resources. They initiate no action of their own; they must wait for problems to be brought to them. If no one brings a case to the Supreme Court involving the use of property taxes to finance the school systems, for example, the Court may not rule on the question. Once the courts are engaged and hand down a decision, they are basically powerless to enforce it, and few decisions are self-enforcing. Enforcement is up to the executive. The legislature must provide funds for enforcement; it often controls the finances of the courts themselves, their number and structure, even their existence. The "nine old men" of the Supreme Court are not likely to overthrow the government. On the other hand, the acceptance of courts as rightful arbiters of disputes by the public does endow the courts with considerable power. As long as most people, however reluctantly, regard as unlawful what the courts say to be unlawful, then the courts can exercise a large measure of influence over public issues. And in the United States there is a remarkably strong tendency to resort to the courts. Virtually every political question becomes a judicial issue at some point.

Courts in the United States are a very complex body of institutions. Federalism produces a dual system of courts, partly but not entirely hierarchical. The two segments are more intertwined than are the dual executive and legislative aspects of American government; the nature and extent of this overlapping leads to conflict and confusion on many occasions.

Jurisdiction often overlaps. Although there are fairly specific rules governing jurisdiction, there may be a choice for a litigant in a civil case, or prosecution in a criminal case, in the matter of the court and legal system invoked. This may have practical advantages for one side or the other;

different courts have been shown to have different records in support of management v. labor, wife v. husband in divorce, and so forth. Thus the first decision in many lawsuits will be to choose a federal or a state court if both have jurisdiction, and to choose a particular court within those systems if there is a choice possible. In criminal law, the number of overlapping offenses is smaller, but a single action can violate both federal and state laws. The prosecutors must then decide, if both are interested, who will prosecute first, following certain protocols. The defense may also attempt to relocate the case, by having it removed to another court on grounds of local prejudice or bias on the part of the judge. In the Algiers Motel trial arising from the shooting of three young black men by white Detroit policemen in 1967, the defense argued successfully for the removal of the trial from Detroit to a small outlying town, which resulted in an all white jury. If prosecution in one court fails and a charge is possible in the other system, the defendant may have to stand trial again. The Fifth Amendment prohibits double jeopardy, or the retrial on the same charge of

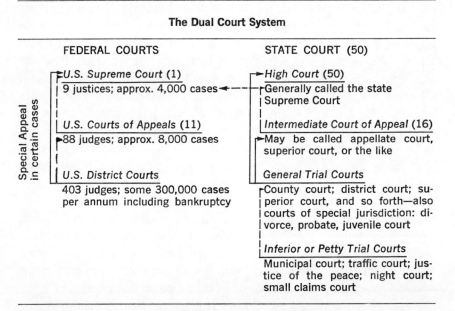

The Dual Court System

	FEDERAL COURTS	STATE COURT (50)
Special Appeal in certain cases	*U.S. Supreme Court (1)* 9 justices; approx. 4,000 cases	*High Court (50)* Generally called the state Supreme Court
	U.S. Courts of Appeals (11) 88 judges; approx. 8,000 cases	*Intermediate Court of Appeal (16)* May be called appellate court, superior court, or the like
	U.S. District Courts 403 judges; some 300,000 cases per annum including bankruptcy	*General Trial Courts* County court; district court; superior court, and so forth—also courts of special jurisdiction: divorce, probate, juvenile court
		Inferior or Petty Trial Courts Municipal court; traffic court; justice of the peace; night court; small claims court

NOTE: Arrows indicate appeal channels; a solid line indicates a right of appeal; a dotted line indicates judicial discretion to grant appeal or review if it so desires.

a person once acquitted. Originally this applied only to the federal courts, and many states did not follow the rule; in 1969, the Supreme Court ruled that the states were included in the prohibition. However, the Court does not interpret trial in both state and federal courts on different charges arising from the same act to constitute double jeopardy.

STATE COURTS.   The state systems vary widely in organization, depending on the size, social environment, and wealth of the state. All of the states have a final court of appeal, or supreme court. The larger and the more urban states have an intermediate level of appellate court as well. The workhorses of the state system are the trial courts at the bottom of the pyramid, which are divided according to jurisdiction and powers. The inferior, or petty, trial courts handle minor civil or criminal matters; a small claims court, for instance, will hear civil issues where the value is less than a set level, usually about $500. A justice of the peace may also have jurisdiction in minor civil cases, generally less than $200, and in misdemeanors, as well as authority to conduct marriages and sentence speed trap violators. The JP is rarely a lawyer, probably not a college graduate, and quite possibly has never even been to high school; he is almost certain to be a "hanging judge." Recent studies show conviction rates on the average in over 96 percent of his cases. The association of the JP with an unthinking and rather sleazy kind of justice is unfortunate; American society needs very badly to develop reputable and attractive minor courts, where people can find help in resolving the tense conflicts that may erupt in a society under pressure. The various municipal courts, such as the small claims courts, are usually headed by men with legal training; their jurisdiction is limited, but not as severely as the JP's. Given careful attention these courts could fill the gap in minor adjudication in the anonymous society. Yet many of them have been allowed to develop into courts which benefit almost exclusively the advantaged in the society; landlords and ghetto stores, for instance, may take over the small claims court and turn it into a collection agency. The original purpose of providing a forum for those who had civil claims but could not afford the expense of a lawyer disappears in distrust and cynicism. The additional factor of the absence of appeal from most of these courts makes the quality of their work even more important, and so more disturbing.

The courts of general jurisdiction handle the great bulk of criminal and civil cases in the United States; the exact number of cases heard each year can only be guessed at, since most states do not publish collected statistics, but the figure is in the millions. Only a small number of these cases will ever be appealed, and only a tiny minority of that group will be appealed and heard by the highest state court; the supreme court can hear at best only a hundredth of a percent of appeals. The quality of the justice administered in the state general trial courts is therefore critical for the quality of justice in America. In most of these courts a crisis exists; the increase in the number of cases has strained the capabilities of the courts almost to breaking point.

THE FEDERAL COURTS.   The federal courts are not yet so overburdened. The number of cases that the federal courts hear is limited by the smaller number of federal statutes in comparison to state laws. The lower level of the federal system, corresponding to state general trial courts, is the district court, where most trials originate. These were established by Congress in the Judiciary Act of 1789. Each state has at least one, and some as many as four; the number of judges varies according to workload. The total workload for the 407 judges is approaching 300,000 cases a year, including bankruptcy proceedings.

The federal appellate courts are the Courts of Appeals, or circuit courts, and the Supreme Court. The former were also established in 1789 and were originally headed by a Supreme Court judge, quite literally "riding circuit." Finally, in 1891 the Courts of Appeals were established, the country divided into 10 circuits plus the District of Columbia, and separate judges provided. Most of the appeals from district courts go to the circuit courts; in a few special cases, when a special "three-judge" district court hears a case in which a federal, state, or local law is challenged as unconstitutional and an injunction sought, the appeal goes directly to the Supreme Court, since an appeals judge is one of the three making up the original court. For most appeals the circuit court is the final court; the Supreme Court will agree to hear few of the cases appealed to it from these courts.

The federal Supreme Court has both appellate and original jurisdiction. If a state sues another state the Supreme Court must be the original court; most original jurisdiction cases are of this kind. Suits by a state against the United States, or suits by one state against another state's citizens or aliens, and those involving ambassadors and other foreign ministers may also originate in the Supreme Court, although they may be heard in lower courts as well. Since the founding of the Court it has decided only a hundred odd original cases; most of its work is in reviewing state and local decisions. Litigants in both state and federal cases may request the Court to review any case, and the Court has discretion to hear the case or not. Theoretically, there is appeal by right to the Supreme Court in cases in which some federal statute or state law or provision of a state constitution has been declared to conflict with federal law, treaty, or Constitution or a state law has been upheld against a challenge of violating federal law, treaty, or Constitution. Yet the Court has many technical grounds on which it can refuse to hear a case. It may find that the federal question raised is not "substantial" or was not raised early enough in the lower proceedings. For example, the Court refused, in *Stover* v. *New York*, to hear the contention of a family that the Rye, N.Y., ordinance that forbade them to keep six lines of clothes hanging in the yard violated the First Amendment because they hung up the clothes to protest taxes. For many years the Court refused to hear cases involving the apportionment of state and federal legislative districts, calling it a "political question" that should be left to the legislatures; suddenly it changed its mind in 1962. In effect, an "insubstantial" or "political" question is whatever the Court says it is, and the right of appeal is not certain.

Other special courts have been established by Congress under its legislative authority: the Court of Military Appeals, head of the military system; the Territorial Courts, roughly equal to District Courts; the Tax Court (which is partly under executive branch control); and, finally, the courts of Customs, Claims and Customs, and Patent Appeals, which are now "constitutional" courts with the same constitutional safeguards as the major federal courts. All of these courts were created primarily to administer certain specified federal laws; their decisions, nevertheless, are as much law as are those of the regular courts.

ORGANIZATION OF THE COURTS.   State and federal judicial systems are hierarchical in form, but the powers of the high courts are limited. Depending on the state, the state supreme court may or may not exercise some supervision over judges and be able to transfer them where needed or even remove them from the bench for cause. In other states the judges are independent of any power except impeachment or defeat at the polls. The decisions of state high courts are binding on lower state courts, but the lower courts may resist, and there is nothing to prevent them from continuing to make decisions inconsistent with high court wishes. The upper courts have no enforcement powers of their own. Each court is for the most part an entity unto itself; with few exceptions there are no uniform requirements of evidence and procedure, each judge determining admissibility, when his court will sit, for how long, and so forth.

The Supreme Court was given authority by Congress some four decades ago to set rules of procedure for federal courts. But some of its recent rules have been set aside by Congress as actually involving questions of substance reserved for Congress, and even with the uniform codes, procedure still varies widely within the general guidelines. The higher federal courts have no controls over lower judges, other than to reverse their decisions. Appointment and removal are not in their powers. Even the Supreme Court cannot enforce its decisions. A decision may be ignored by other parts of the government, or opposed with force. Major examples of this in recent years are the school prayer, school Bible reading, and school desegregation decisions. In many schools throughout the country the day still begins with prayer or Bible reading, and despite *Brown* v. *Board of Education* in 1954 school integration still is not completely accomplished. The lower courts in the state system may rehear a case and come to the same conclusion for slightly different reasons, a process that could go on for years.

The Judges: Selection and Role

There are two major means of selecting judges: appointment and election. A third is a combination of the first two, in which a judge appointed by the executive must be approved by the electorate at least once. (A fourth possibility, a career judiciary with special training, is not found in the United States.) Federal judges are all appointed, under the Constitution, to serve "during good behavior"; effectively, this is a lifetime appointment, since the only means of removal is by impeachment. Nine federal judges have been impeached, and eight others have resigned to avoid impeachment; of the thousands who have held office, only four judges have actually been removed, the last in 1936. In addition, their salaries may not be reduced while they serve. Thus, although the judges are nominated by the President and confirmed by the Senate, once on the bench they are relatively isolated from further political pressures. Even though a President will pick nearly all of his judges from his own party, and from political persuasions congenial to his ideas, the acts of his selections once in office may surprise him. The accidents of history may give one President many more appointments, than others; Franklin Roosevelt made nine appointments, Kennedy two, and in his first term Nixon filled four Supreme Court vacancies. Long after a President has left office, his appointments to the courts, particularly the Supreme Court, will have an impact on the political process. This has been the basis of criticism of the lifetime appointment; the courts may be headed by men whose political views no longer reflect the national reality, and the electorate has no way to hold them responsible. The old quip that Supreme Court judges never die and seldom retire, indicates the problem. Proponents argue that this judicial independence is necessary to enable judges to rule on delicate constitutional matters without fearing that they will be rejected for an unpopular decision.

The elected judiciary, which many of the states have chosen, takes various forms; the length of terms may be as long as eighteen or as short as four years; candidates may run on partisan or non-partisan tickets. Adherents of the system claim greater democracy and greater access to the bench by men of more representative backgrounds. Opponents point to the lack of interest in judicial elections, the difficulty and conflict of interest in raising campaign funds, and possible miscarriages of justice caused by a desire to be re-elected.

Whether elected or appointed, judges may be active or passive, strict or loose constructionists, liberals or conservatives. The last pair of terms refers simply to political philosophy, while the first refers to a belief about the nature of judicial action—whether a judge should seek out or resist opportunities to exercise his policy-making role. (But both "active" and "passive" judges actually do make policy, regardless of their intentions.) Finally, a judge may believe that the Constitution must be interpreted flexibly in order to encompass the changes in politics and society since its adoption, or he may believe that the words must be taken as literally and as closely as possible to eighteenth century meanings. A judge may reflect any combination of these attitudes; a conservative is not necessarily a strict constructionist or a passive judge.

The judge is first an administrator. He must oversee his own court, including its physical plant, and draw up the budget; this may require that he become a lobbyist in state or local government, seeking the funds and personnel needed. The judge and his clerks must establish procedures that will enable him to keep track of the cases filed and keep them moving as

"The Court finds itself on the horns of a dilemma. On the one hand, wiretap evidence is inadmissible, and on the other hand I'm dying to hear it."

Drawing by J. B. Handelsman; © 1972 The New Yorker Magazine, Inc.

smoothly as possible.

Second, the judge is a negotiator and umpire of negotiations. The majority of civil or criminal cases end in settlement without trial; the civil parties agree on a solution, the prosecutor offers the criminal defendant an attractive inducement to plead guilty. The judge may preside over these negotiations in his chambers or simply confirm them afterwards. Either way, he is a participant, helping to weed out cases that do not require a trial for resolution from those matters where the facts or law are unclear and which should receive a hearing. This helps keep the caseload of the court to a manageable level. In most negotiated cases a trial is not in fact needed, but a serious problem exists if the pressures of the caseload cause cases to be settled without trial when a trial should be held.

Third, the judge presides over the hearing when a trial is needed; in the common law system, he is expected to be a neutral party, an umpire, between the two adversary parties arguing the case. When there is no jury, the judge decides both issues of fact and issues of law and then determines the civil settlement or the criminal penalty unless a mandatory penalty is prescribed by the law. When there is a jury he shares some of his authority; the jury determines the facts and may determine the penalty. The judge has considerable control over the jury, however, and may under some circumstances alter its decision on penalty or damages. Finally, in appellate proceedings, the judge or judges always act alone, ruling on the law itself and its ambiguities. Here the policy-making role of the judge comes into focus, and his personal views of the law must guide him.

Lawyers in the Judicial Process

The role of lawyers in the judicial process is pervasive. First, the legislatures that make the laws and the executives whose help in enforcing them is needed are heavily dominated by lawyers; this has been true throughout the history of the United States and has helped to shape American politics, as De Tocqueville pointed out a hundred and forty years ago. Second, lawyers now argue the majority of cases; only a lawyer is legally entitled to argue a case. Nonlawyers who wish to argue their own cases can do so only if the court permits, or if there is statutory provision as there is in the federal system or in small claims courts. There are some courts where lawyers are not often present or even allowed, such as the inferior trial courts. However, recent Supreme Court decisions have expanded the right to counsel in criminal cases until it includes any case that might result in a prison term; the state must now provide a lawyer for those who cannot afford one in almost all cases. The prosecutor is, of course, a lawyer. Third, lawyers constitute the majority of judges. Even though there is no statutory requirement in the federal system for a law degree, no federal judge has been without one (although at the Supreme Court level it could be argued that a nonlawyer might help the Court grapple with the great social problems its decisions involve). Rarely are nonlawyers appointed or elected in state systems, except at the lower, inferior court level. Fourth, lawyers and law schools provide the law reviews that judges often draw upon in writing their decisions; articles on the meaning of certain statutes may have an influence on the outcome of cases; an example is the school segregation cases, which the NAACP won partly because it won the battle of the law reviews.

Reproduced by permission of Johnny Hart and Field Enterprises, inc.

Other Branches of Government in the Judicial Process

THE LEGISLATURE.   The legislature's primary role is, with executive approval, to determine the statutes by which most courts live. It may also shape the courts themselves. In the federal system the Congress determines how many federal courts there will be, other than the Supreme Court: it may create new levels of courts if it wishes, as well as the special "legislative" courts. Congress determines how many judges there will be; the Supreme Court has had as few as five and as many as ten (the figure has stood at nine for a century and will probably remain there). It can control the appellate jurisdiction of the courts; it has on occasion varied the appellate jurisdiction of circuit or Supreme Court. The original jurisdiction of the Supreme Court may also be shared with lower courts if Congress directs. Salaries and other disbursements for the judicial system are under Congress' power; today, as listed in the federal budget, there are 6,691 employees and 407 judges, costing $133 million. Finally, Congress sets up and provides funds for other agencies, such as the Justice Department with its district attorneys; this executive agency spent over four times as much in 1970, $642 million, as did the entire judiciary. State legislatures have varying powers over the courts; some have delegated some controls to the judiciary, but this power can always be revoked or altered. Expenditures approved by the states, including the police, according to federal figures ran over $7 billion in 1970.

THE EXECUTIVE.   This branch is also actively involved. It may have a role in the selection of the judges, acting in some states without legislative confirmation. The federal and state departments of justice, state police and local police departments, agencies such as departments of consumer protection and weights and measures, and the like, play a major part in the system. The executive initiates all criminal and many civil cases, carries out the investigative work, and helps the judge determine sentence. The police in particular are important. The police are the first line in the criminal process; they exercise enormous discretion in making arrests, which brings a problem into the system, and they also do most of the investigation. The executive controls these agencies; sending in police or federal marshals or altering their procedures is ultimately in the hands of mayors, governors, and presidents. Thus the enforcement of decisions is an executive power. In addition the police have a norm enforcement role;

in their decisions to enforce certain laws severely and ignore or play down others, they give preference to certain types of norms, which may have definite class overtones. Crimes committed by upper class whites may go unprosecuted while the street crimes committed by lower class groups are attacked. The attitude of the public to the entire judicial system may be conditioned by the attitude to the police and their manner of operating.

Prisons and jails are another major responsibility of the state and the federal executive branches. Once a judge has sentenced a convicted defendant, his control over him ceases. Probation officers supervise those not sent to prison (although revocation of probation requires a hearing); the prisons and jails are operated by executive bureaus. Early release is determined by parole boards appointed by state and federal executives. The conditions in those jails are under judicial scrutiny only to a point; the Wayne County (Michigan) Jail was recently determined by the county courts to be unconstitutional, as were the state prisons of Arkansas by federal courts. The only remedy available to those judges, however, is to stop sending prisoners to those jails; they may issue an order requiring changes, but they cannot force them to be made. (If changes are not forthcoming the court may order the jail closed, but this has not yet been carried out anywhere.) The choice by the government to organize its prisons as primarily punitive or primarily rehabilitative is not controlled by the courts; it is an executive policy, subject to legislative agreement and willingness to provide funds. The public may also become involved if it is asked to approve bond issues for the improvement of jails and other correctional services.

The Role of the Public: Juries

The Constitution in Amendment Six, since extended to the states, requires that an accused person have the right to confront any witnesses against him and to have assistance in obtaining witnesses for his defense. He has the right to additional public participation if he wishes a jury trial, which is his right in all federal criminal cases (and most federal civil cases). In 1968 the Supreme Court interpreted the Sixth Amendment jury requirement to apply to the states in major criminal cases; all of the states already had some provisions for jury trial. Juries in the federal system are composed of twelve persons; in the states they may be as small as six. Decisions by federal juries must be unanimous;

the Supreme Court has ruled that decisions by state criminal juries may require only the "preponderance of the jurors" if state law so provides.

A second type of jury is the grand jury; this may be either an indicting or an investigating body and may have as few as one or as many as twenty-three persons. Grand juries sit for a year or two, depending on where they are, and then disband, a new grand jury being sworn in. All federal charges of capital offenses (there were thirty-six on the books until the Supreme Court ruled against the death penalty as it had been applied) or "other infamous crimes" must begin with a grand jury indictment, as required by the Fifth Amendment. Other federal charges, and state offenses, are generally brought to court today by the alternative of presenting information to the court, and securing a decision by the judge that there is probable cause to hold the accused for trial. Approximately half of the states have grand juries, most of which are used for the investigation of various public problems or the conduct of public office; they may issue reports that make accusations against specific persons without actually indicting them, leading to many criticisms of grand jury irresponsibility. Yet grand juries in many instances have been the means of eliminating a corrupt official or administration. Both the grand jury and the petit, or trial, jury are generally chosen in the same way: selection by a jury clerk or committee from the voting lists of the area. The selector may rely upon friends and prominent persons in the community to suggest names, tending to exclude the lower socioeconomic strata. Certain occupations are generally barred from service: doctors, lawyers, ministers, teachers, nurses, policemen; in some states a housewife or any woman may be excused. The selector may impose his own prejudices; in a recent Detroit challenge to the jury panel, it was discovered that potential jurors were being excluded on grounds of having long hair, chewing gum, or wearing short skirts. Finally, the lawyers are allowed to excuse a certain number of jurors in each case for no stated reason and an additional number if they can show bias to the judge. The result is that juries are almost never a representative sample of the population.

Other private persons whose work affects the courts are expert witnesses, such as forensic medicine specialists, process servers who serve the papers notifying a person of the suit against him, bail bondsmen, private detectives, and the like. The process servers and bail bondsmen in particular have an important impact. Numerous instances have been discovered of process servers in U.S. cities earning their fees for delivering papers by discarding the papers and reporting to the court that they were served; the person sued for default in payments, not appearing in court, automatically loses the case. The first hint he may have of the situation is when his belongings are repossessed. Similarly, the bail bondsman's role is critical for those who cannot win release simply on their own recognizance, or standing in the community, or who cannot pay the money bail set. The bondsman guarantees the appearance of a defendant in court, and pays his bond if he fails to appear. He is not obligated to take anyone as a client. The accused who cannot find a bondsman to take him will have to remain in jail for trial; his chances of winning acquittal are less than they would be if he were free to assist in the preparation of his defense while awaiting trial, and he may plead guilty if he has to wait for trial longer than the probable penalty. In addition, the bondsman's usual 10 percent fee is not refundable if he returns for trial, while the person who posts his own bond is charged only a tiny fee. Private enterprise thus affects both civil and criminal proceedings; the effect is discriminatory, since those who suffer from these practices are mainly persons of low status.

The jury as an institution goes back hundreds of years to the medieval period in English history. It was formalized in the common law system in the days of Henry II, approximately in 1172, and in the Magna Carta of 1215. From this period come the standard of twelve persons, the idea of a jury of one's peers, and indictment by jury. Essentially the jury became a means of admitting the public to the judicial process as decision makers. The right of the state to try someone was then filtered through a panel of citizens; his fate was also in their hands. Originally this meant nothing more than eliminating control by the king and the aristocracy. Today we interpret "jury of peers" (which is not required by the Constitution; it calls only for an impartial jury) as being composed of at least some persons who have the same or similar social and economic background as the defendant, measured by increasingly precise standards; this is a considerable expansion of the first meaning of peer, as commoner. Jury trials are disappearing in this century; pressure of circumstance has reduced them to about 10 percent of the trials, which is still some 90 percent of the world's jury trials. There are many who argue that justice would be improved by eliminating juries; research in jury behavior has shown that they are generally controlled by the judge and heavily predisposed to believe that the defendant is probably guilty. Yet the withering of the jury system is in some respects a blow against democracy; it closes off another avenue of public participation in, public awareness of, the political process.

Private interest groups use the courts as means of influencing public policy. Suits are often brought by individuals with the backing of a group, which helps to prepare the case and provides financial support. Most of these groups represent the disadvantaged of society; access to the courts is easier in terms of resources and status required than access to the legislatures and executives. In addition the federal courts in particular were the first segment of the political system to show a response to the problems of the disadvantaged in this century. The most dramatic instance of group success in the courts is the NAACP, which has been on the winning side in over 85 percent of the suits in which it took an interest since its founding, culminating in the 1954 *Brown* desegregation case.

The public is entitled to be admitted to a trial; Amendment Six guarantees that trials will be public. Considerations of space can limit the number allowed in; in rare instances a civil trial such as a paternity or divorce suit may be a closed hearing at the discretion of the judges. Some evidence may also be taken *in camera* if considerations of national security are at stake. Otherwise there are no secret trials

Criminal and Civil Justice: Some Political Problems

More attention has been given to the problem of fairness in criminal trials than in civil trials. The criminal trial by its nature is "out of balance"; the full resources of the state against the individual's resources have weighed in the favor of the state for centuries. The Constitution itself contains some provisions for securing a fair trial in a criminal case; half of the Bill of Rights' ten amendments are concerned with judicial proceedings and four of the five with criminal trials. At first these rights applied in the main to federal courts only. In the last thirty years the federal courts have been gradually extending them to the states. Beginning with *Mapp* v. *Ohio* in 1961, which applied the Fourth Amendment guarantees against unreasonable search and seizure to the states by declaring inadmissible any evidence so obtained, the Supreme Court in the following years added a host of new guarantees for the accused in state trials. In 1962 it applied the Eighth Amendment prohibition against cruel and unusual punishment (*Robinson* v. *California*); in 1963 in the important and celebrated *Gideon* v. *Wainwright* case on the Sixth Amendment, it overruled its own 1942 decision and required that states provide counsel to indigents in all major cases (capital cases were already covered). Two cases in 1964 extended the Fifth Amendment right of no self-incrimination to the states (*Malloy* v. *Hogan* and *Murphy* v. *Waterfront Commission*) again overruling an earlier decision. Also in 1964 the Court heard *Escobedo* v. *Illinois*, and in 1966 capped it with *Miranda* v. *Arizona*; these two cases, built upon the *Gideon* case, further guaranteed the Sixth Amendment right to counsel and the Fifth Amendment right not to self-incriminate. In *Escobedo* the Court ruled that a confession obtained when the accused had not been permitted to have counsel present during interrogation was not admissible. In *Miranda*, probably the most controversial and misunderstood decision of the century, the Court issued a set of standards for valid confessions; none would be admissible unless the defendant were informed that anything he said would be used against him, that he had a right to remain silent, a right to have counsel present, and finally that such counsel would be provided if he could not afford to pay it himself. (Both of the two men and a number of others in similar cases were subsequently convicted again without their confessions; in other words, the prosecution can still convict if it can find other evidence, and it *may* use confessions properly obtained.) In 1965 the Court had ruled in *Pointer* v. *Texas* that defendants in state trials were entitled by the Sixth Amendment to confront adverse witnesses; in 1967, in *Washington* v. *Texas*, it added that the state must provide assistance to the defense in obtaining favorable witnesses. In 1967 *Klopferer* v. *North Carolina* guaranteed the Sixth Amendment right to a speedy trial for state defendants. A decision in 1968 brought the same amendment's right to a jury trial (*Duncan* v. *Louisiana*); and 1969 ended the Warren record with *Benton* v. *Maryland*, which finally applied the Fifth Amendment prohibition of double jeopardy to the states, appropriately on the last day of the Warren Court. In 1972 the Burger Court, which had been restricting the impact of some of these rulings (for instance, ruling that inadmissible confessions could be admitted to impeach the veracity of the witness if his trial testimony contradicted that in the confession; 1971 *Harris* v. *New York*), added a new expansion by ruling, in *Argersinger* v. *Illinois*, that counsel must be provided in any criminal case that might result in a prison term, no matter how small.

In the federal courts, all of these rights, plus the additional Bill of

Rights guarantees on matters such as bail and indictment not yet required of the states, are *generally* carried out in a commendable fashion, although there are pockets of resistance here and there, and there are of course problems of circumstance such as the heavy caseloads in some areas such as New York City. The federal courts, however, conduct only a tiny portion of the criminal trials. The adequacy of state action is the critical factor. Obtaining compliance with many of the decisions of the sixties has been difficult; resistance and circumstantial problems are multiplied in the states.

Obtaining police compliance is the first problem. Numerous studies have shown that the *Miranda* warnings are rarely given completely, or in a manner truly comprehensible to a frightened arrestee. Police discretion in arrests and the treatment of those arrested has been shown in other studies to be biased against lower class and minority persons. The prosecutor's office may increase this bias when it determines which cases will be pursued and which will not. Those held are then subject to the mercies of the bail system already described (the Supreme Court has not yet examined this area). The process known as "plea bargaining" then begins.

The increasing case loads, which overburden the capacity of the courts, result in plea bargaining, now the means of disposing of some 90 percent of all criminal cases. The defendant agrees to plead guilty. He may have served more than his probable sentence awaiting trial. He may be guilty or be pressured by a court appointed attorney even though innocent. The attorney may believe that a guilty plea is the best course, or he may be simply interested in earning his fee, which is the same regardless of how long he spends on a case, as quickly as possible and with as little work as possible. The prosecutor may believe the accused to be guilty; he also has to earn a good conviction rate in order to stay in office. In exchange for the agreement to plead guilty, the accused is generally offered a reduced charge, meaning a lesser sentence or perhaps probation; this is the explanation for charges of *attempted* assault when the victim is unconscious in hospital or the logically impossible charge of *attempting* to carry a concealed weapon! The guilty win by this process; they are penalized less severely than they should be. The innocent suffer; both the one who pleads guilty from fear or despair and the community that will be subject to the early return of criminals and possibly also to revenge inflicted by those who go to prison unjustly and are embittered by the experience.

The solutions for this are neither simple nor easy. Crimes without victims—drunkenness, prostitution, drug abuse, gambling, homosexuality, and the like—which constitute half of the criminal cases, could be removed from the courts, lessening the pressure on the courts and police and perhaps improving the treatment of these problems. More judges and courts could be provided. The penal system could be reconstructed so that it is truly rehabilitative, thus eliminating many recidivists or multiple offenders and reducing the fear of the corrections system that partly engenders the guilty plea to get a reduced sentence. Social problems such as racism and poverty that help produce urban and rural crime could be reduced. All of these steps face resistance. Large portions of the society believe that moral crimes must be attacked severely; that the judges are lazy and could work harder; that the penal system is already too "easy"; that society bears no responsibility for crime. Improvements will be expensive, at least in the short run, although in the long run the saving to society in financial and human waste would be incalculable. There can only be more crime and more violence if an educated public and policy-makers cannot overcome these fears.

The standards of fairness in criminal courts have come a long way since the first colony was established in 1607. When the Constitution was written, it was unheard of to guarantee an accused the right to counsel, even when he provided it. Capital crimes encompassed acts such as petty thievery. Death by ordeal, such as pressing to death or, in Europe, burning, was not uncommon for criminals such as witches in colonial days. In many witch trials in Europe, the accused not only had to undergo the ordeal of the trial but paid for the costs of the trial, the judges' entertainment, and his own certain death sentence; his accusers might win his estate! The practice of public execution is barely ended; in the nineteenth century such executions served as a kind of public entertainment, even for children. The last occurred in the United States in the 1930's, witnessed by thousands of persons. By these standards the rights of the accused and the treatment of the convicted have improved enormously. Realizing these rights still remains a problem. There are other issues: Will bail problems be resolved, particularly in the matter of denying bail entirely for preventive detention (i.e., for those whom the judge believes should not be released pending trial)? Will capital punishment be restored to the penal system? Will an effective system for compensating the victims of crimes be developed? What rights will be extended to accused juveniles, who do not receive the procedural safeguards that adults receive?†

In civil trials there has also been a great improvement from the days of imprisonment of debtors. The myth that the civil trial is a match between private parties, and so the state need not concern itself with providing assistance, still pertains. Yet the structure of the law remains strongly in favor of the advantaged; in matters such as landlord-tenant, creditor-debtor problems, the poor, the minorities, the uneducated have little chance against the wealthy and the corporations. If the state does not provide legal assistance for the disadvantaged, and does not alter the laws it writes, then it lends its weight to the bias of civil proceedings. Action has begun in this problem area, but in a halting manner. Many states still leave it to private agencies to provide aid. Others provide assistance only for a few types of cases. The provision of public lawyers for the poor in civil matters has been attacked at both the state and federal level, particularly when those lawyers have won policy victories in court, over-turning government acts or laws, such as the California decision against changes in the welfare system. Strong pressure exists to place such public lawyers under close control and to limit their cases to relatively harmless issues such as credit problems or divorce. The struggle over civil justice is just beginning. The outcome of this struggle and the outcome of the struggle over criminal justice are critical for the continuing hope of eliminating or reducing inequality in America, and so for democracy.

Suggested Readings

Henry J. Abraham, *The Judicial Process* (New York: Oxford University Press, 1968, 2nd. ed.)*; massive bibliography

————, *The Judiciary: The Supreme Court in the Governmental Process* (Boston: Allyn and Bacon, 1969)*

Theodore L. Becker and Vernon G. Murray, eds., *Government Lawlessness in America* (New York: Oxford University Press, 1971)*

Ramsey Clark, *Crime in America* (New York: Pocket Books, 1971)*

Leonard Downie, *Justice Denied* (Baltimore: Penguin Books, 1972)*

Richard Harris, *The Fear of Crime* (New York: Praeger, 1969)*

---

* Available in paperback
† The Supreme Court did rule in 1967 that juvenile courts must follow *some* of the traditional procedural safeguards in order to protect the rights of the accused—see *In re Gault.*

Don Holt, *The Justice Machine* (New York: Ballantine, 1972)*

Morton Hunt, *The Mugging* (New York: Atheneum, 1972)*

Herbert Jacob, *Justice in America: Courts, Lawyers and the Judicial Process* (Boston: Little Brown, 1972, 2nd ed.)*

E. J. Kahn, Jr., "Be Just and Fear Not," *New Yorker*, February 6, 1971

James R. Klonoski and Robert I. Mendelsohn, eds., *The Politics of Local Justice* (Boston: Little Brown, 1970)*

Robert Lefcourt, ed., *Law Against the People* (New York: Vintage, 1971)*

Anthony Lewis, *Gideon's Trumpet* (New York: Vintage, 1964)*

Norval Morris and Gordon Hawkins, *The Honest Politician's Guide to Crime Control* (Chicago: University of Chicago Press, 1970)*

Walter F. Murphy, *Congress and the Court* (Chicago: University of Chicago Press, 1962)

Jerome Skolnick, *Justice Without Trial: Law Enforcement in Democratic Society* (New York: John Wiley and Sons, 1967)*

* Available in paperback

7

THE POLITICS OF PRESSURE GROUPS

Access to Power

Life'd not be worth livin if we didn't keep our inimies.
Mr. Dooley

America is often called "a nation of joiners"; the propensity of the ordinary American to join in voluntary association with others, for an incredible array of purposes, is quite marked in comparison with many other countries. Group associations help tie the society together, uniting the individual members in a network of connections. When the group activity takes on political coloration it helps tie the citizens to the political system. The polity, or political body, is thus not made up only of a great mass of faceless people, persons acting on their own politically. Between the citizens and the political system as a whole are a large number of interest groups, which alter the shape of politics in important ways.

What Is an Interest Group?

Interest groups are associations of individuals. *Primary* associations are the most basic. These are associations based on birth, on family background, on characteristics that generally cannot be changed. Men and women; Northerners and Southerners; Catholics and Jews; Italian-Americans and Chicanos, all are primary associations. For the most part these are unorganized groups, and many are unlikely to form the basis of any organization in the future, such as blondes or redheads. Although a person may occasionally take steps to move out of one of these groups, his past association with it will have some effect on his new primary association.

More important to the political process are the secondary, voluntary associations, organized groups with which the person chooses to affiliate to some extent (although the choice may be limited, as for example taking out membership in a labor union may be a prerequisite for some jobs). The group may have a primarily political purpose, such as a consumer group that is formed specifically to lobby for legislative action. An interest group may have only secondary political purposes; an example is a labor union, which engages in political activity as a consequence of its role in the structure of the economic system.

An interest group may be a wholly private organization, such as the national Association of Manufacturers, the United Auto Workers, the Sierra Club, or the Parent Teacher Association. It may be entirely public. Segments of the government form interest groups that bring pressure on other parts of the government; for obvious reasons the state highway bureaus, the mayors conferences, and the Agriculture Department have all had reason to lobby members of Congress. Interest groups may also represent both public and private members. The "highway lobby," which acts together to obtain highway funding, is a collection of both public and private interests. Education associations may contain both public school administrators and private school officials. Regardless of their public or private character, nearly all interest groups will have political orientation at some point, seeking to obtain some or all of their goals by influencing some part of the political system, at state, local, or federal levels. Not all interest groups act on the political system all the time; but as the scope of political action widens, few groups are able to function effectively in terms of their basic goals without ever turning to the political system for help.

An interest group enables numerous persons to focus their resources on a purpose they hold in common. Organization of resources means that these persons have perceived the goal to be important enough to them to invest some energy in its promotion. In turn, interest group theory of political life is based upon the assumption that, other things being equal, interests supported by organizations are more likely to succeed than those that are not so underpinned. Within those interests backed by organized groups, success is likely to depend upon effective organization, the kind of resources available to the group, and the able mobilization of those resources.

These success factors raise certain political problems. If interests are more successful when organized, the first questions are: What interests are so represented? Who belongs to interest groups? Who are the leaders of these groups? Which interests by their nature are at a disadvantage in the competition for resources and mobilization? Second, we may ask what techniques are available to interest groups in attempting to influence the political system, and which groups within the universe of interest groups are more likely to be able to use these techniques, and thus be more likely to succeed. Finally, we must consider the implications of these problems for democracy in America.

Interest Group Representation

The first characteristic of interest groups in America is that they do cast a fairly wide net over the population. In one recent study, 57 percent of the American respondents identified themselves as members of at least one group, compared to 47 percent in Great Britain, 44 percent in Germany, and 30 percent and 24 percent in Italy and Mexico, respectively.* Though this is a respectable showing, this level of interest group membership from another perspective means that some 43 percent of the sample is not represented in any interest group at all. When the single 57 percent figure is broken down into various groups, some more disturbing statistics appear. Some 68 percent of the men and 47 percent of the women claimed membership in a group; there is a substantial gap between the sexes in participation rates (although the figure for women is low, it is in fact greater than that for women in the other nations, and accounts for most of the difference between the United States and the others.) By occupation, income, education, age, and sex, membership rates vary substantially. As age rises there is greater propensity to join a group; the assumption of the new roles of worker, parent, and spouse tends to create new personal interests that can be advanced in a group of some kind.

The first three are the most significant for the rate of membership; interestingly, they are also the major indicators of socioeconomic status.

* Gabriel A. Almond and Sidney Verba, *The Civic Culture* (Boston: Little, Brown, 1965), pp. 244–65.

Simply stated, membership in groups of any kind is primarily a middle class and upper class activity. In this respect the United States is not alone; it reflects an almost universal characteristic of group membership. In the United States, for example, less than half (46 percent) of the sample with only primary school education in the cited study have any group memberships, compared with 55 percent of those with secondary school training and 80 percent of those with college or university experience. As income rises, so do memberships. And as job status rises, so do memberships; thus, a teacher is more likely to belong to a group than a janitor. The number of memberships held by a single person or family is also affected by these socioeconomic factors. Over half of the professional households in one survey belonged to at least three groups; only 5 percent of the unskilled workers did. A teacher or other professional is much more likely to belong to several groups than is a truck driver, although the truck driver may make more money than the teacher. Within occupations the size of the income is determining; a wealthy farmer is more likely to have several memberships than is a poor farmer.

The second characteristic of American interest group representation is thus a strong class bias, although less marked than in some other Western societies. Lower class persons, women, the young, and minorities are not represented well by the interest groups in the United States, if they hold any memberships at all. In addition, many of these same citizens do not participate on an individual basis by voting. They are in the political system but not of it; they have much less influence than the upper strata and draw little attention unless they riot (joining in a powerful temporary interest group) or in some way strike out violently, whether burning bras or buildings.

Within interest groups, there are additional class pressures. Not all members of interest groups are equal; some are leaders and some are followers. Active participation of any kind is undertaken by only a minority of members. Formal positions of leadership, reflecting the whole political system, are only a small percentage of the membership, thus constituting an elite. There are few interest groups run on a democratic basis, genuinely attempting to reflect the positions of the entire membership. There have been case studies of the few instances of such democratic procedure in order to determine just why it is so rare and why it occurred in that special group. Many social scientists are inclined to believe in what the late Robert Michels called "the iron law of oligarchy"—that all groups, regardless of size or purpose, will be dominated in the end by a small elite that may or may not be benign. If this is true, and it appears to be the case in the great majority of interest groups, then the policy of a particular group, and the way it chooses to press for its goals, will be a more accurate reflection of the wishes of the small group of leaders and their associates (drawn disproportionately from the upper classes even in comparison to the middle and upper class membership of groups in general) than it will be a reflection of the wishes of the membership as a whole.

It comes as no surprise, then, that a substantial number of the actual interest groups in existence in the United States, far more than a majority, is concerned with the representation of business interests, and an even larger proportion of those actively involved in lobbying is made up of business interests. If the interests representing other sources of wealth, such as the rights of property owners as against tenants, are added to the manufacturing and commercial interests, the bias of the interest groups in the United States on the side of the vested or dominant interests, colloquially the "haves," is overwhelming.

Another problem narrows the ability of the interest groups to represent the whole public effectively. Membership in a group may not be the result of support for all, or even most, of that group's activities and purposes. Membership in a union may be a requirement or near requirement for many jobs, thus adding numbers to the labor union who may not agree with its political position. A person may have joined a group such as the Sierra Club or the National Rifle Association when it was not active politically. As the group becomes more politically oriented, a member may not be aware of this side of its activity. Even in groups that are quite busy in the political life of the country, surveys have shown that only half of the membership is informed about this activity. The range of services that the group offers may outweigh its political position in the mind of the member, or indeed may be the only reason for joining. For instance, the great majority of the membership of the American Automobile Association has responded to surveys as being concerned only with the insurance and other car services provided by the society. Few know of its political activity on matters such as mass transit and highway routing. Membership requirements in California allow only 5 percent of the membership to make policy for the remaining 95 percent at general meetings, and those 5 percent voting may be proxies held by the small leadership. Finally, the "connections" that a person can make through a group may be his motivation. Being a doctor or lawyer does not require AMA or ABA membership, but these professional associations provide access to the upper levels of the professions, information useful in his professional life, and so on. At best the membership of these groups can be said not to object to those political activities that they are aware of; membership in the group *per se* does not imply strong agreement with those political activities.

The only exceptions to these comments are the highly political or "ideological" groups, such as the John Birch Society, Common Cause, the Committee for an Effective Congress, the Center for Public Law, and the like. These groups have only one reason for existence, to exert pressure on the political system for certain political actions or to offer the membership a means of expressing their dissatisfaction with the present state of affairs, from either end of the political opinion range. Some of these groups work for tangible results, such as the election of certain candidates or organizational changes in Congress. Others are so disaffected that they can offer only symbolic rewards, on the order of the continuous calls for the impeachment of Earl Warren. The membership of these extreme groups is not likely to find any satisfaction, even in the election of a group member to political office, since the political belief of the group is based on the idea that the forces of evil are winning in any event. Extremists often appear to obtain a kind of perverse satisfaction from thinking that they are losing and all is doomed. Even among these highly concentrated political groups, it cannot be assumed that all of the membership approves of all actions taken by the group, specifically by its leadership.

The third characteristic of interest groups in the political system is therefore their structural tendency to be dominated by an elite, which often does not express the wishes of the whole membership. Far from providing channels for the public to participate in the political system and to articulate individual preferences, the interest groups in fact offer much greater access to power for the elites of American society than they might have as individuals; as leaders of groups, these elites have acquired the resources of others to use for their own purposes.

One counter to this general picture is the growth in recent years of groups that, for the first time, represent directly groups such as migrant farmworkers, welfare recipients, tenants, poor consumers, and the like. While these groups are by no means a match, numerically or financially, for the higher status groups, they do represent a substantial widening of the interest groups, bringing many people into the competition for political power who have been outside the arena until recently. The success or failure of these new groups is important for the future of democracy in America.

Interest Group Resources

An interest group must draw upon one or all of three basic kinds of resource in order to exert political influence. It may have financial power, numerical voter bloc power, or information power. The wealthier groups of course tend to rely upon the first factor rather than the second. The American campaign system offers a wide open field for financial muscle to show itself. In addition, there is the problem of corruption, payments to persons to influence their votes or actions directly. The more important and (at least until the 1972 activities disclosed by the Watergate revelations) the more respectable channel for money is through the financing of campaigns; the parties and candidates are perpetually in need of funds.

Groups not having large checkbooks must turn to their membership lists for influence. A union may be outgunned by corporate funds, but if it is sufficiently cohesive to deliver the votes of a large part of its membership, and also supply numbers of willing campaign workers, that may do as well or better in some circumstances. The mass membership associations thus have an advantage over the wealthy, small groups in situations that call for power in the polling booths. Their influence will depend, of course, on the ability of the leadership actually to spark active campaign work and to get the vote out on election day.

Pressure groups, or lobbies, also offer organizational help and information to assist the executive or legislator to do his job. Much of the work of drawing up bills for legislative consideration is done by interest groups rather than by the lawmakers and their staffs. The executive may rely upon an interest group for information on some subject. For example, for many years the Federal Power Commission has taken its basic information on the availability of various fuels from the power industries themselves. The shortage of heating oil in the winter of 1972–73 that foreshadowed the continuing shortage of petroleum products in general occurred despite oil industry assurances that there would be an abundant supply; the FPC had no way of knowing otherwise. Similarly, the Food and Drug Administration relies upon drug companies themselves to do most of the testing of drugs before they are approved for general distribution. Wealthier groups have an edge here, in terms of the ability to provide this information; however, a group supported by many enthusiastic laymen can put together a great deal of knowledge, and environmental, health, and consumer groups have demonstrated this in the late sixties and the seventies.

Techniques of Influence

The methods of exerting pressure through these three major resources vary enormously. A list of activities engaged in by interest groups includes the following: marshaling of public opinion; contributions to campaigns; provision of workers for campaigns; contribution of support through endorsements; assistance in drawing up bills; advising legislative and executive branches; attempts to obtain government positions for supporters of the group's policies, and initiating court actions.

The choice of technique will depend partly upon the resources of the group and partly upon the choice of target. Although the term most commonly used for pressure group activity, lobbying, refers to influence on the legislative branch (hanging around in the lobby to talk to legislators) this is by no means the only area of government subject to pressure; none is immune.

PRESSURE THROUGH THE JUDICIAL SYSTEM.   Many groups choose to exert influence through the judicial system. A matter of public policy is often greatly affected by court decisions. The effect on policy may be immediate; rather than waiting the long years it may require to persuade dozens of legislators, a single judge or a few judges (only five at the Supreme Court) can make a decision virtually overnight. The resources required are much less than those for activity in other government arenas. Although arguing a case in the Supreme Court will cost several thousand dollars, the expense is a drop in the bucket in contrast to the cost of campaign contributions. No membership of any size is needed; judicial decisions are not supposed to be affected by considerations of majority preference (although an elected judge may be subject to such considerations, he usually is not up for re-election very often). The primary resource required is information, in the form of legal briefs to influence a particular decision.

The interest group seeking political success in the courts must initiate a *test case*; the courts cannot act unless they are "triggered" by some other party. Through a favorable decision in one case, a general policy may be established, or altered. The group will thus pick the most favorable case it can find, perhaps even advertising for litigants. The legal brief for the particular case will of course be part of the strategy, as well as persuasive oral arguments where the courts require or permit them. Two major avenues of influence exist outside of the case itself. One is the submission of supporting arguments directly to the court, in the form of *amicus curiae* briefs, and the other is the influencing of the development of constitutional and statutory interpretation by placing articles in law reviews and other legal periodicals that will support the argument the group is making.

In the first tactic, an outside organization files a brief as "a friend of the court," or *amicus curiae;* if all litigants agree, the brief is automatically accepted. If the parties do not agree, then the group may petition the court for permission to file, and the court may or may not act. The most frequent filers in recent years have been the NAACP, the American Civil Liberties Union, the AFL-CIO, the American Bar Association, the National Lawyers Guild, veterans groups, and the government itself. These organizations have substantial records of success. The government and the NAACP in particular have won most of the cases in which they have taken an interest. To what extent the *amicus curiae* briefs are responsible is hard to measure. Certainly the opinions of the courts in many instances seem to reflect the arguments advanced in the briefs. Unless and until there is confirmation in future publication of judicial papers, it is not possible to know whether the judges came to these opinions on their own or were impressed by the briefs submitted. The organizations in question continue to submit briefs, assuming that at least it does no harm and it may well be determining.

Many of these groups also take measures to obtain support for their position in the legal literature, which judges often cite openly in their opinions as having helped shaped their view of the law. Roughly a quarter of Supreme Court decisions cite some legal periodical, especially those of Harvard, Yale, Columbia, and the University of Michigan. The landmark desegregation decision, *Brown* v. *Board of Education,* in 1954, was heavily supported by references to scholarly literature, much of which had been contributed by supporters of the NAACP anticipating the case.

Other groups in recent years that have resorted to the courts, especially the federal courts, are women's rights groups, minority movements, and homosexual organizations. The common characteristic of most groups that rely heavily on court activity is their disadvantaged status in society. These groups are not likely to have the financial resources or the status to influence the legislature or executive. They often are able to cite the Constitution and other political documents in their favor, obtaining successful results from the appellate courts. Their success is limited by the amount of compliance that the rest of the political system is willing to give. Judicial lobbying thus may eventually require lobbying in the rest of the government to some extent, either to influence the choice of judges (as in the fights over the nominations of Carswell and Haynsworth to the Supreme Court) or to influence the executive and legislative reaction to the opinions won from the bench.

Pressure on the legislature. The most familiar form of interest group activity is that of lobbying, or attempting to influence legislatures. Again the key is the control of information, but in a very different form. Pressure groups seek to mobilize the expression of public opinion by gathering and directing letters and other communications from constituents to legislators. They frequently have persons who work part or full time for their interests in city, state, or national legislatures. Either or both of these methods requires substantial funds and either a large enough membership or a high enough status to impress the lawmakers.

The techniques available to influence legislators in direct contacts are much more varied than those permissible to influence judges. The judge in the American system is not supposed to discuss cases with interested parties at all; his role is the most isolated and impartial in American politics. Legislators, however, are free to listen to arguments from all sides and, indeed, are supposed to. The lobbyist is essentially a full-time advocate, who may work only for one group or act as a "freelance," taking on work for different groups at different times. One of his jobs may be to be a "nice guy," developing friendly contacts with legislators, gradually building up a sense of personal obligation on the part of the legislator. This is known as "wining and dining." The lobbyist is always ready to take a legislator to lunch, to get tickets to the Superbowl, to provide a trip to the home constituency in the company plane, to find a female companion. The staff members close to the legislator are included on a lesser scale because their approval or disapproval may be critical. There is not necessarily any suggestion of bribery in this process, although it is not unheard of at any level. By a simple process of proximity and persuasion, a legislator who is not careful may be brought to feel that the activities the lobbyist friend supports are the ones deserving of his own support. This aspect of lobbying helps to explain why interest groups often hire former congressmen or other legislators to represent them; not only do these men already "know their way around" the legislature, but they are already friends with many of the men still in power. This possibility of a job is a second means of influence, or "deferred bribe"; even though few legislators are able to bring themselves to think seriously of defeat, the increased rates of turnover in recent years mean that many lose or choose to resign. It is often difficult to return to the job held before office, even for lawyers. Most politicians seem to find it difficult to tear themselves away from the seat of their former power. Their staffers may follow them into lobbying as well. Many become freelance lobbyists; others join particular groups that they supported while in office. In the twenty years after World War II for instance, twenty-three senators and eighty representatives remained in Washington as lobbyists after leaving office.

Campaign contributions are a third form of influence. The law prohibits campaign or other contributions specifically in exchange for a vote; that is bribery, and it is a crime as a few legislators have discovered to their sorrow. The law also prohibits contributions by corporations and labor unions, but these restrictions are easily evaded by setting up front groups, and the lobbyist's job is to make sure that the recipients know to whom they are indebted. Even if the money is given ostensibly to a campaign committee collecting for several candidates, it is easy enough to earmark funds for a specific man. The campaign committee in turn will write the check for him, and the lobbyist may "hand deliver" the committee's check. Some of these contributions are illegal, and others come quite close to the line of illegality. In 1973 for instance the Nixon campaign returned some contributions when the donors were discovered to be the targets of possible criminal action in connection with business activities; others, such as illegal contributions from American Airlines, it solicited and retained. This area of political activity is one of the most corruptible and lately has become the subject of great criticism.

Fourth, the lobbyist is a prime collector, dispenser, and publicizer of information; for some, the best known example being Ralph Nader, this is their major role. The individual lobbyist may be valued for his knowledge of whom to seek in Washington to get something done. He and his staff may be a major source of legislative research for the lawmakers. Lobbyists can spend their entire effort compiling facts about sugar production, oil needs, steel needs, or whatever they are promoting. The individual legislator is unlikely to have a staff anywhere as large, and his staff is primarily occupied with service jobs for constituents, preparation of the legislator's schedule, and other logistics. The committees devoted to specific areas of legislation may have larger staffs, which must still divide their attention among many bills; subcommittees often have only one or two staff members for all aspects of the subcommittee's work. Thus the services provided by the lobbyist are valuable. In the state and local assemblies they may greatly improve the quality of the legislative work. Many of these lower level assemblies have virtually no staff at all, such as the Alabama legislature, which in 1970 had only four assistants for all staff work! The legislators choose to rely upon lobbyists rather than increase staff size and perhaps draw public ire over the additional expense. Thus the lobbies may shape the laws in a very direct fashion, by actually writing them.

PRESSURE ON THE EXECUTIVE.   Within the executive branch itself, individual departments and the President's office act as lobbyists in both the legislative and judicial branches, even setting up formal offices for liaison with Congress; mayors, governors, and other state executive heads must also try to build good relations with their assemblies. These executive agency lobbyists, such as police departments, the FBI, or the military, may be some of the most powerful lobbyists at all levels of government.

Congress and the courts, in return, exert much less pressure on the executive, which has been the arena for some very important and sophisticated lobbying in recent years as the scope of executive power and discretion has widened. Most pressures come from private groups or from lower level executives such as the governors' conference. There is again a range of tactics, often greatly favoring high-status, well-financed groups. The vote is not as great a threat here. Only a few executive officers are directly elected; many lower level bureaucrats continue in office regardless of changes in party fortunes. In comparison to legislators, those who are elected are subject to a much larger constituency, and so less subject to pressure from any single group. Campaign contributions are still of great importance for those elected officials, who may need larger campaign chests by virtue of their larger constituencies. Another means of access is, again, through the provision of information, assisting the executive in drawing up legislative proposals. An example is the use of industrial advisory committees by almost all federal executive departments; there are no corresponding consumer or public advisory committees in most instances.

The independent regulatory agencies, which also act as lobbyists on occasion, were originally the product of successful pressure group action in Congress or state legislatures. Today they are subject to powerful and continuing efforts by those whom they regulate to deflect that regulation into favorable channels. The public, which is supposedly protected by these agencies, rarely has an organized lobbying effort on its behalf. It is therefore not surprising that many political scientists speak of the regulatory agencies as protecting business from competition, as the servants of those whom they are to regulate rather than their masters.

SPECIAL AREAS OF ACTIVITY.   The devices of the initiative and the referendum, common in some states, which allow the public to write into or out of the law various proposals, offer additional forums for interest group activity. A great deal of money and organizational effort may back a proposal such as the 1972 California propositions on the control of farm labor organizing, or the mandatory formula for state employee salaries, or the Michigan proposal on abortion law changes. Substantial efforts are needed to place these proposals on the ballot, and then more effort is required to publicize and gather enough votes to pass them (often a two-thirds approval is required). Mass membership groups and wealthy groups are roughly equal in these efforts. Occasionally a group that has neither a large backing of numbers or finances can be successful on the basis of moral appeals, as the farmworkers were in California in 1972.

Attempts to Regulate Lobbying

Lobbying action has been carried out for most of the history of the republic, but efforts by the legislatures and the Congress to control it did not really begin until the mid-nineteen thirties. The laws are shot with loopholes, especially at local levels. Registration by lobbyists is voluntary; if they assert that their primary activity is not lobbying, that it is directing "grass roots" activity rather than directly influencing a legislator, that it is primarily "informational" rather than influential, then by this self-assessment they are excluded. Many of the most active and influential lobbyists do not register and so make no reports of their activities.

Reproduced by permission of Johnny Hart and Field Enterprises, Inc.

The majority of lobbyists, registered or not, are corporate interests known vaguely by such names as oil lobby, highway lobby, dairy lobby, sugar lobby, and so forth. The oil lobby, for example, is headed by the American Petroleum Institute, composed of major oil companies, and spends perhaps $10 million a year. A huge lobby drawn from the government itself is the military lobby, which includes corporations that do business with the Pentagon and employs perhaps 1,500 retired military officers. Labor unions support powerful lobbies, headed by the AFL-CIO through its Committee on Political Education and now the Teamsters Union. Cities and states send lobbyists to Washington and to the state legislatures. Public interest lobbies, such as environmental groups, are not entirely new, but they are far fewer than the corporate and government lobbies. The advantage goes to business with its overwhelming financial resources (ultimately paid for by the consumers in higher prices). The public interest groups and the less powerful government lobbyists such as mayoral delegates must rely upon the marshaling of votes and opinions and the provision of as much information as possible. Additionally these groups often have a wide range of concerns, while corporate groups need worry about only a few problems; the public interest groups may be pressing for change and the business groups trying only to preserve existing policies, and the power of inertia favors the *status quo*. It can not be determined what the structure of government benefits would look like if there were no interest group activities, but few economists will deny that the structure of government subsidies, tax breaks, and the like, is heavily biased to the corporate and wealthier segments of American society, whether they approve of this bias or not.

Interest Groups and Democracy

What can be said about the effect of interest groups on democracy in the United States? First, the power and importance of interest groups in general shifts the focus of political action from the individual to the group. This may be the only way to organize political life in an urban, mobile, and complex society, but it does change the possibility and varieties of participation in this important way.

Interest group activity in the United States appears to support what is known as a competitive elite; unlike some nations whose elite is a unified group, the U.S. elite is stratified and divided among itself on many questions that can be openly fought out. On basic issues about the organization of the economic and political system, however, most are in agreement. Most of these groups are working for only incremental changes, such as reshaping of the tax laws, rather than fundamental and radical changes in the society.

The smaller, more cohesive special interests, which tend to be the wealthier ones, have a greater chance of getting concrete results, while the less cohesive mass groups may get some rhetoric in order to get their votes, but little more. Groups that are disadvantaged by the present arrangements must get concrete change in order to have any success, while those who like things the way they are need only sit tight. As noted earlier, the advantage will generally be with those who sit tight.

The pluralist view supports interest groups as a channel for grass roots influence on leadership, a means of participating that goes beyond voting, and so a contribution to democracy; the upper class, *status quo* bias of interest groups is the price that must be paid for this channel of influence. The critics find that the unrepresentative character of interest group politics seriously detracts from democracy in America and would prefer to see interest group activities brought under much stricter controls and made as open as possible.

Both sides tend to exaggerate the importance of these group activities and the extent of their success. It is unlikely that any single political policy in Washington or in the states can be attributed solely to pressure group activity. Accidents of history can help or hinder; as air pollution rises and breathing becomes less pleasant, the public is less willing to support highway builders and industrialists, regardless of their lobbying efforts. One person may overturn the practice of decades, as John Banzhaf, who brought the suit that led to the removal of cigarette commercials from TV, and Ralph Nader have shown. Madelyn Murray O'Hair single-handedly accomplished changes in the relationship of church and state. Political parties also play important roles, and the groups may find their influence diminished in the competition for influence within the parties. An interest group may try to influence both parties, in order not to lose if one party is thrown out of power, but this places a strain on the resources of most groups. If the membership is divided in party loyalty, the ability to influence either party by votes is reduced, and it is rare for more than 70 percent of any group's members (or a 20 percent majority) to support one party. Conflicting pressures within a party may cancel each other —for example, the splits that existed for years between Southerners and other Democrats over civil rights legislation. In general a party will know which groups support it and which dislike it cordially; shifting loyalties is difficult and rare, perhaps awaiting a traumatic experience such as the Civil War or the Depression. Thus the parties will dominate their interest groups in most cases, rather than the other way around. Party politics is more than just a coalition of interest group politics, although it is partly that; in turn, American politics is often more than the clash of political parties. Interest groups must be recognized as important forces in American political life, and the thrust of interest group activity reinforces the *status quo* more than it does the prospects for change, the advantaged more than the disadvantaged.

Suggested Readings

Murray Edelman, *The Symbolic Uses of Politics* (Chicago: University of Illinois Press, 1967)*; a classic treatment of political symbolism

David Hapgood, "The Highwaymen," *Washington Monthly,* 1:2 (March, 1969)

Helen Leavitt, *Superhighway—Superhoax* (New York: Ballantine, 1970)*

Legislators and the Lobbyists (Washington: Congressional Quarterly, 1968)

Edgar Litt, *Ethnic Politics in America* (Glenview, Ill.: Scott, Foresman, 1970)*

Lester Milbrath, *The Washington Lobbyists* (Chicago: Rand McNally, 1963)

Jack Newfield and Jeff Greenfield, *A Populist Manifesto* (New York: Paperback Library, 1972)*

Michael Novak, *The Rise of the Unmeltable Ethnics* (New York: Macmillan, 1972)

E. E. Schattschneider, *The Semi-Sovereign People: A Realist's View of Democracy in America* (New York: Harcourt Brace Jovanovich, 1960)*; a classic

James S. Turner, *The Chemical Feast* (New York: Grossman, 1970)*

* Available in paperback

Clement Vose, "Litigation as a Form of Pressure Group Activity," *The Annals* (Philadelphia: The American Academy of Political and Social Science, September, 1948); a classic

Harmon Zeigler and Wayne Peak, *Interest Groups in American Society* (Englewood Cliffs, N.J.: Prentice-Hall, 2nd ed., 1972)*

Harmon Zeigler, *Interest Groups in the States* (Boston: Little, Brown, 1965)

* Available in paperback

8

PARTIES

Brokers of Power in America

You may elect whichever candidates you please to office if
you allow me to pick the candidates.

Boss Tweed

The American major political party is essentially an organization for the
winning of elections, unlike many European parties (and some small
American parties), whose primary concern is with refinement and presentation of an ideology or political philosophy. This goal influences most
aspects of the party system in the United States: how parties are organized, how they select candidates for office and conduct campaigns, and
what policies the victorious candidates put into effect.

Like most other American political forms, the present party system developed by historical trial and error. The Framers and early supporters of
the Constitution hoped that there would be no parties, or "factions," as
they pejoratively described them. They perceived the new nation as need-
ing consensus and considered parties to be divisive elements that could
only harm the young republic. Thus the Constitution itself made no provision for the operation of parties. In the first national election the
Electoral College turned unanimously to George Washington, a charis-
matic leader whose prestige and influence were so great that he was virtually beyond criticism. Known as "the Greatest of Good Men and the
Best of Great Men," Washington stayed in office for two terms and then
retired, setting a fortunate precedent for stable succession to office. While
he was President Washington presided reluctantly over the development
of the first parties: the Federalists centered upon the aristocratic Alexander
Hamilton, and the anti-Federalists, or Democratic-Republicans, upon the

Reproduced by permission of Johnny Hart and Field Enterprises, Inc.

multi-talented young Thomas Jefferson. In many respects these two presented the same division of interests that appeared in new nations around
the globe in the twentieth century. The Federalists were a coalition of
local elites of superior status, relying upon the respect of the population
for their "betters"; they tended to be older than their opponents and more
conservative; they were opposed to the expansion of popular participation
in the government and were convinced of their "natural" right to rule.
The Democratic-Republicans set up a strong organization headed by rising young men, with a large popular following that was attracted by the
more democratic proposals of the Jeffersonians and by their opposition to
the growing wealth of the manufacturing elite. The Federalists won the
presidency in 1796, but by 1800 the Democratic-Republicans were strong
enough to put Jefferson in the White House, and the Federalists began to
collapse. They never won national office again and in another decade were
gone. In the death throes of the Federalists, various New England leaders
attempted to secede from the Union but were unable to convince their
states to support these bitter efforts.

The Democratic-Republicans ruled the nation for a quarter of a century, but during this period the internal unity of the party began to crack.
By 1824 the party had split into warring factions; in 1828 these organized
as the Democratic party, under Andrew Jackson, and the National Republican party. (In 1832 the first third party, the Anti-Masons, emerged.
Its narrow advocacy of a single issue was characteristic of the third parties
that would follow.) The National Republicans joined with disaffected
Jacksonians in 1836 to form the Whig Party, which remained until 1856
as the second major party. It adopted, in less aristocratic fashion, many of
the conservative attitudes of the Federalists. The Whigs lacked a strong
leader, and the growing tension of the slavery issue eventually tore the
party apart. The Democrats were also divided on this question, finally
turning against the Jeffersonian heritage as the Southern wing took over
and gathered in the majority of the Whigs. From many former Democrats in the North, the abolitionist movement, the small Free Soil party,
and the ashes of the Whig progressives the Republican party was born,
nominating its first presidential candidate in 1856. The major lines of
party competition were then drawn; the Republicans and Democrats
would continue to dominate the American scene.

The Civil War left its mark on the two parties, a stamp that distorted
the competition and created many of the difficulties of twentieth century

campaigns. The assumption by the Democratic party of the slaveholder's heritage clashed with the liberal estate of Jefferson and Jackson (although the ideas and acts of these two men themselves contained the seeds of the inconsistencies). The party eventually became a divided one, with one foot in the conservative southern states and another in the more liberal urban areas. The Republicans too were divided. Their role as the saviors of the Union and emancipators of the slaves gave them an image of liberality and the loyalty of the ex-slaves that fit poorly with the Republicans' strong association with the enormous concentration of economic and political power in the great trusts of the late nineteenth century. Neither the urban worker nor the rural agrarian worker was represented by the policies of either party. This fueled an attempt by the Populist movement to take over the Democratic party. In 1896 they succeeded but then sealed their own doom by nominating the florid William Jennings Bryan, who would be defeated for the presidency three times. In the process of his defeats the conservatives and Southerners gained complete control of the party. The Republicans continued to support their business associates, and even the much hailed trust busting of Theodore Roosevelt was not to make the Republicans a populist party. The 1896 election marked the end of the enthusiastic participation of the disadvantaged in politics; the figures for voting participation show a marked decline after 1896, which has continued to the present day.

The Republicans controlled the national political scene from 1856 to 1932 with only minor interludes of Democratic resurgence. The Great Depression then brought about a substantial realignment of forces within the parties. The minorities and the poor returned to the Democrats as the party shifted to a more liberally oriented national policy, based upon greater intervention in economic and social affairs by the government. The Republicans in turn became ever more identified as the party of big business and the exponent of rugged individualism, with the role of government to be correspondingly restricted. As the twentieth century aged, both parties appeared to blur their differences, accepting the major outlines of government action as established. Although survey work showed the leadership of the parties to differ strongly in personal ideologies, the activists and officeholders in both parties continued to be dominated by members of upper socioeconomic groups, a fact that was reflected in the similarity of their appeals. The party programs often seemed more alike than different and were perhaps most strongly characterized by ambiguity.

The failure of strong third parties to develop in the United States, and the resulting complex base of the two major parties, also contributes to party ambiguity. Since the end of the Civil War there have been only four substantial national challenges by third parties. In 1896 the Populists won 8½ percent of the votes, followed by Roosevelt's Progressive (Bull Moose) party in 1912 with 27½ percent, LaFollette's Progressives in 1924 with 16½ percent, and George Wallace's American Independent Party in 1968 with 13½ percent. (The Dixiecrat effort of 1948, limited as it was to the Deep South, did not pose a national challenge.) None of these parties lasted long as organizations on a national scale, although they and some of their less successful relatives managed to achieve some power of a local or state nature in many instances. In American politics, third party success nationally can be measured only in terms of the extent to which at least one of the major parties has adopted some of the aims of the third party. Once the third party programs have been partially co-opted by the major parties, the third party dies. The party dies too if it is unable to convince the major parties to take up its goals. In either case the party itself may refuse to read the obituary and carry on, but it ceases to have any electoral effect. The two major parties have thus become to some extent conglomer ates of many different interests. Unendangered by any strong challenges from third parties, they are able to operate without sharply defining their difference with each other or with new parties.

Party Systems and Organization

Yet another reason for lack of party "responsibility"—that is, the failure of strong party doctrines to develop and the additional failure of the parties to enforce conformation to even those vague policies they do espouse—lies in party organization. Unlike most European parties, the American parties, both nationally and on state levels, are decentralized. There is, of course, a national organization, the National Committee, and a national convention. The convention chooses only the presidential and vice-presidential candidates; the other national offices, those of Congressmen, are filled by men nominated by state and local party groups. This tends to drive a wedge between the President and Congress, and some observers have felt that, as a result, there are actually four parties, a congressional party in each major party, and a presidential party in each. The national leaders, with the exception of an incumbent President, have no powers over their party officeholders. With rare exceptions, they cannot deny them nomination, and although they do disburse some funds, the majority of campaign funds are raised at other levels of the party or by the candidates themselves. Thus each officeholder is free of party discipline, at least on a national level. This disjointed structure would have to change if the parties were to move in the direction of "party responsibility," which in turn would be a prerequisite to realigning the parties into more truly ideological liberal and conservative parties. In the early part of the seventies, a number of party affiliation changes took place, with prominent figures moving from one party to another, and groups such as labor shifting slightly from their long adherence to one party. These changes may result in the tightening of party policies along ideological lines, but without party responsibility the two parties will be unlikely to enforce these differences.

The majority of the population associates itself with one or the other party, but not in formal membership. Rather, the majority of party followers in the United States can be termed "identifiers," or *party voters*. They fall into two groups: those who identify with a party, voting for it more frequently than for the other but often splitting their votes, and those who vote for one party consistently in general elections. A more select group consists of those known as *primary voters*, who take the trouble to go to the polls in a primary election (excluding those instances where one party is so dominant that its primary is actually the real election) and are willing to identify themselves as supporters of a particular party in those states that require this registration for primary voting. The active membership of the parties runs between 5 and 10 percent of the adult population (roughly the same percentage of the Russian population are actually card carrying Communists!). Those who are the party leadership are a miniscule group, consisting of the formal officeholders, either in the party or in government, and a few nonofficials who are close to them, plus persons who have either time or money to offer the parties. Those who contribute money tend to have considerable influence. The mix of leadership varies from state to state, and the joining of various state groups in turn gives the national parties their polyglot character. The individual environment of each state affects the nature of the mix; each has a different social, economic, and racial make-up and a different history. The type of state party system present also affects the party leadership, as the leadership affects the development of the party system in the future.

ONE PARTY NON-COMPETITIVE.   A few states in American history have been ruled by political parties that were not internally competitive; while opposition could not be outlawed legally, it could be done informally by men of great power. A case in point is Huey Long, who ruled the Democratic party in Louisiana with an iron hand. Long was able to keep from active roles in the party almost all of those opposed to him, although when he went to Washington as a senator his grasp on the state party began to slip. Governor Wallace in Alabama has had a very substantial measure of personal control over the Democratic party there since early in the 1960's. In such a situation, the party leadership and the state party itself may be distorted; men and interests who would otherwise be included or excluded will be kept out of or brought into the party because of their relationships with the dominant figure or figures. This type of party is fairly rare; it is not consistent with the basic norm of American politics that competition and opposition are not to be suppressed, at least not openly.

ONE PARTY COMPETITIVE.   Many states, by history and tradition, have been governed by one party almost exclusively. The Democrats in the southern states and the Republicans in New England and parts of the Midwest are examples. The other party may exist largely on paper and primarily to receive patronage from the White House if that party should capture it, and it may or may not nominate and campaign for office. Most of the competition that elsewhere would be expressed as interparty struggle is here swept under the single party label. The primary election becomes the effective election; the winner of the dominant party's nomination for the general election has already won. In some states only one or two persons will compete in the primary, but more commonly a number of persons will run, the winner gaining only a small plurality. Particularly in the South, the device of the run-off election (common in the multiple party systems of Europe) was adopted to overcome the deficiencies of this system, in which the public has shown no clear preference and in fact the initial winner may have been successful only because the vote was split among several other popular candidates. If no candidate received a clear majority in the initial primary, the top two or three vote-getters will compete again in the run-off election to produce a winner with a majority. The existence of many states with one-party competitive systems has helped to produce the anomalous national parties. Men who would normally be members of one party will run for office under the other label because first and foremost they wish to win; adherence to the preferred party comes second. The conflict is illustrated by the dilemma that faced John Conally in deciding to shift to the more personally congenial Republicans in the setting of his strongly Democratic home base of Texas.

TWO PARTY COMPETITIVE, WITH ONE PARTY DOMINANT.   Some states with two active parties may nevertheless be dominated overwhelmingly by one of the two. The dominant party does not always win, but it usually does. In this setting the second party has sufficient strength to affect policies, and it has a chance, though slim, of gaining power temporarily.

TWO PARTY COMPETITIVE.   Here the parties are more evenly matched. Neither wins more than 60 percent of the time or loses more than 40 percent of the time. Thus neither can be confident of success or certain of defeat. Party affiliation cannot depend upon simply picking the party that is always the ticket to electoral success. Here the ideological lines may be more clearly drawn between the parties, and the mix of interest groups in the state can coalesce into more natural groupings than in the first three systems. The drive for electoral success will, of course, affect this process; in the appeals to the vast "middle" group of voters who are determining, the two parties will still adopt positions that are similar in more ways than they are different. California and Illinois are examples.

THREE OR FOUR PARTY COMPETITION.   New York State is an example. It has the Democratic and Republican parties and Conservative and Liberal parties as well. The latter two are closely associated with the first two but are not the same. On occasion, as happened in 1970, when James Buckley was elected to the U.S. Senate on the Conservative ticket, one of the smaller parties will actually elect a candidate. Generally, this means that the dominant parties nominated men who were too similar, splitting one segment of the vote, while the third man gathered in all the opposing groups and slipped into office by a plurality. On occasion this happened at the national level as well. In 1968, for instance, the combined vote of the two Nixon opponents was greater than his total. The run-off election is the solution to this problem; a second contest between the top two vote-getters would force the public to decide which general position they really preferred. The winner would have a majority, no matter how slim. The 1972 election has for the time being reduced the concern over this problem, but if a strong third party movement should surface again, the American political system may have to consider introducing a run-off election, particularly if the Electoral College is changed or eliminated.

MULTIPLE PARTY SYSTEMS.   There are few examples of this in American life. Some single party states, such as Florida, have been identified as multiparty systems in disguise; within the one party there were so many factions that the political behavior of the system resembled multiparty activity. These systems are common in Europe and almost inevitably produce the device of coalition government. Rarely does any one party gain enough support to govern alone; it is forced to join with several other parties, sometimes producing odd associations, in order to form a government. The parties in these systems are generally much more clearly based in ideology; their differences are sharper, and the process of forming and maintaining coalitions is difficult. Governments may form and reform easily; France had nearly two dozen after the Second World War until the public finally tired of government inertia and restored De Gaulle to power. Postwar Italy has had nearly forty governments, frequently enduring periods of paralysis while power changed hands. The proponents of this variety of party system argue that these disadvantages are balanced by the representation of clear policy positions and the political sophistication of the public.

Two Party Versus Multiple Party Systems: Choice and Consequences

Although the two party system and the variations of it that exist in the United States are in large part the products of historical circumstances, there are indications that some measure of deliberate choice has always played a part in the maintenance of this system. Various constitutional and statutory arrangements give the two party system an advantage. Foremost among these are the single-member district and the array of legal requirements for the listing of candidates and parties on the ballot. Under the single-member district system, there is only one winning candidate and party in each district. Almost all American elections are conducted on this basis, even the federal ones, although the Constitution does not require it. A few cities have used the alternative, proportional representation, which is favored in Europe. Under proportional representation, each party receives a portion of the seats being filled, roughly approximating its percentage of the vote. This allows minority parties to gain office rather than being forced to merge with a majority party in order to obtain a voice.

A new third party or an independent candidate finds many obstacles on the way to the ballot. The courts have on occasion removed some of these, but most are still in effect. The general practice is to require a new party to obtain the signatures of a percentage of the voters in the last election in order to qualify the party for listing on the ballot. This may be rendered virtually impossible by requiring that only those persons willing temporarily to give up their major party identification for primaries may sign, or by restricting each signer to a petition for one new party only. Even without these limitations, the effort needed to obtain thousands of signatures is substantial. The success of George Wallace in obtaining a place on the ballot in all fifty states was rightly hailed as a major political feat. Filing fees also may discourage some candidates running as independents. The major political parties act as the legal supervisors of elections in many states. Finally, the Electoral College "winner takes all" system of electing the President, and the dominance of that office in the thought of many politicians, work against third parties just as single-member districts do. The only ways a third party could affect the Electoral College vote are if it suddenly had majority support throughout the country or if it carried enough states to prevent any candidate from winning in the Electoral College, thus throwing the election into the House of Representatives. A small swell of support scattered throughout the country is of no use.

The majority of political scientists, and the majority of American politicians, have viewed the disjointed, gangling American parties, and their two-party arrangement, as beneficial for American politics. In the words of one writer, "Vast gaudy friendly umbrellas, under which all Americans, whoever and wherever and however minded they may be, are invited to stand for the sake of being counted in the next election." The theory behind this view may be summarized as follows. The United States is a huge country, with a population that counts representatives of every nationality and race, religion and color, language and culture, on the earth. It has vast economic and social groups, ranging from billionaires to hardscrabble tenant farmers, General Motors to the neighborhood drug store, the Four Hundred families to the lower class. It has huge natural regions with distinct and separate histories. If all these separate groups in American life were to form political parties, they might well shatter the nation and incapacitate its government. Instead, the two major parties have cut across sections, socioeconomic classes, racial and national groups, and by so doing have held the country together. True, a great deal of the compromising and appealing to all groups has been motivated less by any consideration of principle than by the desire to put together the largest majority possible and so get into or stay in office, but such may be the "price of union." The drive to obtain more votes has, in this view, resulted in the expansion of democracy in ways that might otherwise have been impossible. If the opening of the franchise to more voters were motivated not by genuine feelings that these voters were entitled to it but rather by an urge to add this group or that to the totals under the party heading, the outcome in terms of democracy is the same; both the vote and the access to political office were greatly broadened, as parties added candidates to the slates that would appeal to the new groups of voters. Finally, the supporters of the system as it has evolved point to this historical development itself as evidence. Clearly, the American parties are the way they are because the American public prefers them that way; they developed in history in response to the felt needs of the times, and if they were not satisfactory the people would have rejected them. Instead, time and time again the people have rejected the alternatives. For nearly one hundred twenty years the people have given their approval to these two major political parties. To propose to change them, or the party system, radically is to flout the will of the people.

The critics of the American party system find the "unity at any price" no longer compelling, if it ever was. While the country may have stood in danger of civil war a century ago, it is far too unlikely a threat today to justify the continuation of the Tweedledum and Tweedledee system. Second, the expansion of the franchise had little to do with the parties; it was the efforts of the excluded groups themselves with some assistance from dedicated supporters who believed in the principle of democracy that won the vote for blacks, women, young people, American Indians, and so on. Third, the parties may have been adequate to the needs of earlier times, but the pressures of the late twentieth century are too great to be contained with a nineteenth century framework; the inability of the parties to present and act on clear alternatives hinders the ability of the political system to cope with the great challenges facing America today. Finally, the critics raise the question of whether or not the state of the parties may have something to do with the darker aspects of American politics: the demonstrated lack of principle among many politicians, the willingness to exploit fears and prejudices in order to collect votes, the continuing failure to deal with the twin nightmares of racism and poverty, and the apathy and immaturity of much of the electorate, as measured by low turnouts and poor knowledge of politics. The obsession with building a winning coalition sweeps all before it, obscuring the question of "winning for what?" Even though the public may have been satisfied with what was offered in the past, in order to "grow up" it should now be faced with real alternatives and so learn to weigh the consequences of political action more carefully. Some advocate the development of a multiple party system, others the development of the present parties into responsible liberal and conservative parties. In either case, the critics are saying that with greater attention to principles a greater measure of clarity in presenting programs and the discipline necessary to implement those programs, the parties could help to bring the American dream of political freedom and economic welfare closer to realization, and without those changes they will help to delay its realization.

Functions of the Parties in American Politics

Regardless of whose hopes and prescriptions for the party system are filled, the functions that system serves in the American polity are not likely to change. The parties act as brokers, or aggregators, of power, enabling various special interest groups to work together for at least some general common purposes, while at the same time the groups gain some access to power for their particular views. In the process of campaigning and in the presentation of views when in office the party activists help to perpetuate the political culture, offering the public very general "maps" to help sort out their understanding of what happens in government. Loyalty to one or the other party is strong in many families, and often becomes part of the heritage of succeeding generations. Although the child may change his own allegiance as the result of his adult experience, his early political experiences in his family, collectively known as "political socialization," help to determine how and why he reacts to events as he does. His parents' party background is a large factor in this process. Finally, and most immediately and dramatically, the parties recruit and elect the political leadership of the country.

SELECTION AND ELECTION OF THE GOVERNMENT AND THE PARTIES.   The primary form of public participation in politics is through elections, which fill over 600,000 positions in the United States. For some of the lower offices, which may be uninteresting and poorly paid, the party is critical in finding candidates and persuading them to run; although no one may come forward on his own to compete, the party has a great interest in adding to the total of offices it controls and so will search for candidates. The sought-after offices do not need the party as catalyst, but those who seek them turn to the party for assistance, and as a result, with some exceptions, the parties also select the candidates for these offices. To win election as an independent, with the backing of no party organization and funds, is exceedingly difficult and rare; even a person who could finance his own campaign finds that in facing an opponent with party loyalty and support, his chances of wooing the voters from the party nominees are slight. Thus the parties determine the shape of political leadership in America; the public selects its rulers from the alternatives offered by the parties.

Selection of the candidates may be either by primary or convention. The primary involves a greater number of citizens, but both means result in an elite group selecting the nominees. Primary voters generally are drawn from the more active, higher status segment of the electorate. The convention may allow a very tiny group of men to select the nominees, either in the convention itself or by manipulating the selection and agenda of the convention so that it merely ratifies the choice of the inner circle of the party leadership. Certain persons and groups have favored positions in this selection process. The incumbent who wishes to run again almost always is renominated. In a primary his name will be familiar to the voters, and at the convention he occupies a favorable seat. In turn, the incumbent will be reelected more than 90 percent of the time; the party naturally wishes to stay with a winner. When there is no incumbent running, the requirements of an election campaign will still play an important role in selection. The primaries themselves are miniature elections and are subject to all of the influences on general elections discussed below. The selection by convention also depends in part on the party's assessment of each candidate as a campaigner and his campaign resources.

THE CAMPAIGN.   Increasingly the major issue about American political campaigns is their cost. In Lincoln's first election the parties spent

Reproduced by permission of Johnny Hart and Field Enterprises, Inc.

$100,000. By 1928 the total spending at all levels had reached $16.5 million. In 1952, the last major campaign conducted with little television, the two parties spent $140 million, including $11.5 million on the presidential race. Total expenses in 1964 had risen to $200 million, with $60 million spent on the race for President. In 1968 the presidential contest consumed $100 million, and the total rose to $300 million; another $100 million rise occurred in 1972, the presidency alone taking some $150 million of the $400 million. Many congressional races were also costing millions of dollars. Rep. Ottinger spent an estimated $4 million in 1970 in losing to a $2 million dollar opponent; of fifteen candidates for the Senate in the seven major senatorial elections that year, eleven were millionaires themselves, and not one of the seven winners came from the ranks of nonmillionaires. These enormous sums are in turn dwarfed by the recorded $7.7 million spent by Governor Rockefeller in retaining his gubernatorial position in 1970. Even state and local campaigns rose to giddy heights. New York's Mayor Lindsay reported $2 million in 1969; candidates across the country were spending hundreds of thousands on offices that paid less than $20,000. A good deal of the expenditures were incurred in the primary campaigns; the presidential primaries in 1968 cost nearly $50 million. Some major races saw more money spent in primaries than in the general election.

Inflation and rising labor costs have contributed substantially to the increase since Lincoln's day. The population itself is seven times greater, and the proportion of the population that can vote is much greater. New techniques are also responsible, primarily television. In 1968 for instance, the production of political broadcasts and the purchase of broadcasting time took over a quarter of the campaign expenditures.

The implications of these campaign costs and techniques are enormous. The field of potential leaders increasingly becomes restricted to the rich and the friends and allies of the rich; as costs rise, even a millionaire cannot finance his own campaign without bankrupting himself. The role of campaign contributors, the sources of funds, becomes critical. Who are these people? What do they expect from their contributions?

Perhaps 10 percent of the public has contributed to a campaign at some time. Already the field of influentials constitutes an elite. Within the group of contributors, the degree of influence is greatly varied. Most contributors give in small amounts, under $50. Those who contribute over $500 constitute only 10 percent of the whole, a mere 1 percent of the public; these individuals and groups, especially those whose contributions are measured in many thousands, even millions, are the powers behind the parties. Many of the individual contributors appear to act from genuine belief in or friendship for a particular man, or from the satisfaction of being personally connected to an officeholder, and expect no return in policy or patronage. Others expect a stint as ambassador or to be consulted in some way for an appointment or policy decision. Interest groups, corporations, and the like may expect even more. The structure of privileges built into the tax and subsidy system, the policies made that favor the interests of large business and labor organizations, and the host of government arrangements that benefit the vested interests (such as allowing private patents on the results of governmentally financed research or traditionally placing an "oil man" on the House Ways and Means Committee to help protect the depletion allowance that serves to subsidize the oil industry) can all be attributed in part to the system of campaign finance in the United States.

Campaign Reform

There were attempts in the sixties and early seventies to put a ceiling on campaign spending. The federal government passed some legislation in 1971; states and cities are also contemplating new laws. A federal fund was set up, to be financed with income tax check-offs (i.e., one dollar from each taxpayer who designated it on the tax return), for presidential elections. Yet the changes seem to have had little impact. The poorly publicized fund drew few contributions partly because the check-off provision was buried deep within the tax forms. Prosecution of violators continues to be almost nonexistent; and no candidate has been prosecuted. The laws are easily deflected by channeling funds through a host of committees not "authorized" by the candidate. Expenditures on the use of television and radio are controlled by the new federal law; expenditures on new techniques such as computerized, personalized mailings are not. It is not likely that such forms of campaigning can be limited. There will be challenges to the restrictions as limiting freedom of speech. The seriousness of the problem is matched by the difficulty of solution. Yet the revelations in the Watergate investigations of 1973 indicate that the problem must be at least partially solved, even if awkwardly. If the system of campaign finance and control cannot be rigidly supervised by some public agency, trusted by the public, in place of the generally covert and corruptible vesting of power in private hands, the foundations of the political system will be dangerously weakened. It is up to the public and the politicians who perceive the consequences of the present system to seize the initiative and present alternatives. Much of the political history of the seventies will be written in the campaign account books.

A Note on Nonpartisan Elections

Some state offices, including the Minnesota and Nebraska legislatures (Minnesota is now changing to party election), and some city positions are filled through nonpartisan elections. Although the candidates may have long associations with a political party, there is no designation of party on the ballot. This is carried to absurdity in some instances, such as in the Michigan Supreme Court elections, where the two parties nominate candidates who then run as nonpartisan! Most of these elections are the result of earlier reform periods when it was thought that removal of party labels would remove corrupting party influence in municipal and judicial offices. Instead, in most cases there has been no readily identifiable "clean" outcome, and most nonpartisan elections show poor voter turnouts compared to partisan contests. Party designations apparently draw people's attention and involve them in the race. With all of their ugly defects, the parties remain the key to political participation in America; it is in the parties that the hopes for selecting a better leadership and effecting compassionate and intelligent public policies must be realized, or fail.

Suggested Readings

Angus Campbell, *et al*, *The American Voter* (New York: John Wiley and Sons, 1964); a classic study of public opinion

William Chambers, *Political Parties in a New Nation* (New York: Oxford University Press, 1963)*

William Flannigan, *The Political Behavior of the American Electorate* (Boston: Allyn and Bacon, 1968)*

* Available in paperback

V. O. Key, Jr., *Politics, Parties, and Pressure Groups* (New York: Thomas Y. Crowell, 5th ed., 1967); a classic study of American political parties and the party system

————, *The Responsible Electorate* (Cambridge: Harvard University Press, 1966) a study concluding that voters in the mass behave more rationally than often supposed

Seymour Martin Lipset, *The First New Nation* (Garden City: Anchor Books, 1967)*

Gerald Pomper, *Elections in America: Control and Influence in Democratic Politics* (New York: Dodd, Mead, 1968)*

Austin Ranney, *The Doctrine of Responsible Party Government* (Urbana: Illini Books, 1962)*

E. E. Schattschneider, *The Semi-Sovereign People: A Realist's View of Democracy in America* (New York: Holt, Rinehart, and Winston, 1960)*; a classic

Frank Sorauf, *Party Politics in America* (Boston: Little, Brown, 1968)

* Available in paperback

DEMOCRACY IN AMERICA

The Semi-Participatory Society

The problem is not how 180 million Aristotles can run a democracy but how we can organize a political community of 180 million ordinary people so that it remains sensitive to their needs.

E. E. Schattschneider

Definition

The definition and measurement of democracy is one of the most difficult problems in American politics. In the official documents of the nation's founding, the word "democracy" does not appear; the United States is called a *republic*, a public thing, by implication a society governed by and in the public interest if not by the public itself. The dominant voices of American politics in the two centuries since the Revolution have used the language of democracy, although many have been skeptical about the ability of the people to rule wisely. The dream that brought many immigrants to the new land was a democratic vision. What were they pursuing? Was it illusionary?

Literally, democracy, in its Greek roots, means "rule by the people." We obviously cannot measure ourselves by the political conditions of the Greek city-states; can we define the original terms more clearly, in a way that will allow us to examine our own society and compare it with others that claim to be democratic?

Participation

The first question that can be raised is, simply, Who are the "people"? In every society some members will be excluded from the political side the polity, if only those who are not yet able to talk! What other exclusions are made, and how many people do they affect? The significance of this question can be recognized by examining the situation in the prototype of democracy, the Greek states. Here there were many inhabitants of the society who were not members of the polity; slaves and noncitizens often outnumbered the citizens, and women too were excluded. Many present day societies have only recently abolished their barriers to female participation.

Other nations that are self-proclaimed democracies or republics in their constitutions are undone by statistics. In the Republic of South Africa, for instance, whose constitution on its face incorporates many democratic elements, only some 15 percent of the adult population is ever admitted to the polity, and the methods adopted for enforcing that 85 percent exclusion bring South Africa at least to the verge of dictatorship. One dimension of democracy, then, may be formulated as the proportion of the society that is qualified as the polity.

RESTRICTIONS ON PARTICIPATION: FORMAL.   What restrictions are there on participation in the United States? The simplest way to answer this question is to examine the legal and constitutional restrictions on the franchise, the right to vote. Without the vote, a person is not entirely excluded from political participation, but many political rights such as running for office depend upon the vote. The two centuries of independence have seen the abolition of many restrictions and the addition of others; the balance is on the side of democracy.

The Constitution in Article I gives primary responsibility for voting rights to the states; the federal franchise is largely dependent upon the right to vote in a particular state, with certain recent exceptions. In the early nineteenth century, the state property qualifications began to fall. Eventually the only remnant left for general elections was the requirement in the southern states that a tax be paid upon registration, which effectively disenfranchised the poor white and, more pertinently, most of the black population. It took national action to eliminate this, in the form of the Twenty-fourth Amendment in 1964, which banned the tax as an impediment to voting in federal elections; two years later the Supreme Court extended the ban to state elections. The only elections today in which a property requirement may be imposed are those special elections in some states for changes in the property tax millage or for water districts and the like. The Supreme Court has ruled on several occasions, including a deci-

QUALIFICATIONS	ABOLITION
Property	By state action, and the Twenty-fourth Amendment
Race	By state action, and the Fifteenth Amendment
Sex	By state action, and the Nineteenth Amendment
Age	Lowered by state action, and by the Twenty-sixth Amendment
Residence in Washington	By the Twenty-third Amendment, for the office of President only
Literacy	For national offices by the 1970 Voting Rights Act; suspended in some states by the 1965 Voting Rights Act
Citizenship	————
Length of residence	Limited by the 1970 Voting Rights Act for national offices
Presence at the polls on election day	Provision in some elections for absentee ballots with advance notice
Good character and mental capacity requirements	Suspended in some states by the 1965 Voting Rights Act
Registration	New requirement in most states

sion in the 1972–73 term, that such elections are not unconstitutional, even if they impose weighted voting on the basis of property size. This might be paraphrased as "no representation without taxation."

The extension of the franchise to the black population (originally, of course, only to black men) took a Civil War, followed by the Fifteenth Amendment in 1870. Subsequent to the amendment, the states adopted other legal means of disenfranchising the Negro; the poll tax was one, and literacy tests were another. Eventually, in 1965, the literacy test was forbidden to those states and counties that had less than half of the adult population registered; this did not outlaw the literacy test elsewhere, and it may be permitted again where it is now suspended if the Justice Department agrees. In federal elections, however, literacy was abolished as a requirement by the 1970 Voting Rights Act.

Women, whether black or white, did not receive the right to vote on a national scale until 1920 and the Nineteenth Amendment; a few states, such as Wyoming, had already extended them the franchise. Four years later the one remaining ethnic exclusion began to be lifted when Indians were given a statutory right to vote in 1924. This was part of the long delayed process of bestowing citizenship on the Indians; by 1948 most Indians had been included, although Indians living on federal reservations were often not admitted to state politics.

The next major changes in voting rights occurred in the 1960's. In 1961 the Twenty-third Amendment to the Constitution granted the residents of Washington, D.C., the right to select electors for the presidential election. The federally controlled city government and the absence of any voting District representatives in Congress were not altered, leaving District residents with barely a toehold on the franchise (finally, in 1974, Congress did provide home rule for the District). The poll tax amendment and civil rights changes noted above followed; in 1970 Congress passed a voting rights bill that attempted to alter by statute the age, literacy, and residence requirements set by the states. The Supreme Court ruled that the new act applied only for federal elections and left the states with the option of running two sets of polls. The states chose instead to ratify the Twenty-sixth Amendment, lowering the voting age for all elections to eighteen. Few states other than those already controlled by the 1965 law imposed any literacy tests. Most states did have residence requirements exceeding thirty days, the limit established for eligibility for federal elections. The federal courts have since struck down some of the longer requirements, and the apparent upper limit will be in the vicinity of sixty days.

A number of restrictions still exist. Temporary absence from home may prevent someone otherwise qualified from voting unless he is able to comply with the often complicated absentee ballot provisions, including the necessity of knowing weeks in advance of the absence. Some elections, such as primaries, may have no absentee provisions. Problems such as being held in jail while awaiting trial (but not yet convicted) do not qualify as permissible circumstances of absence. Those who are insane (not necessarily all residents of mental hospitals) or mentally incapable ("idiots" in most state constitutions), convicted felons, and those resident in prisons are not eligible to vote. A certain length of time after attaining citizenship may be required before one is eligible to vote: citizenship itself is imposed in the federal and state constitutions as a requirement. A host of other qualifications based on the idea of "good character" may be imposed, although many states are forbidden by the 1965 Voting Rights Act from using these qualifications unless they are granted approval. Disqualification on "character" grounds may be a result of fighting a duel or otherwise participating in the duel, having a dishonorable discharge, pauperism, improper lobbying, living in a common law marriage, and so forth. Other disqualifications, such as marriage of a Caucasian to an Oriental, are still on the books in some states but are presumed unconstitutional.

Finally, there is the requirement of registration, which began to develop after the Civil War and came into vogue in the early twentieth century as a means of fighting some of the corruption in the cities controlled by political machines. Prior to the use of registration, most voters were simply handed ballots by poll workers who knew them personally, but the growth in size of the population made this personal identification impossible, and electoral fraud mushroomed. Other states not burdened with urban growth found that the registration procedures, coupled with literacy and good character tests, were a useful device for limiting the numbers and nature of eligible voters to those approved by the incumbents. Not all states found it necessary to adopt registration; eight states today have no requirements, leaving it up to local jurisdictions.

In numerical terms, the combination of age limits and required registration today constitutes the greatest barrier to voting. In 1972 it was estimated that there were 139 million persons eligible to vote, of a population of 207 million. Perhaps 5 percent of the 139 million were rendered ineligible by the various temporary or permanent qualifications imposed by the states. Within the eligible population, 25–30 percent had not registered and so on election day were unable to participate in that round of democracy.

The question we now raise is deceptively simple: Which of these requirements may be considered not to detract from democracy? In other words, which are justifiable demonstrations of "competence to participate"? Which are wounds in a democratic body politic? Each requirement has its supporters and opponents. Nearly all societies, at least informally, have some minimum age level requirement. In contemporary American society, many of those excluded from voting turn to supporting their political beliefs in other ways, and in addition demand a greater share of participation in the government of the schools. A second common requirement, sanity, seems justifiable in principle. Yet a scrutiny of the standards used in most states for commitment raises some question about this requirement as well, which greater care to safeguard the rights of those whose sanity is questioned could help reduce. Many of the other existing requirements work as barriers primarily for the less advantaged in American society, and in addition they have the ugly character of permanent disenfranchisement for a single mistake, such as a bad conduct discharge or a felony, making a mockery of any rhetoric of rehabilitation. It is of interest here to note that the California Supreme Court has just become the first court to rule that denial of the franchise after the term of the sentence or after release from parole is unconstitutional.

Finally, the American system in comparison to other Western systems, does not do much to encourage participation. Few states offer any registration by mail or set up registration booths in easily accessible places. Many states purge a voter from the rolls if he does not vote in a certain period of time. This tends to eliminate those who vote primarily in federal elections but not in state contests, from either noninterest or frequent moving, and tends to work to the disadvantage of the Democrats. No state makes election day a holiday to enable the working population to vote more easily. Registration procedures in most instances are complex and discouraging to people pressed for time or who have little education. (Attempts to enable national registration by mail have been frustrated in the Congress; conservatives and Republicans have tended to view ease of registration as a threat to them, since most of those who might become voters in those circumstances would probably be Democratic and liberal, at least on economic issues.) And finally, the residence requirement itself disenfranchises a large number of people in a highly mobile society; some 20 percent of the population moves every year in America, crossing voting residence lines in most instances; those who move within a month or two of the election will not be eligible.

RESTRICTIONS ON PARTICIPATION: INFORMAL.   In defining "the people," we also have to consider informal barriers to participation. Do all groups in the eligible population participate to the same extent? Is the total turnout satisfactory? The answer, quite simply, must be *no*. The effects of various cultural and political encouragements and discouragements to voting (which are examined below), combined with the discriminatory factors of the legal bars to voting, produce substantially higher turnouts among some segments of the population: the better educated, those who have higher status jobs, men, whites, Republicans, urban dwellers, Northerners, older persons (up to age sixty-five), the employed, and so forth. The total participation is not particularly impressive when contrasted to

Copyright © 1950 by Walt Kelly. Courtesy Publishers-Hall Syndicate.

almost any other Western society. The highest turnout for a recent presidential election is 64 percent in 1960; in 1972 the figure was 54 percent, only partly because of the inclusion of the 18 to 21 year olds. In nonpresidential federal elections, the participation is even less; deprived of the drawing power of the presidential race, federal candidates can generally muster only 42–45 percent of the voters. In state and local elections the percentage may slip into the twenties, with the rare exceptions of dramatic contests for mayor such as the 1969 election in Detroit, which pitted a black man against a white, with the city almost evenly divided in racial terms. The low local turnouts are a paradox for anyone who believes that the governments closest to the people should be the most responsive and the most representative; subject to control by so few voters, such governments are instead more likely to slip into corruption and manipulation by the privileged few while the national candidates engage the attention of the majority.

The low turnout, coupled with the low level of support for democratic principles commonly discovered in survey research (see page 178), is symptomatic of another paradox. The rhetoric of politics in the United States is strongly supportive of participation; the system is often spoken of as deriving its legitimacy from the mandate offered up by the electoral process. Yet a sizeable group of Americans never participate in elections at all, and an even larger group, possibly a majority, participate only in the presidential election. In surveys, those who do not vote indicate a very low level of knowledge about the system and a high degree of alienation from it, expressed in a sense that the system is not responsive to them, does not act in their interest, and does not offer any choices in candidates or policies that are relevant to them. Most of those not voting are at the bottom of the socioeconomic standings; they have low-paying jobs or none at all, little education, and low status in general. Moreover, most are not participants in the system through membership in interest groups of any kind. This is not a surprising set of findings; yet the implications for the system, even if expected, are serious. What are the effects over the long run of such a huge group remaining outside the political system? Might they someday constitute support for a home grown fascist or, acting on their own, bring the prevailing "middle class order" into sudden chaos? In the short run, incorporating such citizens into the system as voters may have "negative" effects on social policy; elections on the local level with a very high turnout offer some evidence that many of the alienated will vote against social programs, such as school funds, that they themselves need the most. Is the political system or the social system as a whole capable of educating the abstainers to believe in and act upon democracy? These are hard questions, but they need to be answered.

FORMS OF PARTICIPATION.   There are a number of ways of participating in the political system in the United States, most of which flow from the vote and are built around the election of officers in the government. Some are based on the expression of individual and group opinion, influencing policy-makers; these are primarily in interest group activities, examined in Chapter 7. Electoral participation, based on the parties, is of a more public character and, potentially at least, subject to greater public control and encouragement. The voting and "joining" population is about the same size, roughly three-fifths of the population. Beyond voting and joining, a person may become active in support of his beliefs by encouraging others to vote or join groups; this is roughly one-third of the population, who may be called "opinion leaders." The percentages decline rapidly as one moves on; activism in party, group, or campaign work engages the efforts at most of a tenth of the population, including those who contribute to campaigns. Only about 1 percent of the public will ever run for political office. Significantly, as the percentages dip, the class basis of the groups becomes clearer. Very few persons of low socioeconomic status ever work in campaigns, contribute to a candidate or party, or run for office; even fewer are elected. The leadership as a whole, although it is more representative today than in the past, still consists heavily of middle and upper class white men. Blacks have less than 1 percent of the elected offices; women are represented in approximately the same number (though they are more than half of the population); other groups are likewise inadequately represented or even unrepresented. Thus in the vertical, or leadership, dimension of democracy, the United States does not measure as well as it does on the horizontal, or franchise, dimension.

A second aspect of participation in the United States is the strong orientation to the selection of others to lead. Forms of participation in which the citizen himself is actually involved in governing are quite limited. Most are found at the local level, which is a natural result of size and the location of responsibilities for various activities, such as schools. These local governing bodies, however, are frequently subject to the same problems of corruption and unrepresentativeness as the larger local governments. The demands for decentralization of school boards, the proliferation of block clubs, and other proposals intending to promote greater participation for each person in the government of the basic aspects of his and his children's lives, nevertheless indicate the powerful, if unconscious, attraction that the idea of participation has for many people. Even though there is often an undercurrent of reactionary motivation, such as using local government as a means of censorship or discrimination, the demand for community control is more than that. It would have come as no surprise to Thomas Jefferson; early in the nineteenth century Jefferson predicted that one urgent need for the success of the American experiment was to find some means for the ordinary citizen to *be* his government as well as simply having greater freedom in selecting others to govern. Jefferson advocated a system of wards, which would be linked to the upper levels of government, partially selecting them; the wards themselves would be the basic units of government. Nothing came of his idea. Moreover, as the cities increased in size, the boroughs and neighborhoods ceased to have any real political meaning; the cities were often stripped of the powers they needed to govern themselves, becoming fiefs of the state legislatures and governors. As the second century of the experiment nears its end, the local governments, city, township, county, and the special districts such as schools, are badly in need of reform. The local level is the natural level for individual participation in government; if Jefferson's hope is ever to be realized, it must be here.

A third characteristic of participation in the political system is the difficulty of determining how much, if any, impact the electoral process has on policy-making. Even when groups focus on particular issues, as some interest groups do, it is difficult to trace their influence on that issue through the policy maze. The electoral system as a whole is diffuse in its relation to issues. The policy stands of the parties, as noted in Chapter 8, are generally vague; in addition, in the loose structure of American party politics, the candidates may not support the party stand at all. The voter must therefore turn to the campaigns for his information on the policy stands of the candidates. We have seen that the American campaign is poorly suited for this purpose; often it is consciously planned to disguise the policy beliefs of the candidate, to blur them around the edges. Even if the voter is able to discern clearly and accurately the candidate's position, perhaps armed with his past voting record, it is unlikely that he will find a nominee who supports all of his own views; more often, each candidate will take some stands congenial to the particular voter and others that are displeasing. The voter must then determine which candidate offers the most favorable combination of views. Possibly there will be one with a close approximation. At other times one issue may be so important that a voter will be driven away from his otherwise preferred candidate because of that one stand. In 1964 for example a number of voters who favored most of Goldwater's positions deserted him for fear that he would destroy the social security system or start World War III. In 1972, their flight was paralleled by Democrats, frightened by McGovern's stand on a guaranteed income or on guaranteed income taxes for the wealthy.

The result is that it is very difficult to interpret election results, which often are votes cast for personalities, in terms of support for policies and ideas. What were the voters in 1968 saying in New Hampshire when they gave their approval to McCarthy? Curiously, many of them seem to have been voting for McCarthy to express their disapproval of Johnson for *not* giving the military its way in Vietnam. What were the voters saying in 1972 when they gave the President a substantial re-election margin, and at the same time increased the number of his opponents in the Congress? Which issues led to success for the two sides? All too often votes are cast to express dissatisfaction with the incumbent's performance, regardless of the challenger's views; or from misunderstanding of one candidate's platform; or for reasons of party loyalty, partly but not entirely related to issues; or for considerations of personality or ethnic origin or good looks or family background of the candidate; or for any one of dozens of non-ideological, nonissue-oriented reasons. The voter who is concerned with issues, and who finds himself voting for men who take one stand and then do the opposite (or for men who take no stands) or who cannot find candidates supporting his views at all, is likely to become disaffected.

In some states there are opportunities to express opinions, at least on some matters, through the electoral devices of the initiative and the referendum. In the former, the public can petition to place on the ballot a proposed law or sometimes an amendment to the state's constitution, and the public is then able to vote on that specific issue; in the latter, an enacted law is subject to approval by the electorate, again voting specifically for that issue, if a petition campaign succeeds in forcing it onto the ballot. Even though poorly written proposals sometimes blur the effectiveness of these two issue votes, they do offer the public some chance to express opinions of major issues. Nationally there is no such channel for opinions; even the ratification of constitutional amendments is filtered through the state legislatures (or, rarely, through state conventions) rather than set before the public.

The Levels of Democracy in Society

Another set of measures of democracy may be developed by looking at the different levels of political life in the United States, examining what support for democracy exists in the political culture. What do persons in the society think and believe about politics? How are the mechanics of the system arranged? What kind of distribution of resources does it produce?

THE INDIVIDUAL: POLITICAL CULTURE, POLITICAL SOCIALIZATION.   In the past two decades political scientists and sociologists have undertaken a good deal of research to try to depict the political beliefs, feelings, and values of the various groups that make up political culture. The discoveries so far are not encouraging for the proponents of democracy. Abstract statements of political freedom win support from most of the public. However, when principles are translated into concrete problems, such as freedom of speech in the local community for atheists, employment of homosexuals in the schools, rights of persons accused of crime, rights of minority group members to live in the next house, support for these ideals plummets. People in positions of political leadership in general take much more tolerant views on concrete problems than the average respondent does. Even so, a substantial minority, in some cases close to a majority, even of the leadership, take the intolerant outlook. The majority of the "masses" reject the tolerant position. This has been translated by one analyst as "working class authoritarianism." The citizen often will take liberal stands on economic matters such as support of trade unions, but on "non-economic" issues such as freedom of speech he assumes a rigid posture against those he regards as holding views opposing his own, especially if they are in a position to influence his children. The leadership is able to escape this authoritarianism to some extent because it has benefited from greater education and may have a somewhat happier personal situation; greater income, greater leisure, greater personal satisfaction with one's work often translates into a less jaundiced view of the world.

A second factor in American political culture is the strong alienation from the political system expressed by the majority of the public. The common view of politics is that it is a "dirty" business, and mothers do not dream of their children growing up to be politicians, although they would not mind if Johnny became President someday. The common referent for the government is "it" or "them"; few people speak of the government as something that belongs to them, and even fewer conceive of the government as an activity of which they are truly a part. The outcome is a substantial sense of isolation and helplessness. On occasion this can flare into rage, and acts of individual destruction or group violence, such

Copyright © 1957, 1961, 1962 by Walt Kelly. Courtesy Publishers-Hall Syndicate.

as a riot, may result. In this sense a riot is a political act; the participants are generally responding to some felt need. There may be some manipulation of this latent political fury, but riots generally do not require an agitator; and even with an agitator on the scene, anger cannot be sown where the seeds do not exist.

The attitudes and values about the political system that form the political culture and subcultures of the United States are passed on to the rising generations through a process known as *political socialization;*

the society perpetuates itself and its political ideas through the gradual learning of those ideas by the young. The key areas of influence in this process are the family, the schools, and the experience of early adulthood; peer groups also play some role.

From a very early age, the political attitudes of children are shaped by their parents and by older children. The patterns of authority that are established in a family, the attitudes that the parents express to outward authority, the opinions expressed directly, and, more significantly, the general pattern of the parents' beliefs all form the background for the child's growing perceptions of society and his attempts to relate himself to it. The economic and social standing of the family also contribute to the environment influencing the child's developing political attitudes. By the time a child enters school, he has already acquired some knowledge of what the political system is all about and what the "correct" attitude toward politics is. His contacts with other children and their parents have also begun to influence his views.

From the point of entry into the school system, political socialization is then shaped considerably by the education the child receives. Here a major distinction generally occurs, with serious implications for future political attitudes. Those who go through grade school and high school only, particularly in a vocational track, receive a different kind of education and socialization from those who are expected to go on to college, and the difference is generally reinforced by home and peer group experiences. For the group as a whole, public schools rarely offer any serious discussion of political and economic realities. History courses rarely mention the blemishes on the American past or the seriousness of its social problems today, rooted in past actions. How many high school students discover such things as the political role of the police in the development of American cities, the dark history of the American policies toward Indians, the internment of Japanese-Americans in World War II, or the anti-labor Red Scare after the First World War, which culminated in the trial of Sacco and Vanzetti and the deportation of thousands of aliens? The information conveyed by the teacher and the impact of the relationship between teacher and student that often condemns open intellectual inquiry and stresses deference for authority keeps open the gaps in information in the texts. Some school districts or schools or classrooms may escape from rote. In most, the end result is at best loyalty to symbols: the flag, the salute, the national anthem. Later, if these symbols are challenged, as some in the peace movement unwisely did with the flag and some black athletes have done with the anthem, the response may be frighteningly violent and seemingly out of proportion to the provocation. It is true that there is an emphasis on the value of participation as the political right of each citizen and on his civic duty to exercise his right by voting. In lower class and minority areas this belief in the value of participation is not much taught, or absorbed, however; only those students whose personal experiences outside of these schools draw them to the system, such as membership in a labor union, are likely to become participants.

A third period of socialization is the post high school years, during which over half of the population leaves the school system, many never to return, and the rest go on to college. The size of this second group today is well over a third of the total age group and should approach 50 percent by the end of the decade. Many of the college-bound young receive a more open discussion of American politics in high school, in college preparatory programs, or simply attend better high schools, and many were encouraged by peers or family in the development of a more tolerant and questioning attitude. The college experience can help to reinforce this, and it can also help students break with the prejudices of their parents. Although college level education in the past has been associated with more conservative attitudes on economic matters, partly as a result of the higher incomes commanded by college graduates, this conservatism is not the same kind of conservatism identified as "working class authoritarianism." The life experiences of the group that does not go to college, both men and women, have produced in the past, and continue to produce, a split *within* generations that is as great as any *between* the generations.

The rapid spread of college education, and the development of ferment in the labor force over the nature of work, plus the slow revolt among housewives unleashed by the women's movement, make this an exciting and unpredictable time. For the first time in history more than half the population soon will be able to go to college. Will this produce a more democratic public? Or will the sudden explosion of the college-bound group, met on an *ad hoc* basis by the development of massive institutions, overcrowded classes, reduction of entrance requirements without much provision of help for poorly trained high school students, simply result in the reduction of the college experience to an additional four years of high school for higher pay on the job? Certain kinds of college training in the past have shown little evidence of promoting open or tolerant views of the world; college *per se* is not enough. On the other hand, the return to school and the interest in taking courses that do not simply fill requirements for higher income jobs is encouraging. If a higher education becomes as widespread and as much a part of life as public libraries have been, without the obsession with grades and the economic consequences, then a true revolution may well occur in American politics.

THE POLITY: THE MECHANICS OF MAJORITY RULE AND PLURAL SOCIETY.   A second problem for examination is the extent to which the people, in terms of the majority, are actually admitted to power, and the implications of this in terms of minority rights in a diverse society.

Simply viewed, democracy must mean at least the consent of the majority of "the people" to their government. In some respects this is too broad; nearly all societies must be so defined, since few governments if any are powerful enough to sustain themselves over the active opposition of the majority of the public. A more demanding definition, then, requires that some form of popular consultation be part of the system, with some alternative to the present incumbents or policies as a choice. This is generally accomplished through elections, with some competitive element. The observer looking for democracy in the system may then ask: To what extent does the majority view as ascertained in elections hold sway? To what extent are the mechanics of government based upon majority rule?

In the American system, the answer is complex. The Framers of the Constitution feared executive tyranny, and so they made the legislature more powerful, as they saw it. They also feared legislative power, and so they developed a system of checks within the legislature that grew over the years into a powerful force restricting majority opinion. More than anything they feared the tyranny of the majority; as De Tocqueville later pointed out, the majority tyranny is the most frightening because it is so difficult to overthrow and so suffocating to the minorities. Thus the entire government was constructed to make clear majority rule difficult.

The legislature was split into two houses, partly modeled upon the two houses in colonial rule, the royal council and the colonists' assembly. In the Senate the states were accorded equal representation, regardless of size or population, and so the votes of a majority of senators may represent only a minority of the population. This can prevent action desired by a majority from being undertaken and even lead to passage of minority sponsored legislation, although the House of Representatives, apportioned by population, can counter such measures. If the House is composed of men whose primary constituents are local elites and interests, it may fail to exercise this check; and even the House is not completely representative since every state has at least one member, no matter how small it is. Otherwise, the Supreme Court ruled in the 1960s that districts may not vary significantly in population within a state.

The office of President, under the Electoral College system, also may not represent the votes of a majority. Fifteen presidents have been elected with less than a majority, twelve on occasions when more than two candidates were running and the winner had only a plurality; three when the Electoral College vote actually gave the nod to the loser in the popular vote: Jackson in 1824, Hayes in 1876, and Harrison in 1888.

In turn, the President (with Senate confirmation) chooses the federal judiciary. Once on the bench, the judiciary by tradition is not to respond to public sentiment; if a majority feels that segregation is a good thing, that is not binding on the judiciary. The public has no means of removing a federal judge short of the rare and difficult impeachment process.

State governments may be clearly based on majority rule. The Supreme Court ruled in the sixties that both houses of a state assembly must be apportioned by population rather than by counties or other political divisions. Even though recent decisions have allowed some deviation from numerical equality in districts for one house, to take into account dividing lines, the ties to majority rule are still tight. State executives are elected directly by majority vote rather than filtered through an electoral college device. In addition states frequently have popularly elected judges, subject to removal by the electorate. Many of the same checks that dilute majority rule at the federal level operate also in the states, however, particularly in the division of power between two houses. (Only Nebraska has a single assembly, a unicameral legislature.)

Regardless of the degree of majority influence, in a society composed of many different subpopulations the problem of minority rights arises. A plural society is one composed of at least two self-consciously different groups; race, religion, nationality, language, region, even life-style can divide a nation. Few plural societies have been democratic; most are seized by either the single dominant group or a coalition of groups, or by one tiny minority that has a monopoly on the means of force. Both China and Russia are plural societies dominated by one or two large groups; South Africa's plural society is controlled by the white minority, and even within the white minority one group, the Afrikaans-speaker of Dutch heritage has come to dominate those of British background. Switzerland and Canada are two of the small group of plural democracies.

The United States is particularly burdened with the problem of minority rights, since it is subject to so many kinds of division; within the nation is a vast array of groups. The problem of preventing one coalition from dominating the rest is critical. The Framers of the Constitution and the sponsors of the Bill of Rights placed many checks on majority rule in order to protect minority rights. Preventing the more privileged minorities from using these restrictions on majority rule to aggrandize their own position is another problem. As the ideal of the melting pot has disappeared in the last decade while many groups reassert their differences, the difficult job of reconciling majority rule and minority rights has become ever more necessary and more difficult.

The question of majority rule is a procedural issue; provisions for majority rule and the restrictions on majority rule in themselves guarantee nothing in terms of the substance, or the kind and quality of policies made in that political system. Policy results from an interaction of the mechanics of the system with the political culture of the society and the resources available to that society. The final question for democracy is the extent to which the outcome of political action helps to reduce or to magnify the differences in resources available to various groups and individuals.

POLICY OUTCOMES: THE DISTRIBUTION OF RESOURCES AND DEMOCRACY.   The question of distribution of resources may be approached as a political question in two ways. The first perspective is the problem of poverty in the most basic sense, the absence of sufficient food, clothing, and shelter for even the most minimal participation in the society. There can be little argument that such poverty exists in the United States. Senate committees and executive researchers have uncovered evidence that millions of people, a large number of them children, suffer from serious malnutrition because of their poverty. For an adult, this can result in a state of anemia, depriving him of even the physical energy to participate. A child who suffers from a lack of basic nutrients in his early years may be mentally and physically retarded for the rest of his life, with adverse effects on his social and political role in comparison with those who had adequate nutrition. There has been some reduction in the most severe malnutrition in the United States, but it continues to be a major problem; as long as it does the quality of democracy, particularly in the world's most affluent nation, will be damaged.

Beyond this basic problem, a further issue of distribution exists. The

distribution of both income and ownership of resources is heavily concentrated in the upper levels of society. The top 5 percent of the population gets over 20 percent of the income, while the bottom 20 percent
gets 5 percent; the share of the top 5 percent is equal to that of the bottom
40 percent of the population. Ownership of resources is even more concentrated, most of it falling within the top tenth of the nation. This distribution has not altered much over time, and in some analyses it appears
to be growing less rather than more equitable.

Government action in the form of taxes has little if any impact; the
combined tax bite of all taxes in the United States is about 30 percent of
income, regardless of the size of that income. Many of the very wealthy,
the upper 10 percent, are able to reduce this by taking advantage of ex-
emptions or simply by failing to report all income. Wage earners have
few such opportunities; their income is subject to taxation before they
receive it, and most "loopholes" are of no value to those with small incomes. The poor also pay taxes, and they are subject to sales taxes that
often take a greater proportion of their incomes than of those of the rich;
property taxes also are independent of income. Social security payroll
taxes are another notorious example of a levy that affects those with low
earnings considerably more than others.

By contrast, the structure of government benefits tends to favor the
advantaged. Benefits available to the disadvantaged, such as Social Security
and welfare, and the provision of services, such as public schools, are
greatly outweighed by the vast array of subsidies provided to various
activities, and the greater quality of schools, fire protection, roads, police,
and so forth provided by wealthier communities to their residents. (Some
of these discrepancies have been attacked in the courts; although it ruled
a few years ago that discrimination in some services such as roads was not
permissible, the Supreme Court has recently ruled that discrepancies in
public schools based on property taxes do not violate the Constitution.)
One example of the structure of subsidies favoring the "haves" is the
complex of farm benefits. The bottom 40 percent of farmers, by income,
have an average income of $800 and receive a total of $300 in subsidy. The
wealthiest 7 percent have an average income of $13,400 supplemented by
federal benefits of $14,000, putting this group of farmers into the top 5
percent of all families by their income!

The distribution of income affects to a marked degree the participation
of the citizen in the polity, his attitude toward politics, and his support
for democracy in particular. As long as the distribution of resources in

America remains so badly skewed, participation is likely to be limited in numbers and in quality, keeping the roots of democracy shallow. To the extent that the government could re-order its programs and taxes and does not, to that extent its policies are not supportive of democracy. Whether or not the advantages that are claimed for these policies (rewarding initiative, building self-reliance, and the like) are justifications for their retention is a question that each observer must answer for himself. How valuable is wider participation in the system?

Suggested Readings

Walter Adams and Horace Gray, *Monopoly in America* (New York: Macmillan, 1955)

Taylor Branch, "The Screwing of the Average Man: Government Subsidies: Who Gets the $63 Billion?" *Washington Monthly*, 4:2 (March, 1972)

Robert Dahl, *Preface to Democratic Theory* (Chicago: University of Chicago Press, 1956)*

Roland Delorme and Raymond McInnis, eds., *Antidemocratic Trends in Twentieth Century America* (Reading, Mass: Addison-Wesley, 1969)*

Murray Edelman, *The Symbolic Uses of Politics* (Chicago: University of Illinois Press, 1967)*; a classic treatment of political symbolism

Robert Hess and Judith Torney, *Development of Political Attitudes in Children* (Garden City: Doubleday, 1968)

Gabriel Kolko, *Wealth and Power in America* (New York: Praeger, 1962)

Ralph M. Kramer, *Participation of the Poor* (Englewood Cliffs, N.J.: Prentice-Hall, 1969)

Seymour Martin Lipset, *Political Man* (Garden City: Anchor Books, 1963)*

Michael Novak, *The Rise of the Unmeltable Ethnics* (New York: Macmillan, 1972)

Gerald Pomper, *Elections in America: Control and Influence in Democratic Politics* (New York: Dodd, Mead, 1968)

E. E. Schattschneider, *The Semi-Sovereign People* (New York: Holt, Rinehart, and Winston, 1960)*

Philip Stern, *The Rape of the Taxpayer* (New York: Random House, 1973)

* Available in paperback

10 CONCLUSION

Democracy is a theory that the common people know what they want, and deserve to get it good and hard.

H. L. Mencken

It is clear from the foregoing chapters that the American political system displays real stréngths, but that it also contains definite problem areas. Some of these may be dealt with by tinkering with the structures and mechanisms of government, but others might require fundamental revisions of the thought and reactions of the people themselves; still others may be beyond the capability of a political system to eliminate. In an imperfect world it is helpful to work for improvement, but it is futile to expect perfection. Without attempting to judge which weaknesses of the system may be inevitable, we can identify some of the inadequacies that appear to present the greatest difficulties. They seem to stem from three interrelated causes; apathy, ignorance, and a gross imbalance in the distribution of power.

Maldistribution of power is apparent whether the subject under consideration is private power versus the public interest, the power of the affluent versus the poor, the power of mainstream groups versus minorities (especially racial and ethnic minorities), or even the distribution of power within the government itself. Implicit in the nature of constitutional democracy is that the majority shall hold the bulk of the power but that majority power shall not extend to invasion of certain minority rights; in practice, there often are powerful minorities of elites who are able to restrict some of the rights of the majority, often in an unrecognized manner. In a form of government organized basically upon democratic principles, the majority permits this only because of lack of concern or lack of knowledge. The government often displays inadequate responsiveness to the people, but it would be of little help if the government were to respond to public pressure that is unenlightened. The problem is one of education.

The federal system is built upon a tenuous balance between national and state power. It is important to recognize that either level of government can be a progressive force and that either can be regressive; neither an all-powerful national government that swallows the states nor a retreat to the reactionary and discredited theories of "states' rights" provides any answer to the questions -posed by modern conditions. It is doubtful whether any form of organization can insure a specific result. Those who develop solutions probably will have to investigate methods of political education as well as revisions of structures. They probably also will have to be unconcerned with political labels, because the most promising solutions are likely to be those that will involve considerable innovation, and those who advocate innovation often are the targets for name-calling. Arrogance in high places is destructive, regardless of the form of government, just as national arrogance is destructive on an international basis. It will require something innovative to revise the attitudes that are responsible for both kinds of arrogance.

There is much that can be said about each of the three branches of government. It is painfully obvious that Congress must become more efficient and more courageous. Either would be small improvement without the other. In order to begin to redress the present imbalance of power between the legislative and executive branches, Congress must become more assertive on important matters. In order to accomplish this, it must first equip itself in terms of staff and research resources to place itself more nearly on an equal basis with the executive. All of the government must become more responsive to the people if the system is to retain its democratic basis, and this is especially true of Congress. It is not enough to be responsive, however; Congress also must pay careful attention to its function of assisting in the political education of the nation. A pandering to prejudice does not constitute effective political response. When the Presidential Commission on Pornography issued its report in 1970 and declared that it could find no evidence that pornographic literature is harmful, the President immediately condemned the report, saying that he knew such things to be harmful regardless of the experts' findings; the

U.S. Senate, on the other hand, had no official relation to the report whatever, since it was produced by a presidential commission. Nevertheless, the Senate voted overwhelmingly to "reject" the report and its findings, even though no one had asked the Senate to "receive" it. This was an inexpensive way to build support with the voters, but it is doubtful whether most of the senators cared particularly about the issue and still more doubtful whether most of them had bothered to read or even to look at the report. This well-publicized action appears to be an instance of using responsiveness to public opinion as a means of evading the responsibility to help educate the public. This is not to cast judgment upon the merits of the report but to point out that neither the Senate nor the public was well informed. The Senate gave publicity to its actions, not to an examination of the issues involved. Other things it prefers to do quietly, such as maintaining tax loopholes for the benefit of special interests.

An even greater tendency to restrict the ebb and flow of information is evident in the executive branch. According to some who have been close to presidents, the Presidency provides much more leisure than the popular myth would indicate, and it is less of a "killing" job. Therefore, even that slim basis for the dangerous and increasing isolation of the President from all public contact and review is specious. It is not the Congress alone but also the President and his executive branch that need to provide more information to the public and to be more responsive to the popular will.

In the judiciary, the dangers are the slowness of the system, the possible impact of political considerations at the expense of justice, and, here also, the tremendous advantage that accrues to those of wealth. The greatest dangers of all are probably those least recognized by the public: the fragility of the courts themselves, of the judicial system, and of constitutional guarantees. A courageous judge and a much-publicized court case in which justice triumphs over great odds are likely to receive the publicity; the many instances of injustice, large and small, many of them occurring routinely, day in and day out, rarely do. And when they do, who cares?

The corruptive nature of campaign financing, the power of wealth throughout the system, and the relative powerlessness of the individual citizen are some of the most obvious factors in need of change. One of the answers may be through party reform. The parties, above all other institutions, should be responsive to the people. Both parties have made efforts at reform, but more are necessary. The Republicans have tended to be somewhat more democratic in their internal proceedings than have the

Democrats, but in the 1972 campaign, the Democrats made a major break-through in attempting to reach the grass roots and gain the participation of the "man in the street." The results demonstrated that party reform alone is insufficient. The Democrats held open meetings throughout the country as the first step in delegate selection to the Democratic National Convention; in some wards, because of corrupt party officials, lack of interest, or some other reason there were no attempts to hold meetings (although delegates later appeared from some of the meetings that were not held!). In other wards, the officials were there, but no one else came. Probably the typical ward was one in which a few dozen citizens appeared but in which there were possibly a hundred times that many Democratic voters. This was not caused by lack of publicity; the meetings were an-nounced publicly and well in advance. The lack of interest in public affairs that this illustrates is one of the strongest indicators that all is not well with the American political system and that its future may not be bright.

It is one of the basic contentions of this book that, despite the con-trary opinions of some writers, political apathy is one of the greatest dangers facing American constitutional democracy, immediately following the foremost danger, political ignorance. Citizens in a popular govern-ment must maintain a sense of vigilance and of responsibility for the political actions of their nation if they are to prevent the erosion of liber-ties and halt the decay of popular institutions. Moreover, citizens must retain a desire for freedom and a confidence in their ability to govern themselves. Otherwise, the burdens of freedom will appear too difficult for them to bear. More than thirty years ago, Erich Fromm wrote, in *Escape from Freedom*, of the manner in which many persons and nations seek the security and certainty of authoritarianism as an escape from the trials and uncertainties of the free life.*

Apathy is not the only threat to constitutional democracy, but it com-bines with the others to make them even more threatening. Various totalitarian ideologies contend with the ideals of freedom for the affection of the citizens. Some are obvious, some subtle. Frequently the plea of necessity will be sufficient to convince many that they should suffer re-strictions on their personal lives in order to advance national security, or to preserve law and order. Everyone who is convinced that he should refrain from criticism of governmental policies because those in power have access to more information than have the people weakens the cause of constitutional democracy.

* New York: Holt, Rinehart & Winston, 1941.

Also threatening constitutional democracy is our lack of concern with the language. Advertisers constantly tell us that every product is better than every other; politicians, similarly, more often than not speak with a view toward obtaining emotional reactions rather than seeking to enlighten or educate. George Orwell long ago wrote of the decay of language and of the deleterious effects that linguistic decay has on the quality of political life. Today, it often is difficult to tell if politicians wish to speak the truth or not. They tend to speak in formulas, saying the same things and repeating the same patterns over and over. The hearers have come to expect just this, and, far from being outraged, they accept it as normal. The extraordinary politician who speaks out tends often to offend, to enrage, or to confuse. Many office seekers, both "conservative" and "liberal," appear to believe that the quickest path to office is to repeat the same clichés and to shy away from reasoned and critical analysis. Whether they intend it or not, such speakers are engaging in deception, and often are deceived along with their listeners.

Constitutional democracy depends on an enlightened citizenry and a free flow of information to the government, and from and about the government. A major tendency of government is to wish to protect itself from criticism. One of the easiest ways to accomplish this, and one of the ways most destructive to a free society, is to conduct governmental operations in secrecy. Governments that are cut off from criticism tend to become arrogant, and arrogant governments consider themselves justified in treating their citizens as children, rather than as free adults. Thomas Jefferson recognized long ago that a free press was an absolute necessity if free government is to exist.

One danger to constitutional democracy is that the right of the press to criticize as it sees fit, even unfairly, often seems to be a bigger issue than the governmental policies themselves. Many Americans seem to have lost sight of the true function of the news media in a free society. If they perform their functions well, they will inevitably irritate those in power; that is their job, "to comfort the afflicted and afflict the comfortable." All adminstrations, regardless of party, intention, or persuasion, need constant criticism and overseeing by an unrestricted press to encourage the degree of humility proper to the servants of the public. Unfair, even vicious, criticism, is vastly preferable to too little. No newspaper has ever overthrown a government, but many governments have overthrown freedom of the press! Regardless of the reason, when there is a dearth of criticism, whether the lack results from apathy, inadequate searching for information, or official intimidation, it is potentially fatal to free and open government. Such considerations led Jefferson to conclude that if forced to choose, he would prefer a free press with no government to a government with no free press.

Constitutional democracy in the United States has withstood many determined assaults. It is now under much more subtle attack than, for example, the attacks from those professing totalitarian ideologies of both the right and the left during the period of the Great Depression. Neither the Communist party, the John Birch Society, the Minutemen, the Weathermen, the Ku Klux Klan, the American Nazis, nor any other extremist group has ever been the major threat to American democracy. The greatest dangers are less dramatic, but they are stronger than ever. One of the most salient features of modern America is that the citizen's life is affected more and more by decisions made elsewhere and over which he has no control. The pressures of increasing population, the effects of a technologically oriented industrial society, the availability of ever newer and more sophisticated techniques for the invasion of privacy, public apathy, and political ignorance and misinformation all combine to cast doubt upon the future. It is the privilege, right, and obligation of us all to see to it that constitutional democracy survives even these troubles and grows to meet the new challenges, in freedom. It can be done. The price is commitment—commitment to knowledge, and commitment to the use of that knowledge.

A Note on Watergate

The Constitutional Convention produced the basic outlines of the American political system. In a sense, a second convention has been in session ever since, as Americans have worked out the details of the Constitution in experience and struggled to protect and preserve it. From time to time this struggle has assumed the proportions of a national emergency; for this generation, that emergency is "Watergate." After World War II a number of imbalances developed in the American political system as a result of the new American role in world affairs; changes in American society produced additional problems in the political system. Eventually, perhaps inevitably, these imbalances led to actions by government and campaign officials that threatened to upset the Constitution itself. The revelations of the events collectively known as Watergate, and the simultaneous if unrelated investigation of the financial affairs of the Vice President, produced a spirited public debate. Many of the issues discussed in this book made the headlines, and edged out soap operas and prime time detective programs.

The first problem so clearly illustrated by the Watergate scandals is the centrality of money in American political campaigns and the inability of either government or political parties to control the raising and spending of campaign funds. Vast sums of money underlay the activities of the Watergate conspirators. Campaign funds are the root of the Vesco case in which two former Cabinet members stand indicted, and of the resignation in disgrace of a Vice President. The problem is not the amount of money spent. In comparison with the advertising budgets for toothpaste, detergent, and cereals, the amounts spent on election advertising are hardly excessive. The problem is that this money must be raised from private sources by men who are not responsible to the public and who, in practice, are not controlled by the laws.

Second, the Pentagon Papers dimension of the Watergate complex of issues shows the extent to which the argument of national security has come to dominate the public and private consciousness. Indeed, the Watergate burglars themselves had been told that they were protecting national security against the onslaughts of the Democrats. A failure to understand the strengths of America led some government officials to take actions that were in themselves far greater threats to the survival of constitutional democracy in the United States than any real or imagined threats put forward as justification. This calls to mind the comment that the village in Viet Nam had to be destroyed in order to save it.

Third, the Watergate affair illustrates that the greatest threat to the existence of law and public order is government lawlessness. Murder and muggings can be fought, but when the highest law officers in the land stand indicted or self confessed to illegal conduct, including conspiracy to prevent the discovery of crimes, the fight to prevent private lawlessness is damaged, if not lost.

Finally, all of the Watergate events were made possible, if not caused by, the "Imperial Presidency" that has emerged in this century. Belief in the omnipotence and omniscience of the modern presidency led public officials to contemplate and undertake lawless acts, and the developments since World War II have given the President and the executive the necessary powers. Public trust in the presidency made these acts possible, as well as producing a climate in which the attempt to cover up the degree of government complicity succeeded for many months.

The investigation into Watergate itself has brought more problems into focus. The cultural role of the press in American politics shows clearly. Without the determined investigation and reporting of Watergate, notably by the Washington *Post*, there might have been no judicial or congressional inquiry. The importance of an independent judiciary is marked by the contribution of Judge Sirica to the investigation. Moreover, the failure of Congress to act until nearly a year had passed after the break in points out the need for Congress to re-assert itself in the political process. The struggle over the Senate investigation and the powers of the Special Prosecutor indicate the necessity to define more clearly the power of the executive in general, and the President in particular, in relationship to the legislature and the judiciary. What are the limits of executive privilege? Is the President subject to the law under the courts? Does the separation of powers prevent judicial or legislative inquiry into crimes committed by members of the executive branch?

Other cases that have shaken the American nation have served in the end to strengthen it; different leaders have come forth and have won anew the support of the public for the Constitution. It should be remembered that the Watergate affair has again shown the importance of individual actions for good or ill in the American system. It was not *all* judges, but one courageous judge, who asked searching questions; it was not *all* reporters, but two determined reporters in Washington, who kept digging. Neither was it *all* politicians who broke the law, but a small group; there were others who came forward to uphold the law and the Constitution. In point of fact, it was *one* watchful security guard alone who uncovered the burglary that led to all the subsequent disclosures. It is these persons, judges, congressmen, reporters, editors, public officials, and sometimes private citizens, who can preserve and strengthen the American experiment in free government.

APPENDIX A
Notes on Political Science as a Discipline

Approaches to Political Science

Political science is the systematic study of government and politics. It encompasses such concerns as the processes of political continuity and change, the development and nature of the modern state system, the various forms that modern governments can take, and the relationships of individual civil rights and liberties to the state.

Modern political science embraces two distinct approaches. The more traditionally oriented stress governmental structure, institutions, and constitutional frameworks—i.e., the form and organization of the use of power; the other, newer approach has come to be called "behavioralism." Behavioralism represents an attempt to make political science more truly "scientific" in the current sense of the word. It stresses empirical studies, mathematical techniques, and, insofar as possible, the separation of fact from value. Above all, it limits its formal statements to description and prediction rather than prescription. The behavioral approach has influenced the development of systems theories that direct attention to politics as a dynamic and ongoing process. Political philosophy, although separate from both of the above approaches, is not so much a third approach as a complementary subject. It deals with the history of political ideas; with the study of values, doctrines, and goals in politics; and with the analysis, interpretation, and criticism of both political reality and research methods.

For some time there was intense controversy between the adherents of behavioralism and its opponents. Most scholars appear now to accept a variety of approaches as valid. Some of the most prominent behavioralists, in fact, now speak of the "post-behavioral revolution" and seek to arrive at an accommodation that admits the impossibility of a value-free social science. In point of fact, no science is value free.

Effects of Political Science

A second argument in the discipline is aimed at more than methodology and cuts directly to the heart of political science. Essentially, the charge is that the discipline is uncritical and that most political science literature implicitly, if not explicitly, supports and preserves the *status quo*. Certainly those political science studies that analyze American government critically are rare; rarer still are those that criticize the fundamentals of the system itself. In their efforts to establish themselves as true scientists, many political scientists have refused completely to involve themselves in value judgments and have attempted to emulate the natural sciences. By concentrating only upon those questions that lend themselves to scientific study, they have ignored some of the most pressing questions of the day. There is, to be sure, a need for the collection of evidence and the formulation of hypotheses; the discipline should be subject to rigorous standards. But this does not exclude values; indeed, the amassing of facts without reason or philosophy is a sterile exercise. If political scientists make no judgments about the American system, the critics argue, they are depriving political science of the major reason for its existence.

APPENDIX B

The Declaration of Independence*

The Unanimous Declaration of the Thirteen United States of America

When in the Course of human events, it becomes necessary for one people to dissolve the political bands, which have connected them with another, and to assume among the powers of the earth, the separate and equal station to which the Laws of Nature and of Nature's God entitle them, a decent respect to the opinions of mankind requires that they should declare the causes which impel them to the separation.—We hold these truths to be self-evident, that all men are created equal, that they are endowed by their Creator with certain unalienable Rights, that among these are Life, Liberty and the pursuit of Happiness.—That to secure these rights, Governments are instituted among Men, deriving their just powers from the consent of the governed,—That whenever any Form of Government becomes destructive of these ends, it is the Right of the People to alter or to abolish it, and to institute new Government, laying its foundation on such principles and organizing its powers in such form, as to them shall seem most likely to effect their Safety and Happiness. Prudence, indeed, will dictate that Governments long established should not be changed for light and transient causes; and accordingly all experience hath shewn, that mankind are more disposed to suffer, while evils are sufferable, than to right themselves by abolishing the forms to which they are accustomed. But when a long train of abuses and usurpations, pursuing invariably the same Object evinces a design to reduce them under absolute Despotism, it is their right, it is their duty, to throw off such Government, and to provide new Guards for their future security.—Such has been the patient sufferance of these Colonies; and such is now the necessity which constrains them to alter their former Systems of Government. The history of the present King of Great Britain is a history of repeated injuries and usurpations, all having in direct object the establishment of an absolute Tyranny over these States. To prove this, let Facts be submitted to a candid world.—He has refused his Assent to Laws, the most wholesome and necessary for the public good.— He has forbidden his Governors to pass Laws of immediate and pressing importance, unless suspended in their operation till his Assent should be obtained; and when so suspended, he has utterly ne-

* As it reads in the parchment copy

197

glected to attend to them.—He has refused to pass other Laws for the accommodation of large districts of people, unless those people would relinquish the right of Representation in the Legislature, a right inestimable to them and formidable to tyrants only.—He has called together legislative bodies at places unusual, uncomfortable, and distant from the depository of their public Records, for the sole purpose of fatiguing them into compliance with his measures.—He has dissolved Representative Houses repeatedly, for opposing with manly firmness his invasions on the rights of the people.—He has refused for a long time, after such dissolutions, to cause others to be elected; whereby the Legislative powers, incapable of Annihilation, have returned to the People at large for their exercise; the State remaining in the meantime exposed to all the dangers of invasion from without, and convulsions within.— He has endeavoured to prevent the population of these States; for that purpose obstructing the Laws for Naturalization of Foreigners; refusing to pass others to encourage their migrations hither, and raising the conditions of new Appropriations of Lands.—He has obstructed the Administration of Justice, by refusing his Assent to Laws for establishing Judiciary powers.—He has made Judges dependent on his Will alone, for the tenure of their offices, and the amount and payment of their salaries.—He has erected a multitude of New Offices, and sent hither swarms of Officers to harrass our people, and eat out their substance.— He has kept among us, in times of peace, Standing Armies without the Consent of our legislatures.— He has affected to render the Military independent of and superior to the Civil power.—He has combined with others to subject us to a jurisdiction foreign to our constitution, and unacknowledged by our laws; giving his Assent to their Acts of pretended Legislation.—For quartering large bodies of armed troops among us:—For protecting them, by a mock Trial, from punishment for any Murders which they should commit on the Inhabitants of these States:—For cutting off our Trade with all parts of the world:—For imposing Taxes on us without our Consent:—For depriving us in many cases, of the benefits of

Trial by Jury:—For transporting us beyond Seas to be tried for pretended offenses:— For abolishing the free System of English Laws in a neighboring Province, establishing therein an Arbitrary government, and enlarging its Boundaries so as to render it at once an example and fit instrument for introducing the same absolute rule into these Colonies:—For taking away our Charters, abolishing our most valuable Laws, and altering fundamentally the Forms of our Governments:—For suspending our own Legislatures, and declaring themselves invested with power to legislate for us in all cases whatsoever.—He has abdicated Government here, by declaring us out of his Protection and waging War against us.—He has plundered our seas, ravaged our Coasts, burnt our towns, and destroyed the lives of our people.—He is at this time transporting large Armies of foreign Mercenaries to compleat the works of death, desolation and tyranny, already begun with circumstances of Cruelty & perfidy, scarcely paralleled in the most barbarous ages, and totally unworthy the Head of a civilized nation.—He has constrained our fellow Citizens taken Captive on the High Seas to bear Arms against their Country, to become the executioners of their friends and Brethren, or to fall themselves by their hands.—He has excited domestic insurrections amongst us, and has endeavoured to bring on the inhabitants of our frontiers, the merciless Indian Savages, whose known rule of warfare, is an undistinguished destruction of all ages, sexes and conditions. In every stage of these Oppressions We have Petitioned for Redress in the most humble terms: Our repeated Petitions have been answered only by repeated injury. A Prince whose character is thus marked by every act which may define a Tyrant, is unfit to be the ruler of a free people. Nor have We been wanting in attentions to our British brethren. We have warned them from time to time of attempts by their legislature to extend an unwarrantable jurisdiction over us. We have reminded them of the circumstances of our emigration and settlement here. We have appealed to their native justice and magnanimity, and we have conjured them by the ties of our common kindred to disavow these usurpations, which would inevitably interrupt our connections and correspondence. They too have been deaf to the voice of justice and of consanguinity. We must, therefore, acquiesce in the necessity, which denounces our Separation, and hold them, as we hold the rest of mankind, Enemies in War, in Peace Friends.—

We, therefore, the Representatives of the United States of America, in General Congress, Assembled, appealing to the Supreme Judge of the world for the rectitude of our intentions do, in the Name, and by the Authority of the good People of these Colonies, solemnly publish and declare, That these United Colonies are, and of Right ought to be Free and Independent States; that they are Absolved from all Allegiance to the British Crown, and that all political connection between them and the State of Great Britain, is and ought to be totally dissolved; and that as Free and Independent States, they have full Power to levy War, conclude Peace, contract Alliances, establish Commerce, and to do all other Acts and Things which Independent States may of right do.—And for the support of this Declaration, with a firm reliance on the protection of divine Providence, we mutually pledge to each other our Lives, our Fortunes and our sacred Honor.

APPENDIX C

The Constitution
of the United States of America

We the People of the United States, in Order to form a more perfect Union, establish Justice, insure domestic Tranquillity, provide for the common defence, promote the general Welfare, and secure the Blessings of Liberty to ourselves and our Posterity, do ordain and establish this Constitution for the United States of America.

Article. I.

SECTION. 1. All legislative Powers herein granted shall be vested in a Congress of the United States, which shall consist of a Senate and House of Representatives.

SECTION. 2. The House of Representatives shall be composed of Members chosen every second Year by the People of the several States, and the Electors in each State shall have the Qualifications requisite for Electors of the most numerous Branch of the State Legislature.

No Person shall be a Representative who shall not have attained to the age of twenty five Years, and been seven Years a Citizen of the United States, and who shall not, when elected, be an Inhabitant of that State in which he shall be chosen.

Representatives and direct Taxes shall be apportioned among the several States which may be included within this Union, according to their respective Numbers, which shall be determined by adding to the whole Number of free Persons, including those bound to Service for a Term of Years, and excluding Indians not taxed, three fifths of all other Persons. The actual Enumeration shall be made within three Years after the first Meeting of the Congress of the United States, and within every subsequent Term of ten Years, in such Manner as they shall by Law direct. The Number of Representatives shall not exceed one for every thirty Thousand, but each State shall have at Least one Representative; and until such enumeration shall be made, the State of New Hampshire shall be entitled to chuse three, Massachusetts eight, Rhode-Island and Providence Plantations one, Connecticut five, New-York six, New Jersey four, Pennsylvania eight, Delaware one, Maryland six, Virginia ten, North Carolina five, South Carolina five, and Georgia three.

When vacancies happen in the Representation from any State, the Executive Authority thereof shall issue Writs of Election to fill such Vacancies.

The House of Representatives shall

chuse their Speaker and other Officers; and shall have the sole Power of Impeachment.

SECTION. 3. The Senate of the United States shall be composed of two Senators from each State, chosen by the Legislature thereof, for six Years; and each Senator shall have one Vote.

Immediately after they shall be assembled in Consequence of the first Election, they shall be divided as equally as may be into three Classes. The Seats of the Senators of the first Class shall be vacated at the Expiration of the second Year, of the second Class at the Expiration of the fourth Year, and of the third Class at the Expiration of the sixth Year, so that one third may be chosen every second Year; and if Vacancies happen by Resignation, or otherwise, during the Recess of the Legislature of any State, the Executive thereof may make temporary Appointments until the next Meeting of the Legislature, which shall then fill such Vacancies.

No Person shall be a Senator who shall not have attained to the Age of thirty Years, and been nine Years a Citizen of the United States, and who shall not, when elected, be an Inhabitant of that State for which he shall be chosen.

The Vice President of the United States shall be President of the Senate, but shall have no Vote, unless they be equally divided.

The Senate shall chuse their other Officers, and also a President pro tempore, in the Absence of the Vice President, or when he shall exercise the Office of President of the United States.

The Senate shall have the sole Power to try all Impeachments. When sitting for that Purpose, they shall be on Oath or Affirmation. When the President of the United States is tried the Chief Justice shall preside: And no Person shall be convicted without the Concurrence of two thirds of the Members present.

Judgment in Cases of Impeachment shall not extend further than to removal from Office, and disqualification to hold and enjoy any Office of honor, Trust or Profit under the United States: but the Party convicted shall nevertheless be liable and subject to Indictment, Trial, Judgment and Punishment, according to Law.

SECTION. 4. The Times, Places and Manner of holding Elections for Senators and Representatives, shall be prescribed in each State by the Legislature thereof; but the Congress may at any time by Law make or alter such Regulations, except as to the Places of chusing Senators.

The Congress shall assemble at least once in every Year, and such Meeting shall be on the first Monday in December, unless they shall by Law appoint a different Day.

SECTION. 5. Each House shall be the Judge of the Elections, Returns and Qualifications of its own Members, and a Majority of each shall constitute a Quorum to do Business; but a smaller Number may adjourn from day to day, and may be authorized to compel the Attendance of absent Members, in such Manner, and under such Penalties as each House may provide.

Each House may determine the Rules of its Proceedings, punish its Members for disorderly Behaviour, and, with the Concurrence of two thirds, expel a Member.

Each House shall keep a Journal of its Proceedings, and from time to time publish the same, excepting such Parts as may in their Judgment require Secrecy; and the Yeas and Nays of the Members of either House on any question shall, at the Desire of one fifth of those Present, be entered on the Journal.

Neither House, during the Session of Congress, shall, without the Consent of the other, adjourn for more than three days, nor to any other Place than that in which the two Houses shall be sitting.

SECTION. 6. The Senators and Representatives shall receive a Compensation for their Services, to be ascertained by Law, and paid out of the Treasury of the United States. They shall in all Cases, except Treason, Felony and Breach of the Peace, be privileged from Arrest during their Attendance at the Session of their respective Houses, and in going to and returning from the same; and for any Speech or Debate in either House, they shall not be questioned in any other Place.

No Senator or Representative shall, during the Time for which he was elected, be appointed to any civil Office under the Authority of the United States, which shall have been created, or the Emoluments whereof shall have been encreased during such time; and no Person holding any Office under the United States, shall be a Member of either House during his Continuance in Office.

SECTION. 7. All Bills for raising Revenue shall originate in the House of Representatives; but the Senate may propose or concur with amendments as on other Bills.

Every Bill which shall have passed the House of Representatives and the Senate, shall, before it become a Law, be presented to the President of the United States; If he approve he shall sign it, but if not he shall return it, with his Objections to that House in which it shall have originated, who shall enter the Objections at large on their Journal, and proceed to reconsider it. If after such Reconsideration two thirds of that House shall agree to pass the Bill, it shall be sent, together with the Objections, to the other House, by which it shall likewise be reconsidered, and if approved by two thirds of that House, it shall become a Law. But in all such Cases the Votes of both Houses shall be determined by yeas and Nays, and the Names of the Persons voting for and against the Bill shall be entered on the Journal of each House respectively. If any Bill shall not be returned by the President within ten Days (Sunday excepted) after it shall have been presented to him, the Same shall be a Law, in like Manner as if he had signed it, unless the Congress by their Adjournment prevent its Return, in which Case it shall not be a Law.

Every Order, Resolution, or Vote to which the Concurrence of the Senate and House of Representatives may be necessary (except on a question of Adjournment) shall be presented to the President of the United States; and before the Same shall take Effect, shall be approved by him, or being disapproved by him, shall be repassed by two thirds of the Senate and House of Representatives, according to the Rules and Limitations prescribed in the Case of a Bill.

SECTION. 8. The Congress shall have Power To lay and collect Taxes, Duties, Imposts and Excises, to pay the Debts and provide for the common Defence and general Welfare of the United States; but all Duties, Imposts and Excises shall be uniform throughout the United States;

To borrow Money on the credit of the United States;

To regulate Commerce with foreign Nations, and among the several States, and with the Indian Tribes;

To establish an uniform Rule of Naturalization, and uniform Laws on the subject of Bankruptcies throughout the United States;

To coin Money, regulate the Value thereof, and of foreign Coin, and fix the Standard of Weights and Measures;

To provide for the Punishment of counterfeiting the Securities and current Coin of the United States;

To establish Post Offices and post Roads;

To promote the Progress of Science and useful Arts, by securing for limited Times to Authors and Inventors the exclusive Right to their respective Writings and Discoveries;

To constitute Tribunals inferior to the supreme Court;

To define and punish Piracies and Felonies committed on the high Seas, and Offences against the Law of Nations;

To declare War, grant Letters of Marque and Reprisal, and make Rules concerning Captures on Land and Water;

To raise and support Armies, but no Appropriation of Money to that Use shall be for a longer Term than two Years;

To provide and maintain a Navy;

To make Rules for the Government and Regulation of the land and naval Forces;

To provide for calling forth the Militia to execute the Laws of the Union, suppress Insurrections and repel Invasions;

To provide for organizing, arming, and disciplining, the Militia, and for governing such Part of them as may be employed in the Service of the United States, reserving to the States respectively, the

Appointment of the Officers, and the Authority of training the Militia according to the discipline prescribed by Congress;

To exercise exclusive Legislation in all Cases whatsoever, over such District (not exceeding ten Miles square) as may, by Cession of Particular States, and the Acceptance of Congress, become the Seat of the Government of the United States, and to exercise like Authority over all Places purchased by the Consent of the Legislature of the State in which the Same shall be, for the Erection of Forts, Magazines, Arsenals, dock-Yards, and other needful Buildings;—And

To make all Laws which shall be necessary and proper for carrying into Execution the foregoing Powers, and all other Powers vested by this Constitution in the Government of the United States, or in any Department or Officer thereof.

SECTION. 9. The Migration or Importation of such Persons as any of the States now existing shall think proper to admit, shall not be prohibited by the Congress prior to the Year one thousand eight hundred and eight, but a Tax or duty may be imposed on such Importation, not exceeding ten dollars for each Person.

The Privilege of the Writ of Habeas Corpus shall not be suspended, unless when in Cases of Rebellion or Invasion the public Safety may require it.

No Bill of Attainder or ex post facto Law shall be passed.

No Capitation, or other direct, Tax shall be laid, unless in Proportion to the Census of Enumeration herein before directed to be taken.

No Tax or Duty shall be laid on Articles exported from any State.

No Preference shall be given by any Regulation of Commerce or Revenue to the Ports of one State over those of another; nor shall Vessels bound to, or from, one State, be obliged to enter, clear or pay Duties in another.

No Money shall be drawn from the Treasury, but in Consequence of Appropriations made by Law; and a regular Statement and Account of the Receipts and Expenditures of all public Money shall be published from time to time.

No Title of Nobility shall be granted by the United States; And no Person holding any Office of Profit or Trust under them, shall, without the Consent of the Congress, accept of any present, Emolument, Office, or Title, of any kind whatever, from any King, Prince or foreign State.

SECTION. 10. No State shall enter into any Treaty, Alliance, or Confederation; grant Letters of Marque and Reprisal; coin Money; emit Bills of Credit; make any Thing but gold and silver Coin a Tender in Payment of Debts; pass any Bill of Attainder, ex post facto Law, or Law impairing the Obligation of Contracts, or grant and Title of Nobility.

No State shall, without the Consent of the Congress, lay any Imposts or Duties on Imports or Exports, except what may be absolutely necessary for executing its inspection Laws: and the net Produce of all Duties and Imposts, laid by any State on Imports or Exports, shall be for the Use of the Treasury of the United States; and all such Laws shall be subject to the Revision and Controul of the Congress.

No State shall, without the Consent of Congress, lay any Duty of Tonnage, keep Troops, or Ships of War in time of Peace, enter into any Agreement or Compact with another State, or with a foreign Power, or engage in War, unless actually invaded, or in such imminent Danger as will not admit of delay.

Article. II.

SECTION. 1. The executive Power shall be vested in a President of the United States of America. He shall hold his Office during the Term of four Years, and, together with the Vice President, chosen for the same Term, be elected, as follows

Each State shall appoint, in such Manner as the Legislature thereof may direct, a Number of Electors, equal to the whole Number of Senators and Representatives to which the State may be entitled in the Congress: but no Senator or Representative, or Person holding an Office of Trust or Profit under the United States, shall be appointed an Elector.

The Electors shall meet in their respective States, and vote by Ballot for two

Persons, of whom one at least shall not be an Inhabitant of the same State with themselves. And they shall make a List of all the Persons voted for, and of the Number of Votes for each; which List they shall sign and certify, and transmit sealed to the Seat of the Government of the United States, directed to the President of the Senate. The President of the Senate shall, in the Presence of the Senate and House of Representatives, open all the Certificates, and the Votes shall then be counted. The Person having the greatest Number of Votes shall be the President, if such Number be a Majority of the whole Number of Electors appointed; and if there be more than one who have such Majority, and have an equal Number of Votes, then the House of Representatives shall immediately chuse by Ballot one of them for President; and if no Person have a Majority, then from the five highest on the List the said House shall in like Manner chuse the President. But in chusing the President, the Votes shall be taken by States, the Representation from each State having one Vote; a quorum for this Purpose shall consist of a Member or Members from two thirds of the States, and a Majority of all the States shall be necessary to a Choice. In every Case, after the Choice of the President, the Person having the greatest Number of Votes of the Electors shall be the Vice President. But if there should remain two or more who have equal Votes, the Senate shall chose from them by Ballot the Vice President.

The Congress may determine the Time of chusing the Electors, and the Day on which they shall give their votes; which Day shall be the same throughout the United States.

No Person except a natural born Citizen, or a Citizen of the United States, at the time of the Adoption of this Constitution, shall be eligible to the Office of President; neither shall any person be eligible to that Office who shall not have attained to the Age of thirty five Years, and been fourteen Years a Resident within the United States.

In Case of the Removal of the President from Office, or of his Death, Resignation, or Inability to discharge the Powers and Duties of the said Office, the Same shall devolve on the Vice President, and the Congress may by Law provide for the Case of Removal, Death, Resignation or Inability, both of the President and Vice President, declaring what Officer shall then act as President, and such Officer shall act accordingly, until the Disability be removed, or a President shall be elected.

The President shall, at stated Times, receive for his Services, a Compensation, which shall neither be encreased nor diminished during the Period for which he shall have been elected, and he shall not receive within that Period any other Emolument from the United States, or any of them.

Before he enter on the Execution of his Office, he shall take the following Oath or Affirmation:—"I do solemnly swear (or affirm) that I will faithfully execute the Office of President of the United States, and will to the best of my Ability, preserve, protect and defend the Constitution of the United States."

SECTION. 2. The President shall be Commander in Chief of the Army and Navy of the United States, and of the Militia of the several States, when called into the actual Service of the United States; he may require the Opinion, in writing, of the principal Officer in each of the executive Departments, upon any Subject relating to the Duties of their respective Offices, and he shall have Power to grant Reprieves and Pardons for Offenses against the United States, except in Cases of Impeachment.

He shall have Power, by and with the Advice and Consent of the Senate, to make Treaties, provided two thirds of the Senators present concur; and he shall nominate, and by and with the Advice and Consent of the Senate, shall appoint Ambassadors, other public Ministers and Consuls, Judges of the supreme Court, and all other Officers of the United States, whose Appointments are not herein otherwise provided for, and which shall be established by Law; but the Congress may by Law vest the Appointment of such inferior Officers, as they think proper, in the President alone, in the Courts of Law, or in the Heads of Departments.

The President shall have Power to fill up all Vacancies that may happen during the Recess of the Senate, by granting Commissions which shall expire at the End of their next Session.

SECTION. 3. He shall from time to time give to the Congress Information of the State of the Union, and recommend to their Consideration such Measures as he shall judge necessary and expedient; he may, on extraordinary Occasions, convene both Houses, or either of them, and in Case of Disagreement between them, with Respect to the Time of Adjournment, he may adjourn them to such Time as he shall think proper; he shall receive Ambassadors and other public Ministers; he shall take Care that the Laws be faithfully executed, and shall Commission all the Officers of the United States.

SECTION. 4. The President, Vice President and all Civil Officers of the United States, shall be removed from Office on Impeachment for, and Conviction of, Treason, Bribery, or other high Crimes and Misdemeanors.

Article. III.

SECTION. 1. The judicial Power of the United States, shall be vested in one supreme Court, and in such inferior Courts as the Congress may from time to time ordain and establish. The Judges, both of the supreme and inferior Courts, shall hold their Offices during good Behaviour, and shall, at stated Times, receive for their Services, a Compensation, which shall not be diminished during their Continuance in Office.

SECTION. 2. The judicial Power shall extend to all Cases, in Law and Equity, arising under this Constitution, the Laws of the United States, and Treaties made, or which shall be made, under their Authority;—to all Cases affecting Ambassadors, other public Ministers and Consuls; —to all Cases of admiralty and maritime Jurisdiction;—to Controversies to which the United States shall be a Party;—to Controversies between two or more States; —between a State and Citizens of an-

other State;—between Citizens of different States;—between Citizens of the same State claiming Lands under Grants of different States, and between a State, or the Citizens thereof, and foreign States, Citizens or Subjects.

In all Cases affecting Ambassadors, other public Ministers and Consuls, and those in which a State shall be Party, the supreme Court shall have original Jurisdiction. In all the other Cases before mentioned, the supreme Court shall have appellate Jurisdiction, both as to Law and Fact, with such Exceptions, and under such Regulations as the Congress shall make.

The Trial of all Crimes, except in Cases of Impeachment, shall be by Jury; and such Trial shall be held in the State where the said Crimes shall have been committed; but when not committed within any State, the Trial shall be at such Place or Places as the Congress may by Law have directed.

SECTION. 3. Treason against the United States, shall consist only in levying War against them, or in adhering to their Enemies, giving them Aid and Comfort. No Person shall be convicted of Treason unless on the Testimony of two Witnesses to the same overt Act, or on Confession in open Court.

The Congress shall have Power to declare the Punishment of Treason, but no Attainder of Treason shall work Corruption of Blood, or Forfeiture except during the Life of the Person attainted.

Article. IV.

SECTION. 1. Full Faith and Credit shall be given in each State to the public Acts, Records, and judicial Proceedings of every other State. And the Congress may by general Laws prescribe the Manner in which such Acts, Records and Proceedings shall be proved, and the Effect thereof.

SECTION. 2. The Citizens of each State shall be entitled to all Privileges and Immunities of Citizens in the several States.

A Person charged in any State with Treason, Felony, or other Crime, who shall flee from Justice, and be found in another State, shall on Demand of the executive Authority of the State from which he fled, be delivered up, to be removed to the State having Jurisdiction of the Crime.

No Person held to Service or Labour in one State, under the Laws thereof, escaping into another, shall, in Consequence of any Law or Regulation therein, be discharged from such Service or Labour, but shall be delivered up on Claim of the Party to whom such Service or Labour may be due.

SECTION. 3. New States may be admitted by the Congress into this Union; but no new State shall be formed or erected within the Jurisdiction of any other State; nor any State be formed by the Junction of two or more States, or Parts of States, without the Consent of the Legislatures of the States concerned as well as of the Congress.

The Congress shall have Power to dispose of and make all needful Rules and Regulations respecting the Territory or other Property belonging to the United States; and nothing in this Constitution shall be so construed as to Prejudice any Claims of the United States, or of any particular State.

SECTION. 4. The United States shall guarantee to every State in this Union a Republican Form of Government, and shall protect each of them against Invasion; and on Application of the Legislature, or of the Executive (when the Legislature cannot be convened) against domestic Violence.

Article. V.

The Congress, whenever two thirds of both Houses shall deem it necessary, shall propose Amendments to this Constitution, or, on the Application of the Legislatures of two thirds of the several States, shall call a Convention for proposing Amendments, which, in either Case, shall be valid to all Intents and Purposes, as Part of this Constitution, when ratified by the Legislatures of three fourths of the several States, or by Conventions in three fourths thereof, as the one or the other Mode of Ratification may be proposed by the Congress; Provided that no Amendment which may be made prior to the Year One thousand eight hundred and eight shall in any Manner affect the first and fourth Clauses in the Ninth Section of the first Article; and that no State, without its Consent, shall be deprived of it's equal Suffrage in the Senate.

Article. VI.

All Debts contracted and Engagements entered into, before the Adoption of this Constitution, shall be as valid against the United States under this Constitution, as under the Confederation.

This Constitution, and the Laws of the United States which shall be made in Pursuance thereof; and all Treaties made, or which shall be made, under the Authority of the United States, shall be the supreme Law of the Land; and the Judges in every State shall be bound thereby, any Thing in the Constitution or Laws of any State to the Contrary notwithstanding.

The Senators and Representatives before mentioned, and the Members of the several State Legislatures, and all executive and judicial Officers, both of the United States and of the several States, shall be bound by Oath or Affirmation, to support this Constitution; but no religious Test shall ever be required as a Qualification to any Office or public Trust under the United States.

Article. VII.

The Ratification of the Conventions of nine States, shall be sufficient for the Establishment of this Constitution between the States so ratifying the Same.

done in Convention by the Unanimous Consent of the States present the Seventeenth Day of September in the Year of our Lord one thousand seven hundred and Eighty seven and of the Independence of the United States of America the Twelfth In witness whereof We have hereunto subscribed our Names,
GO. WASHINGTON—PRESIDT.
    and deputy from Virginia

Amendments to the Constitution
Amendment [I.]*

Congress shall make no law respecting an establishment of religion, or prohibiting the free exercise thereof; or abridging the freedom of speech, or of the press; or the right of the People peaceably to assemble, and to petition the Government for a redress of grievances.

Amendment [II.]

A well regulated Militia, being necessary to the security of a free State, the right of the people to keep and bear Arms, shall not be infringed.

Amendment [III.]

No Soldier shall, in time of peace be quartered in any house, without the consent of the Owner, nor in time of war, but in a manner to be prescribed by law.

Amendment [IV.]

The right of the people to be secure in their persons, houses, papers, and effects, against unreasonable searches and seizures, shall not be violated, and no Warrants shall issue, but upon probable cause, supported by Oath or affirmation, and particularly describing the place to be searched, and the persons or things to be seized.

Amendment [V.]

No person shall be held to answer for a capital, or otherwise infamous crime, unless on a presentment or indictment of a Grand Jury, except in cases arising in the land or naval forces, or in the Militia, when in actual service in time of War or public danger; nor shall any person be subject for the same offence to be twice put in jeopardy of life or limb; nor shall be compelled in any criminal case to be a witness against himself, nor be deprived of life, liberty, or property, without due process of law; nor shall private property be taken for public use, without just compensation.

Amendment [VI.]

In all criminal prosecutions, the accused shall enjoy the right to a speedy and public trial, by an impartial jury of the State and district wherein the crime shall have been committed, which district shall have been previously ascertained by law, and to be informed of the nature and cause of the accusation; to be confronted with the witnesses against him; to have compulsory process for obtaining witnesses in his favor, and to have the Assistance of Counsel for his defence.

Amendment [VII.]

In Suits at common law, where the value in controversy shall exceed twenty dollars, the right of trial by jury shall be preserved, and no fact tried by a jury, shall be otherwise re-examined in any Court of the United States, than according to the rules of the common law.

Amendment [VIII.]

Excessive bail shall not be required, nor excessive fines imposed, nor cruel and unusual punishments inflicted.

Amendment [IX.]

The enumeration in the Constitution, of certain rights, shall not be construed to deny or disparage others retained by the people.

Amendment [X.]

The powers not delegated to the United States by the Constitution, nor prohibited by it to the States, are reserved to the States respectively, or to the people.

Amendment [XI.]

The Judicial power of the United States shall not be construed to extend to any

* Brackets enclosing an amendment number indicate that the number was not specifically assigned in the resolution proposing the amendment.

suit in law or equity, commenced or prosecuted against one of the United States by Citizens of another State, or by Citizens or Subjects of any Foreign State.

Amendment [XII.]

The Electors shall meet in their respective states and vote by ballot for President and Vice-President, one of whom, at least, shall not be an inhabitant of the same state with themselves; they shall name in their ballots the person voted for as President, and in distinct ballots the person voted for as Vice-President, and they shall make distinct lists of all persons voted for as President, and of all persons voted for as Vice-President, and of the number of votes for each, which lists they shall sign and certify, and transmit sealed to the seat of the government of the United States, directed to the President of the Senate;—The President of the Senate shall, in the presence of the Senate and House of Representatives, open all the certificates and the votes shall then be counted;—The person having the greatest number of votes for President, shall be the President, if such number be a majority of the whole number of Electors appointed; and if no person have such majority, then from the persons having the highest numbers not exceeding three on the list of those voted for as President, the House of Representatives shall choose immediately, by ballot, the President. But in choosing the President, the votes shall be taken by states, the representation from each state having one vote; a quorum for this purpose shall consist of a member or members from two-thirds of the states, and a majority of all the states shall be necessary to a choice. And if the House of Representatives shall not choose a President whenever the right of choice shall devolve upon them, before the fourth day of March next following, then the Vice-President shall act as President, as in the case of the death or other constitutional disability of the President—The person having the greatest number of votes as Vice-President, shall be the Vice-President, if such number be a majority of the whole number of Electors appointed, and

if no person have a majority, then from the two highest numbers on the list, the Senate shall choose the Vice-President; a quorum for the purpose shall consist of two-thirds of the whole number of Senators, and a majority of the whole number shall be necessary to a choice. But no person constitutionally ineligible to the office of President shall be eligible to that of Vice-President of the United States.

Amendment [XIII.]

SECTION 1. Neither slavery nor involuntary servitude, except as a punishment for crime whereof the party shall have been duly convicted, shall exist within the United States, or any place subject to their jurisdiction.

SECTION 2. Congress shall have power to enforce this article by appropriate legislation.

Amendment [XIV.]

SECTION 1. All persons born or naturalized in the United States and subject to the jurisdiction thereof, are citizens of the United States and of the State wherein they reside. No State shall make or enforce any law which shall abridge the privileges or immunities of citizens of the United States; nor shall any State deprive any person of life, liberty, or property, without due process of law; nor deny to any person within its jurisdiction the equal protection of the laws.

SECTION 2. Representatives shall be apportioned among the several States according to their respective numbers, counting the whole number of persons in each State, excluding Indians not taxed. But when the right to vote at any election for the choice of electors for President and Vice President of the United States, Representatives in Congress, the Executive and Judicial officers of a State, or the members of the Legislature thereof, is denied to any of the male inhabitants of such State, being twenty-one years of age, and citizens of the United States, or in any way abridged, except for participation in rebellion, or other crime, the basis of representation therein shall be reduced in the proportion which the number of such male citizens shall bear to the whole number of male citizens twenty-one years of age in such State.

SECTION 3. No person shall be a Senator or Representative in Congress, or elector of President and Vice President, or hold any office, civil or military, under the United States, or under any State, who, having previously taken an oath, as a member of Congress, or as an officer of the United States, or as a member of any State legislature, or as an executive or judicial officer of any State, to support the Constitution of the United States, shall have engaged in insurrection or rebellion against the same, or given aid or comfort to the enemies thereof. But Congress may by a vote of two-thirds of each House, remove such disability.

SECTION 4. The validity of the public debt of the United States, authorized by law, including debts incurred for payment of pensions and bounties for services in suppressing insurrection or rebellion, shall not be questioned. But neither the United States nor any State shall assume or pay any debt or obligation incurred in aid of insurrection or rebellion against the United States, or any claim for the loss or emancipation of any slave; but all such debts, obligations and claims shall be held illegal and void.

SECTION 5. The Congress shall have power to enforce, by appropriate legislation, the provisions of this article.

Amendment [XV.]

SECTION 1. The right of citizens of the United States to vote shall not be denied or abridged by the United States or by any State on account of race, color, or previous condition of servitude.

SECTION 2. The Congress shall have power to enforce this article by appropriate legislation.

Amendment [XVI.]

The Congress shall have power to lay and collect taxes on incomes, from whatever source derived, without apportionment among the several States, and without regard to any census or enumeration.

Amendment [XVII.]

The Senate of the United States shall be composed of two Senators from each State, elected by the people thereof, for six years; and each Senator shall have one vote. The electors in each State shall have the qualifications requisite for electors of the most numerous branch of the State legislatures.

When vacancies happen in the representation of any State in the Senate, the executive authority of such State shall issue writs of election to fill such vacancies; *Provided*, That the legislature of any State may empower the executive thereof to make temporary appointments until the people fill the vacancies by election as the legislature may direct.

This amendment shall not be so construed as to affect the election or term of any Senator chosen before it becomes valid as part of the Constitution.

Amendment [XVIII.]

SECTION 1. After one year from the ratification of this article the manufacture, sale, or transportation of intoxicating liquors within, the importation thereof into, or the exportation thereof from the United States and all territory subject to the jurisdiction thereof for beverage purposes is hereby prohibited.

SEC. 2. The Congress and the several States shall have concurrent power to enforce this article by appropriate legislation.

SEC. 3. This article shall be inoperative unless it shall have been ratified as an amendment to the Constitution by the legislatures of the several States, as provided in the Constitution, within seven years from the date of the submission hereof to the States by the Congress.

Amendment [XIX.]

The right of citizens of the United States to vote shall not be denied or abridged by the United States or by any State on account of sex.

Congress shall have power to enforce this article by appropriate legislation.

Amendment [XX.]

SECTION 1. The terms of the President and Vice President shall end at noon on the 20th day of January, and the terms of Senators and Representatives at noon on the 3d day of January, of the years in which such terms would have ended if this article had not been ratified; and the terms of their successors shall then begin.

SEC. 2. The Congress shall assemble at least once in every year, and such meeting shall begin at noon on the 3d day of January, unless they shall by law appoint a different day.

SEC. 3. If, at the time fixed for the beginning of the term of the President, the President elect shall have died, the Vice President elect shall become President. If a President shall not have been chosen before the time fixed for the beginning of his term, or if the President elect shall have failed to qualify, then the Vice President elect shall act as President until a President shall have qualified; and the Congress may by law provide for the case wherein neither a President elect nor a Vice President elect shall have qualified, declaring who shall then act as President, or the manner in which one who is to act shall be selected, and such person shall act accordingly until a President or Vice President shall have qualified.

SEC. 4. The Congress may by law provide for the case of the death of any of the persons from whom the House of Representatives may choose a President whenever the right of choice shall have devolved upon them, and for the case of the death of any of the persons from whom the Senate may choose a Vice President whenever the right of choice shall have devolved upon them.

SEC. 5. Sections 1 and 2 shall take effect on the 15th day of October following the ratification of this article.

SEC. 6. This article shall be inoperative unless it shall have been ratified as an amendment to the Constitution by the legislatures of three-fourths of the several States within seven years from the date of its submission.

Amendment [XXI.]

SECTION 1. The eighteenth article of amendment to the Constitution of the United States is hereby repealed.

SEC. 2. The transportation or importation into any State, Territory or possession of the United States for delivery or use therein of intoxicating liquors, in violation of the laws thereof, is hereby prohibited.

SEC. 3. This article shall be inoperative unless it shall have been ratified as an amendment to the Constitution by conventions in the several States, as provided in the Constitution, within seven years from the date of the submission thereof to the States by the Congress.

Amendment [XXII.]

SECTION 1. No person shall be elected to the office of the President more than twice, and no person who has held the office of President, or acted as President, for more than two years of a term to which some other person was elected President shall be elected to the office of the President more than once. But this Article shall not apply to any person holding the office of President when this Article was proposed by the Congress, and shall not prevent any person who may be holding the office of President, or acting as President, during the term within which this Article becomes operative from holding the office of President or acting as President during the remainder of such term.

SEC. 2. This Article shall be inoperative unless it shall have been ratified as an amendment to the Constitution by the legislatures of three-fourths of the several States within seven years from the date of its submission to the States by the Congress.

Amendment [XXIII.]

SECTION 1. The District constituting the seat of Government of the United States shall appoint in such manner as the Congress may direct:

A number of electors of President and Vice President equal to the whole number of Senators and Representatives in Congress to which the District would be entitled if it were a State, but in no event more than the least populous State; they shall be in addition to those appointed by the States, but they shall be considered, for the purposes of the election of President and Vice President, to be electors appointed by a State; and they shall meet in the District and perform such duties as provided by the twelfth article of amendment.

SEC. 2. The Congress shall have power to enforce this article by appropriate legislation.

Amendment [XXIV.]

SECTION. 1. The right of citizens of the United States to vote in any primary or other election for President or Vice President, for electors for President or Vice President, or for Senator or Representative in Congress, shall not be denied or abridged by the United States or any State by reason of failure to pay any poll tax or other tax.

SECTION 2. The Congress shall have power to enforce this article by appropriate legislation.

Amendment [XXV.]

SECTION 1. In case of the removal of the President from office or his death or resignation, the Vice President shall become President.

SEC. 2. Whenever there is a vacancy in the office of the Vice President, the Presi-dent shall nominate a Vice President who shall take office upon confirmation by a majority vote of both houses of Congress.

SEC. 3. Whenever the President transmits to the President pro tempore of the Senate and the Speaker of the House of Representatives his written declaration that he is unable to discharge the powers and duties of his office, and until he transmits to them a written declaration to the contrary, such powers and duties shall be discharged by the Vice President as Acting President.

SEC. 4. Whenever the Vice President and a majority of either the principal officers of the executive department or of such other body as Congress may by law provide, transmit to the President pro tempore of the Senate and the Speaker of the House of Representatives their written declaration that the President is unable to discharge the powers and duties of his office, the Vice President shall immediately assume the powers and duties of the office as Acting President.

Thereafter, when the President transmits to the President pro tempore of the Senate and the Speaker of the House of Representatives his written declaration that no inability exists, he shall resume the powers and duties of his office unless the Vice President and a majority of either the principal officers of the executive department or of such other body as Congress may by law provide, transmit within four days to the President pro tempore of the Senate and the Speaker of the House of Representatives their written declaration that the President is unable to discharge the powers and duties of his office. Thereupon Congress shall decide the issue, assembling within 48 hours for that purpose if not in session. If the Congress, within 21 days after receipt of the latter written declaration, or, if Congress is not in session, within 21 days after Congress is required to assemble, determines by two-thirds vote of both houses that the President is unable to discharge the powers and duties of his office, the Vice President shall continue to discharge the same as Acting President; otherwise, the President shall resume the powers and duties of his office.

Amendment [XXVI.]

SECTION 1. The right of citizens of the United States, who are 18 years of age or older, to vote shall not be denied or abridged by the United States or any state on account of age.

SEC. 2. The Congress shall have the power to enforce this article by appropriate legislation.

Proposed Amendment [XXVII.]

SECTION 1. Equality of rights under the law shall not be denied or abridged by the United States or by any State on account of sex.

SEC. 2. The Congress shall have the power to enforce, by appropriate legislation, the provisions of this article.

SEC. 3. This amendment shall take effect two years after the date of ratification.

INDEX

Palmer Raids, 46
Parent Teacher Association, 132
Parliamentarian (House), 67
Parliamentary form of government, 12, 18–19, 52–53, 54, 83
Participation, political, 2, 3, 8–10, 51, 136, 161, 167–186
Parties, political, 22, 38, 57, 67, 84, 116, 146, 149–165, 176, 189–190
Party: competition, 153–160; discipline, 67, 71, 154; functions, 160–164; leadership, 152, 154; offices (Congress), 68; programs, 152–153; responsibility, 153, 154; systems, 153–160; voters, 154
Patriotic symbols, 180–181
Pentagon. See Military
Pentagon Papers, 110, 193
Philadelphia Convention. See Constitutional Convention
Philippines, 46, 47
Pilgrims, 4
Plato, 4
Plea bargaining, 127
Plessy v. *Ferguson*, 38–39
Pluralism, 8–10, 145–147
Plymouth Colony, 4
Pocket veto, 79
Pointer v. *Texas*, 126
Police powers, 36, 121–122
Policies: control of, 1, 43; discussion of, 3; federal-state, 39–41; formation of, 8–9, 90, 98–99; implications of judicial decisions for, 111; initiation of, 56–57, 92
Political questions, 115
Political socialization, 160, 178–182
Political thought, American, 5, 7, 17, 46
Political trials, 109–110
Politics, 2–4; definition of, 2; operation in U.S., 8–10; understanding of, 1
Poll tax, 168
Popular sovereignty, 16–17, 167–186, 187–194
Population size, 10, 29
Populists, 152, 153
Pornography, Presidential Commission on, 188
Poverty, 3, 160, 184–186, 184–192
Power, 5, 7, 16–17, 24, 29, 34, 152, 160, 187–192; access to, 9, 136, 138–143; geographic distribution of, see federalism; growth of national, 42–44; growth of presidential, 56–57, 85–86, 94–97, 98–99; limitations on, 7–8, 14, 19, 40, 56–57, 182–184
Power elite, 8

"Power of the purse." See Appropriations
President, 17, 18–20, 22, 38, 39, 69, 79, 83–104, 107, 116, 153, 183, 189; growth in power of, 56–57, 193–194
Presidential aides, 61–62; indictment of Nixon's former, 193
Presidential form of government, 17, 19, 52–53, 54
Presidential terms, 22–23, 28, 52, 149
President of the Senate. See Vice president
President *pro tempore* (Senate), 67–68
Press, freedom of, 191–192; role of, 191–192
Primary elections, 154–157, 161, 163
Primary, Joint Committee on, 69
Privacy, 3, 29–31, 102–103
Privileged reports, 78
Process, serving of, 123–124
Progressive (Bull Moose) Party, 153
Prohibition, 23, 28
Property taxes, 39, 111
Proportional representation, 157–158
Prosecutors, 108–109, 112, 118
Protest, 7
Public good, 10
Public Health Service, 9
Public opinion, 55
Puritans, 4

Racism, 3, 7, 44, 48, 160
Realism, 9–10
"Red scare," 180
Referendum. See Initiative and referendum
Regional groupings, 41
Registration, voter, 171, 172
Regulatory agencies, 87, 143
Representation, 51, 53–55, 182–184
Republic, 167, 168
Republican Party, 151, 152–157, 172, 189–190
Reserved powers, 34
Resources, distribution of, 184–186
Revenue bills, 74
Rhode Island, 4, 13
Rider, legislative, 92
Rights, 7. See also Civil rights *and* Bill of Rights
Riots, 178–179
Robinson v. *California*, 125
Rockefeller, Nelson A., 163
Roosevelt, Franklin D., 87, 117
Roosevelt, Theodore, 85, 152

Rule XXII, 66
Rules, Committee on (House), 77–78

Sacco and Vanzetti, 180
Scandinavian countries, 59
Schattschneider, E. E., 167
Search and seizure, 25, 26
Secession, 43, 151
Secrecy, 189–190
Security, national, 193–194
Sedition Act of 1917, 7, 48
Segregation, 37, 38, 39, 41, 48, 119, 183
Self-interest, 9
Senate, U.S., 17, 37, 48, 60, 61, 62, 63–66, 72–73, 87, 90, 95, 96, 97, 116, 156, 182–184, 189
Senatorial courtesy, 61–62
Seniority, 67, 70–73
Separation of powers, 17–20, 52–53, 61, 63, 83, 91, 182–184, 188–189, 193–194
Sierra Club, 132, 135
Single member district, 157
Sirica, John, 194
Slavery, 5, 12–13, 27, 151, 152
Smith, Adam, 9
Social Security Act, 40, 176
South, the, 5, 28, 38, 41, 71, 151, 153, 155, 168
South Africa, Republic of, 168, 183
Sovereignty, 34
Spain, 46, 96
Speaker of the House, 67, 68, 73
Special courts (U.S.), 115
Special prosecutor (Watergate), 194
Speech, freedom of, 7
State: constitutions, 34, 106–107; courts, 113–114, 117; executives, 84, 183; governments, 34–36, 39, 41, 84, 145, 183, 188; laws, 38; legislatures, 65–66, 84, 142, 177; revenues, 36
State, power of the, 4, 14
States, admission of, 12–13
Status quo, 9, 73, 145–147
Stover v. New York, 115
Strict construction, 42–43
Students, 7
Supreme Court (U.S.), 25, 36, 39, 41, 43, 61, 91, 97, 106, 107, 111, 113, 114–115, 117, 119, 122, 123, 125–129, 140, 168–169, 170, 183; See also Courts
Switzerland, 41, 183

Taft, William Howard, 85
Tanzania, 53
Taxation, 34, 36, 168–169, 176

Teamsters, 145
Technology, 44, 86, 94, 192
Television. See Campaign financing
Territories, 12
Test Ban Treaty, 9
Texas, 41, 45, 156
Third parties, 153, 157, 158
Tobacco, 9
Tocqueville, Alexis de, 119, 182
Treasury, Department of the, 94
Treaties, 36, 43, 58, 93, 95, 96, 107, 115
Trial Courts, 113–116
Truman, Harry S, 97
Turner, Frederick Jackson, 45
Turnout, voter, 2, 172–174
Twain, Mark, 47, 51
Tweed, Boss, 149
Tyler, John, 22

Unicameralism, 63–66
Union, federal. See Federalism
Unitary form of government, 33, 34, 38, 42
United Auto Workers, 132
Urban problems, 6–7
U.S.S.R., 16, 42, 48, 59, 98, 154
U-2 incident, 98

Values, 16
Vanzetti, 180
Vermont, 41
Vesco, Robert, 193
Veto, 21–22, 58, 62, 79, 91, 92, 95; item veto, 84, 92
Vice president, 17, 22, 29, 67, 68, 84, 87–88, 193
Vietnam, 44, 47, 95, 177, 193. See also Indochinese War
Violence in the political system, 105–106, 178–179
Virginia Declaration of Rights, 25
Voters, 2, 154, 161, 167–186
Voting Rights Act, 9, 169, 170

Wallace, George, 153, 155, 158
War, declaration of, 95
Ward politics, 190
Warmaking powers, 95, 98–99
Warren, Earl, 126, 136
Washington, D.C. See District of Columbia
Washington, George, 42, 94, 149
Washington Post, 194
Washington v. Texas, 126
Watergate, 19, 56, 60, 137, 164, 192–194

About the Authors

Max J. Skidmore is currently Head of the Department of Political Science at Southwest Missouri State University. He received his Ph.D. from the University of Minnesota, and specializes in American politics and political thought, and political rhetoric and symbolism. From 1965 to 1968 he was Director of American Studies and Associate Professor of Political Science at the University of Alabama. Earlier, he held various positions with the Department of Health, Education, and Welfare in Washington, D.C., including Administrative Assistant in the Office of the Commissioner of Social Security and Program Review Officer in the U.S. Office of Education. Among his publications are *Medicare and the American Rhetoric of Reconciliation*, University of Alabama Press, 1970, and *Word Politics: Essays on Language and Politics*, Freel, 1972.

Marshall Carter Wanke is currently Lecturer in Government at Ahmadu Bello University in Zaria, Nigeria. She received her Ph.D. from the University of Wisconsin, where she was a Ford Fellow from 1965 to 1967, a University Fellow from 1967 to 1968, and an Emma Perry Ogg Fellow in 1968. Her specialties are comparative judicial process (especially the Third World), public law, political justice, and political change in Africa. She was an Assistant Professor at Wayne State University from 1969 to 1972 and taught at California State University at Long Beach in 1972 and 1973.